# THE
# POLITICS
## OF
# CULTURE

## Edited by
# BRETT WILLIAMS

SMITHSONIAN INSTITUTION PRESS
WASHINGTON AND LONDON

© 1991 by the Smithsonian Institution

Editor: Norman Rudnick
Designer: Linda McKnight

The Smithsonian Institution Press publishes a series of
significant volumes in anthropology edited by the
Anthropological Society of Washington. The Society, the
oldest continuously functioning anthropological
association in the United States, was founded at the
Smithsonian Institution in 1879. Each volume in the
series collects essays written by leading scholars on
aspects of a central topic and originating in a program of
lectures sponsored by the Society.

Library of Congress Cataloging-in-Publication Data
The Politics of culture / Brett Williams, editor.
p.   cm.—(Anthropological Society of Washington
series)
Includes bibliographical references.
ISBN 0-87474-931-X
1. Political anthropology.   2. Culture.   I. Williams,
Brett.   II. Series.
GN492.P66   1991
306.2—dc20                                    90-9610

British Library Cataloguing-in-Publication Data is
available

Manufactured in the United States of America

98 97 96 95 94 93 92 91    5 4 3 2 1

♾ The paper used in this publication meets the minimum
requirements of the American National Standard for
Permanence of Paper for Printed Library Materials
Z39.48-1984

# THE
# POLITICS
## OF
# CULTURE

ANTHROPOLOGICAL SOCIETY OF WASHINGTON

# Contents

# Contributors

DALLAS L. BROWNE
Department of Social Sciences
York College
City University of New York
Jamaica, NY 11451

MICAELA DI LEONARDO
Department of Anthropology
Yale University
New Haven, CT 06520

RICHARD HANDLER
Department of Anthropology
University of Virginia
Charlottesville, VA 22903

LAURA HENLEY
Department of Anthropology
Catholic University of America
Washington, DC 20001

JOHN LEE
Traditional healer
Moncure, NC 27559

ARVILLA C. PAYNE-PRICE
Department of Sociology and
   Anthropology
Howard University
Washington, DC 20059

WILLIAM ROSEBERRY
Department of Anthropology
New School for Social Research
New York, NY 10003

DAVID ROSEN
Department of Anthropology
   and Sociology
Fairleigh Dickinson University
Teaneck, NJ 07666

ROBERT VERREY
Department of Anthropology
University of Hawaii
Honolulu, Hawaii 96822

DAVID E. WHISNANT
Department of English
University of North Carolina at
   Chapel Hill
Chapel Hill, NC 27514

BRETT WILLIAMS
Department of Anthropology
The American University
Washington, DC 20016

# Introduction

*Brett Williams*

T his book began with the annual program that the Anthropological Society of Washington (ASW) presented during its 1986–87 season. The program included individual lectures, a panel discussion about the politics of the past, and a daylong, multimedia celebration of Washington's ties to southern cultural traditions. The program was very much a collective endeavor, as is this book, and I thank the ASW Board members who made both possible: Emlen Myers, Laurie May Trippett, William Leap, Joan Chase, Laura Henley Dean, Patricia Gindhart, Shedd Williams, Grier Greene, Dorothy Angel, Ann Webster, Victor Golla, and Allison Brooks. Jolene Jesse and Michelle Lewis assisted with meticulous editing, and Beth Chambers tactfully and skillfully guided the volume to publication.

We are fortunate to include in this collection the two authors, David Whisnant and Richard Handler, who invented the phrase "politics of culture" and used it early on. In 1983 Whisnant, in *All That Is Native and Fine,* pioneered in both the use of the phrase and the now widely shared ethnographic recognition that seemingly traditional cultures are, in many ways, historical human inventions. Describing cultural intervention in Appalachia, Whisnant argued that settlement workers, folklorists, and other elite northeasterners ignored devastating economic and political change in Appalachia while they romanticized, sanitized, and fed back to residents culture that was not really there. Handler (1988) also explored the politics of culture in earlier work. He has documented the struggle among citizens of Quebec to bound and claim their identity and their past, often through recovering and defining cultural property.

This book is intended to serve two complementary purposes. One is to pay tribute to a year of work and sociability during which ASW members gathered to talk about some of the ways people imagine, mystify, and contest culture for political ends, and invited speakers to engage these topics from many different angles. Anthropologist Geoffrey Burkhart suggested that the subject of discussion was "who gets to say what." The second purpose transcends commemorating a notable year and addresses the interests of a wider audience in preserving and presenting questions of enduring concern to anthropology.

These questions include the following: How do elites invent and inscribe cultural meanings that ordain fractured political realities? How do less powerful groups cross-reference such meanings with their own confusing and possibly contradictory experiences? How do people construct and use the past? How do people compare images of self and community against or with other images received from the outside? How, in short, does politics use, reshape, and express cultural meanings?

I had hoped that each paper included here, representing a revised version of a public lecture, would neatly treat one of the questions. Of course this is not the case: the writers explore topics that reach out to tease, challenge, and bounce off each other. Reality is too messy and the questions too complicated to stay within well-defined bounds. The organization of the book reflects this: Papers interweave, often taking up threads introduced elsewhere, but I have placed them so that each picks up on a provocative theme that emerged in the paper before. In this introduction I want to highlight these themes and also indicate broader questions.

William Roseberry's paper appropriately opens this collection, for he suggests ways to think about culture as a human creation in the context of politics, power, and unequal access to cultural production. He asks us to imagine culture as part of the material world. We are born into circumstances that include culture as it is produced and transmitted through such institutions as mass media and the public schools. Cultural meanings may validate our social experiences, appear to connect to our lives, or inspire confusion, resentment, or resistance. As actors, humans may inscribe meanings in culture, stretch meanings to fit circumstances where they no longer work, and build new meanings as well. Some people have more power than others to shape who gets to say what: Thus, leaders may evoke the Statue of Liberty or remake Martin Luther King to stand in retrospect for varied personal experiences of history.

Part of the power of Roseberry's analysis comes from his emphasis on complexity and disjunction. Members of the same society have different experiences, and attach different meanings to those experiences by generation, time, place, race, gender, class, and ethnicity. Some common understandings and sensibilities emerge, but meaning does not connect directly to the experiences of work, family, and community. Through cultural inscription, selective traditions survive as possible sources of group identity, old language presents history as nature and domination as equality, and narrow definitions bound the ways we value our changing, ambiguous, and often contradictory experiences. Public symbols and cultural meanings thus reflect differences in political and economic power, but elites cannot dominate all cultural production. Roseberry's paper stands as a challenge to ethnographers to probe problematic connections between experience and meaning, politics and culture.

David Rosen's paper, which follows, aptly answers Roseberry's challenge since Rosen discusses the law. The law precisely exemplifies inscription, which refers to the ways by which meanings become lasting and supple enough to accommodate varied circumstances. Many jurists have written that the law transcends petty concerns, personal idiosyncrasies, and social class, framing their decisions with expansive claims of promoting proper social goals and values while remaining within the technical limits of the law.

Rosen tests the jurists' claims by looking at slavery law in North and South Carolina in the years just before the Civil War. He examines a fundamental contradiction of slave society: that a *person* can be a piece of *property*. Because the law protects property rights, judges faced difficulties when individual owners sought to emancipate individual slaves. The humanity of their property paradoxically undermined the owners' rights to dispose of it as they wished. When some emancipated slaves wanted to remain near kin and a familiar community in the Carolinas, judges worried that a growing population of free blacks might increase the possibility of civil unrest and rebellion. Thus, they had to reconcile the technicalities of the law with an ideology that valued the preservation of a slave society.

Rosen's analysis underlines Roseberry's caution against overestimating the ideological unity of the elite. He discovers not a unified, effective resolution of slavery's dilemmas but rather inchoate fragments of case law that tried but miserably failed to give meaning to the actions of judges. He finds conflicts among emancipators, their would-be heirs, trustees who collaborated in transparent scams to free enslaved people through mock trusts, lawmakers who sought similar scams to invalidate those trusts, and slaves who might be kin to some of the above, all over whether to revere individual property rights or to oblige individuals to use their property in certain ways. South Carolina judges emerge as relatively paternalistic, respectful of property, and inclined to regard the human character of such property as a source of strength for the slave system. North Carolina judges in general were concerned about the social control of potentially free slaves and consequently tried hard to perpetuate their status as property rather than people.

Richard Handler's paper also considers the "shelf life" of cultural meanings beyond the originating circumstances and social groups. He discusses a widespread but internally contradictory assumption in the West that individuals are separate, autonomous, and self-sufficient, but also identified and valued by the property they acquire. Individuals are, thus, intrinsically complete yet perpetually incomplete, pressured always to progress and possess. Handler argues that we extend this paradoxical logic of possessive individualism to people in groups and embody the logic in a tired, lame, irrelevant metaphor that encourages both nations and ethnic groups to think in terms of "having" a history or "having" a culture.

This sense that a nation "has" a past elides the conquest, colonialism, revolution, and re-creation that underlie today's continually re-drawn nation-states and proposes instead that each is as bounded, unique, static, and homogeneous as it appears on a color-coded map. Yet this odd formulation seems to dominate ideology and debate about nationalism, history, and culture. Handler traces it through international disagreements about the return of valued museum pieces by First World museums that now possess them to Third World states in whose territory they were found. Handler maintains that cultural-integrity arguments to return these pieces make very little sense because the claimant nations can symbolize only a map-fantasy past of bounded uniqueness through shared property. However, he says, because Western nations exported the metaphor, with its far-flung implications for citizenship, cultural identity, and nationhood, they should also give back the objects.

Handler shows the intensity of the disjunction between some peoples' desire for a shared and enduring identity and the more fractured contours of political history. He argues persuasively against naturalizing today's social groups and inventing static identities projected back into the past.

Robert Verrey and Laura Henley turn our attention from a broad discourse among national elites to narratives and struggles within neighborhoods to construct a unified local identity, reimagine a satisfying and recoverable past, and preserve that imagined past through property. In three communities in and around Washington, D.C., they document disagreements between residents and archeologists over when neighborhood history began, how it proceeded, and how it should be marked. In one case, a neighborhood group chooses a nineteenth-century mansion as its community symbol, remakes its slave-owning resident into a quaint, benevolent, Victorian gentleman, and places the breakup of his estate at the center of its community creation myth. In contrast, archeologists would like to fill out the story with the experiences of indigenous Americans and enslaved blacks and the way a landowner essentially purchased his status as neighborhood icon. In another case, the leaders of an African American community celebrate the founding of their neighborhood by men of color and a long-standing, continuous African American presence in the area, while archeologists would like to depict a more disruptive and problematic past.

In both cases, different groups used material culture to evoke and fight for the past. Verrey and Henley thus remind us that, even on a small scale, the images people build of self and community reflect a dialogue involving other, possibly contending images produced outside, that many feel they must contest undesirable representations of their history and identity, and that we must be aware of whose version emerges.

Verrey and Henley touch also on issues that plague historic preservation in several neighborhoods. They note that visions of cultures as isolated, bounded, and distinct also guide some historical activists. Activists may want a neighborhood history that sets their own community apart, but other versions of the past picture a web of connections to other places and political groups. Neighborhood life reels from (1) changing land-use patterns; (2) fluctuating ownership of agricultural, industrial, and human property; (3) migration, displacement, and the relocation of labor and elites; and (4) national housing policy and the decisions of investors and developers to raze, redline, or introduce devalued development. How do public archeologists reconcile their understandings with some residents' wishes for a more satisfying, identity-bestowing neighborhood story? How do they weigh the history of buildings against the history of people? How do they balance some residents' desires for a simple, homogeneous past and stately procession of events and individuals against the rights of other residents to be included in a more conflicted flow of time or not to "have" any history at all?

Finally, what are the political implications of such icon-ridden, detail-free visions of normative neighborhood history? Verrey and Henley note some positive results: the successful antifreeway movement in Washington in the early 1960s and the current celebration of black community and tradition at a time when much of black Washington is labeled a hopeless pathological wasteland. While these communities never existed in the form some citizens want to re-create, such efforts seem on the surface to harness the politics of culture to useful concepts of communities as more than just commodities. Yet in many parts of Washington, and increasingly all over the world, historic preservation movements and the celebration of a more tasteful and homogeneous past accompany and encourage gentrification, the escalation of property values, and massive displacement and homelessness. How is it that seemingly oppositional ideas about community, identity, and neighborhood are used against neighborhoods? How are cultural resource specialists implicated in these processes? How can the specialists measure the politics of their cultural resource management activities?

Like Verrey and Henley's, my work concerns how people in Washington cast images of community against other images imposed from the outside. As part of a larger study, I examined a neighborhood undergoing gentrification and for a short time integrated with regard to ethnicity, race, and class (Williams 1988). I was interested in the varied ways that residents saw and used the same urban space and especially in the transmission by network television—in the abstract a unifying purveyor of national culture—of skewed but dramatic images of people of one social class to viewers of another. Like other anthropologists today, I believe strongly in exploring a culture by investigating how people reengage and reproduce public culture as it encounters their semi-indigenous traditions (see Appadurai and Breckenridge 1988; Ulf Hannerz, personal communication).

My article here deals with an exception to the strange cross-class role played by television. It examines a brief, but broad, wave of syndicated television cartoons and cartoon character toys, blatantly gendered, that featured banal relational shows for girls and warring teams for boys. Aware of the power of such programming to present straightforward culture for children, I was surprised by the contrary responses. Children used them, ironically, to cross boundaries and form unexpected ties and often remodeled games and play in ways that sabotaged the intentions of advertisers. As William Roseberry argues early in this book, the producers of cultural meanings can neither agree on nor control how the meanings connect with peoples' life experiences. I was struck by a paradox: As children seemingly learned to become slavish consumers of odious toys and television programs, they also drew on that consumption as the source of a subtly liberating generational identity. I could not decide whether to deplore their identification with the cartoon toys or to applaud the ways they exploited the toys to undermine and upend mass culture and adult authority. My article concludes with an expression of appreciation for the contradictions and complexities of at least this version of folk culture.

The next two linked papers, by Arvilla Payne-Price and by Payne-Price and John Lee, continue this concern with folk culture. Anthropologists and folklorists have shown recent enthusiasm for the political possibilities of folk culture, arguing, in part, that folk traditions can enable people who are not dominant or powerful to preserve and celebrate alternative values and customs (Limón 1983; see also Menchu 1983; Recinos 1988; and the more cautious argument in Sider 1986).

Arvilla Payne-Price and John Lee have collaborated for several years. Payne-Price worked on an ethnographic team from Howard University that surveyed African American medical beliefs and practices throughout the U.S. Southeast Lowlands. Through history and the political and economic experiences of blacks in the South, her paper traces the philosophy underlying these traditions. She documents an expansive, entrenched medical system that preserves the past, defines a group, and offers alternative diagnoses, cures, practitioners, and social connections.

In the second paper, with John Lee, Payne-Price helps give voice to Lee's intricate knowledge of traditional healing. The detail and texture of Lee's account testify to the creativity and resilience of folk culture. Lee is a highly regarded and skillful practitioner, firmly rooted in a community that preserves its own meanings within an alien, dominant medical system. Lee and Payne-Price do not argue that the folk practices are heroic or oppositional or that folk culture has here provided a political voice to articulate personal troubles as public issues. The folk medical traditions they describe are not connected to demands for the future or an analysis of the past. Some people are embarrassed to take part in traditional medicine and deny doing so. Also, Lee and Payne-Price do not characterize the folkways as a politically grounded counterculture; they simply portray a rich alternative medical system constructed by people without significant access to dominant institutions.

On the other hand, the former Sandinista government of Nicaragua made a forceful argument for the political possibilities of folk culture. David Whisnant looks at both the cultural desolation wrought by centuries of bitter politics in Nicaragua and the cultural politics that engaged the revolutionary government. He sees a past of great devastation, first, of the indigenous peoples, then of the emerging Catholicized, Hispanicized, urban working classes and peasantry. He discerns many divisions: between classes, between east and west, between urban centers and the countryside; among literary figures who expressed a stifled nationalism, collaborated with Somoza, or identified with the U.S. Beats; and among Nicaraguans enticed by Hollywood, liberal positivism, anticlericalism, or the search for personal wealth.

Whisnant carefully documents this fragmented, global-village past and its bleak cultural harvest for the Sandinistas. Yet he also respectfully records the Sandinistas' search for an indigenous counterculture that served as a source of will and strength during 450 years of mutilating rule. The Sandinistas enlisted folk culture as a vibrant political force in support of the revolution and as the soul of a new "revolutionary culture," believing that the political strength deriving from ties of kin, godparenthood, and community allowed the revolution to succeed in the first place. They traced a heroic, folk-cultural, and political past of indigenous nationalist writers. Their focal Ministry of Culture sponsored poetry workshops, music classes, symphonies and choruses, experimental theater, eulogies, and epics; preserved heroes' homes, supported literacy crusades, libraries, museums, and the celebration of festivals; and encouraged the use of traditional foods and herbal medicines and a reencounter with all things old.

Whisnant thus portrays a vital, energetic effort to draw on the power of the politics of culture to construct a more just society. Yet he measures that energy against the risk that in reconstructing the past the Sandinistas selected democratic, anti-imperialist, and populist traditions, but covered over experiences that were stratified, factionalized, and collaborative. Although the Sandinistas stressed the genius and vigor of folk tradition, Whisnant feels that they may have obscured some persistent divisions and injustices. Thus, the politics of culture both enables and impedes efforts to build a revolution. The Sandinistas mined the new myths for energy but risked being stultified by them.

Of course the Sandinistas were not alone in seeking revolutionary support in a somewhat romanticized and politicized sense of culture. Micaela di Leonardo examines the invented tradition of original matriarchy and the seductive notion that an oppositional women's culture has sustained women during years of patriarchy and nurtured in women patriarchy's opposites: moral maternal connectedness, benevolent loving sexuality, and cooperative social relations. Women's culture theorists argue that women's culture crosses boundaries of race, time, and class, spiritually elevating women above men.

This invented tradition stems in part from intertextuality; readers from a number of disciplines have applied many-layered interpretations to anthropological texts. They have seen in the concept of culture, and in some feminist ethnographies, a way of interpreting women's writing, women's thought, women's morality, and women's folklore. They have seen in some discussions of hierarchy, labor, kinship, and childcare inspiration for a women's culture that transcends history, societies, races, classes, and cultural domains. Di Leonardo is concerned that this transformation of the culture concept denies divisions and differences among women and offers false witness belying a variety of scurrilous female behaviors. She sees this transformation's affinity to the widespread use of cultural symbolism to label complicated human activities. In one example, she discusses the ethnic cultural symbolism that labels Italian American women as moral mothers who nurture large, warm, white ethnic families. Both the transformation of cultural concepts and ethnic cultural symbolism are used to attach moral and political worth to gendered experiences.

Di Leonardo suggests an alternative way to examine gendered experiences: We might acknowledge the male dominance that shapes women's experiences without assuming that patriarchy thus reduces women to a common denominator. For example, Italian American women bear the burden of responding to the moral mother stereotype and to the ways that men embrace it: Often the men believe that they achieve ethnic identity through the labor of the women in their lives who perform the rituals of holidays and feasts and foster family and ethnic fellow feeling. The alternative enables one to examine what women actually do to respond to that gendered burden. Some embrace the stereotype and variously try to gain control and power through "kin work," others refuse to do kin work at all, and many exhibit a complex blend of resistance and consent. The label "Italian moral mother," like the label "women's culture," glosses over the complications and contradictions of what women actually do. One can observe women's agency within the constraints on their lives without approving of all that they do, for example, to perpetuate prejudiced values or manipulate adult children. In short, we must be alert to meaningful differences among women without forgetting that those differences emerge under widespread domination by men.

Finally, di Leonardo points to the larger problem of the failure of culture theory to give adequate consideration to gender as a social force. Like Roseberry's, her article challenges ethnographers to go beyond reporting male privilege, to take note of female agency, and to refine our analyses of culture by taking different perspectives seriously rather than assuming that culture is wholeheartedly shared. Just as notions of power enter into constructions of culture, cultures are rich in different perspectives and subject to many struggles over interpretation as part of larger struggles over social power.

These issues of perspective, agency, and struggle lie at the heart of the problematic topic raised by Dallas Browne, in the last paper of this book. Browne considers the current controversy over female circumcision in Middle Eastern and African societies and confronts those in the West who have expressed concern about the experiences and consciousness of women in those societies who defend the custom. Browne's paper, in a way, fittingly ends the book by touching on many topics previously introduced: the connection between experience and meaning, the politics of the past, the reinvention of tradition, and the extent to which women and men share cultural perspectives. Some feminists in the West have tried to enlist support for women in the Third World who have undergone what appears from the outside to be genital mutilation. Some people—apparently both men and women—in the countries in question have argued for the continuation of such practices; Browne arouses indignation on behalf of those arguments for two reasons.

One reason has to do with the role of circumcision in traditional culture. Among the Kikuyu, where Browne worked, women and men pass from childhood to adulthood through elaborate, culture-rich ceremonies by which they both demonstrate and learn about their adult powers. Although male-dominated, Kikuyu women have found various means of acquiring power and prestige, such as woman marriage, women's councils, managing their husbands' lands, and trading. Female circumcision, by paralleling male circumcision, opened the way to improved status and affirmed a young girl's feeling of participation in and loyalty to the responsible roles and communal duties of her lineage and her culture.

A second reason, however, has to do with history. Browne writes of the double bind imposed on women by British colonialism in Kenya. Colonialism created political and economic opportunities for elite men but excluded women. At the same time British politicians and missionaries helped to deprive women of other avenues to status by attacking as barbaric cultural practices involving gender and family, such as polygyny, bridewealth, and clitoridectomy. An underground counterworld nurtured some of these practices, kept alive a sense of Kikuyu identity under colonial rule, and ultimately spurred rebellions and nationalist passions in the midtwentieth century. Female circumcision became traditional, partly in opposition to missionaries' efforts to westernize Kikuyu families, and has recently come to symbolize revolutionary nationalism and self-determination. Kikuyu women today may be divided in their opinions, but even those who advocate abolition of the custom seem to resent outside criticism of it. Kikuyu women, who do not live in the privileged world of Western education and economic opportunity, face a difficult dilemma: their narrow dual paths to opportunity probably require that they honor their elder kin and embrace tradition.

Browne's discussion raises important questions: Do Kikuyu leaders defend clitoridectomy because it is traditional or because it is historically linked to nationalism? Why has female sexuality become a political boundary marker? Why do Kikuyu *women* have to bear the burdens of tradition and nationalism? How can we know to what extent women and men agree on political practices and alternatives?

I have brought away from my encounter with these papers a somewhat confused sense that the politics of culture seemed simpler before ASW's year of talks. This collection does not conclusively show how culture and politics act on each other, but rather exposes four great cracks in politics-of-culture studies. The cracks seem rich, murky, and treacherous, but life-filled, and I close this introduction by indicating what they suggest for future examination: the messy disjunction between meaning and experience; the schisms between different cultures within a single society; the abyss between the straightforward culture many people apparently want to "have" and the untidy culture pictured by anthropologists; and the chasm between the appeal of the culture concept itself and anthropology's postmodern angst that there is no such thing.

William Roseberry's opening paper traces the tricky gaps and connections among the material world, the production of culture, people's social relations and life experiences, and the meanings that people reach for and that create difficulties for them. My paper on syndicated cartoons reveals, perhaps most tangibly, how culture is indeed part of the material world but, intriguingly, not completely encapsulated by that world. Little boys turn G.I. Joes into dolls; little girls demand a fighting female counterpart to He-Man. Yet, toy manufacturers ultimately sweep all these action-fashion figures from the market. Many of the other papers yield richer interpretations when read in the light of Roseberry's caution that we live our lives within systems of meaning that we both do and do not make or even understand. Imagine, for example, a slave in the late 1850s evaluating her options against the backdrop of a court battle that pits her father's right to place her in trust against her half-brother's claim that to do so would effectively remove her from his proper use. Imagine a Kikuyu girl, in a social world that knows and partly values consumer-oriented global modernity, reviewing her relatives' insistence that clitoridectomy can symbolize tribal tradition and identity.

These papers help to disclose the shifting reins joining meaning to experience and point the way to phenomena needing further interpretation: both the inscription of cultural meanings and the ways meanings can fall apart. David Rosen lays bare the frantic efforts of southern judges to bind unraveling fragments of slaveholding ideology, and David Whisnant presents the Sandinistas hard at work on cultural inscription. Think of the transformed interpretations available for the life experiences of contemporary Nicaraguans surrounded first by U.S. mass culture, then by a revolutionary celebration of the politics of folk, in the counter-context of grinding poverty and an inexorable world system. Whisnant is more concerned with the production of inscription than with how people play ball. However, we need to know still more about how these processes work in peoples' lives. For example, in 1989 Chinese students engaged in one of the most richly mediated political struggles ever, as they tantalized journalists with language and icons from many parts of the world and periods of history (*The Nation* 1989). As we uncover the connections between meaning and experience we face the possibility of joining the study of symbols with the examination of the material world.

These papers also show inescapably that modern societies house many cultures, and that meanings, rather than being static and shared, exist in a video-game world for social groups who play and work with them in struggles for power. Di Leonardo voices this concern in her call for studies of culture that assume multiple voices and disagreements over values. In another and different example, Whisnant writes of many kinds of cultures—folk, traditional, vernacular, indigenous, national, revolutionary, imperialist, and hegemonic—at work in Nicaraguan politics (see also Keesing 1987).

The collection explores incongruent and seriously contested versions of social relations. The papers show that political elites may build and control a great deal of cultural knowledge in modern societies, but they also show the difficulties elites face as they encounter ever-changing historical problems, fight among themselves about solutions, and fend off challenges from outside and below, sometimes rooted in the very meanings the elites have created (see Appadurai and Breckenridge 1988; Lears 1985; Sederberg 1984; Sider 1986).

Many intriguing questions arise: Where, when, how, and why do people fight for and through culture and to what ends? How do people reengage transnational media and help to create a global public culture when both national leaders and dissidents use symbols, metaphors, and language that transcend their immediate political arenas? Lee and Payne-Price describe a strikingly separated medical system kept alive by an otherwise well-encapsulated social group in the Southeast Lowlands of the United States. It seems eminently reasonable to claim for folk culture a prepolitical oppositional status since it honors the social relations we create ourselves, lays claim to shared origins and values rooted there, and bounds a group through profoundly renegotiated cultural meanings. When do people use shared tradition to lay claim to a future? When does culture find a political voice?

What kinds of voices do these culture-based political groups find? Are they always tired, nostalgic, and somewhat retrograde, aping Disneyland versions of gender, nation, community, family, and personal heroism? When do traditions become self-mocking, and when are they used against those who reclaim them? How does the politics of culture go awry so that, for example, a concept that radically criticizes perceived male ways of seeking prestige and power seems to reduce women to biologically determined talents and goals? When does the moment of incorporation come for a once oppositional cultural story that could stop a freeway but can also be used to displace the poor? How are new oppositional identities fashioned out of old, failed quests for an invigorating politics of culture? How, in fashioning identities for ourselves, in finding political uses for our own histories, do we also respect cultural differences and imagine the histories of exotic "others"? Is the politics of culture just a distraction, and would we be better off tackling political issues politically? Why and how does it matter who gets to say what?

These papers also reveal dramatically the chasm between the kinds of cultures various groups seem to want and the kinds ethnographers think they actually "have." The papers show examples where people, for good and bad reasons, fight with historians, ethnographers, other nations, and members of their families to have a fairly straightforward culture. Often these cultural disputes evoke the past. Ethnographers may argue that the primeval matriarchy, Samoa, and the urban village never existed; that cultures are not billiard balls, history not a parade; and that it is intensely problematic to speak of the true meaning or essential character of a culture.

However, the evocation of First World possessive nationalism in Third World states, the Sandinistas' replay of submerged but resistant folkways, the Kikuyu's political recall of female rites of passage, and Deanwood residents' claims to sit atop an enduring African American community, all point to even more interesting questions. What do people think culture is, and why? How do cultural labels get attached to social realities, and how do labeled people deal with value-heavy cultural markers? Who gets to label what, and for what ends? How do *some* decide to speak for the culture of a diverse neighborhood, country, ethnic group, or gender? I believe that we should investigate further the processes by which experiences are loaded with specific meanings called cultural. Lest this sound as if anthropology must become a profession of unmaskers and debunkers, consider the final dilemma.

Another crack lies between anthropology today and the concept of culture itself, which seems to have captured the popular imagination just when many anthropologists hope to abandon it. James Clifford (1988) and many others write convincingly that cultures are ethnographic inventions, even allegories. Kathleen Stewart (1988:229) claims we are "threatened with a deadening pluralism that makes us all just an 'other' among others, in which difference erases into an utter indifference."

Yet we see in this collection of papers that another culture of culture underlies much modern discourse, and we see it elsewhere as well: in the frenzied festival-building of small towns and urban neighborhoods throughout the United States in the 1980s, in the gentrification that now reaches beyond ethnic neighborhoods into the metropolitan countryside; in the specialty shoppes of neo-regional, neo-ethnic malls that occupy old post offices and railroad stations; and in the folk foods that fill supermarket shelves. Conversely, much current discussion on the urban poor seems to assume the existence of an inexorable, pathological "cycle" despite evidence to the contrary. For example, families that do not exhibit an enduring tangle of deviant behaviors are portrayed as having "broken" the imagined cultural cycle.

What can we say about anthropology's stance on the other side of the crack from the concept of culture now that we have helped to inflict our most fundamental construct on the rest of the world? Perhaps one of our tasks must be to understand that there is an important culture of culture and that it both emerges in and evades the global production of culture, the ways people try to recast that culture, and the multiform expressions of culture in political life. As people in many parts of the world grasp the concept of culture and put it to political use, the authors of these papers provide sharp, persuasive evidence that it is important to know precisely who creates what culture, and to what ends. "Who gets to say what" matters.

REFERENCES

Appadurai, Arjun, and Carol A. Breckenridge
    1988    Why Public Culture? *Public Culture* 1(1): 1–4.

Clifford, James
    1988    *The Predicament of Culture.* Cambridge, Mass: Harvard University Press.

Handler, Richard
    1988    *Nationalism and the Politics of Culture in Quebec.* Madison: University of Wisconsin Press.

Keesing, Roger
    1987    Anthropology as Interpretive Quest. *Current Anthropology* 28 (2): 161–74.

Lears, T. J. Jackson
    1985    The Concept of Cultural Hegemony: Problems and Possibilities. *American Historical Review* 90(3): 567–93.

Limón, Jose
    1983    Western Marxists and Folklore. *Journal of American Folklore* 96(379): 34–52.

Menchu, Rigoberta
    1983    *I . . . Rigoberta Menchu.* London and New York: Verso Press.

*The Nation*
    1989    248 (June 12): 800–01.

Recinos, Harold
    1988    *Hear the Cry.* Louisville, Ky: Westminster/John Knox Press.

Sederberg, Peter
    1984    *The Politics of Meaning.* Tucson: University of Arizona Press.

Sider, Gerald
    1986    *Culture and Class in Anthropology and History.* Cambridge: Cambridge University Press.

Stewart, Kathleen
    1988    Nostalgia—A Polemic. *Cultural Anthropology* 3(3): 227–41.

Whisnant, David
    1983    *All That Is Native and Fine: The Politics of Culture in an American Region.* Chapel Hill: University of North Carolina Press.

Williams, Brett
    1988    *Upscaling Downtown.* Ithaca, N.Y.: Cornell University Press.

# CHAPTER I

# Marxism and Culture

*William Roseberry*

The history of anthropology can be written in terms of a series of theoretical oppositions, or antinomies—evolutionism and particularism, science and history, explanation and interpretation, materialism and idealism, and so on. Such expressions are useful in that they help us to organize a mass of material and quickly see what was at issue at a particular moment. They point to areas of tension, irresolvable conflicts between investigators making mutually exclusive sets of assumptions—between, for example, those who take a science of society as their goal and seek precise explanations of social processes and those who deny that such an explanatory science is possible and seek instead an interpretive understanding of social life.

But antinomic thinking carries its own problems. The most obvious is that the presentation of theory in terms of opposed paradigms may oversimplify the actual movement of social thought. More complex or problematic work may be lost or underemphasized, while work that more easily fits the oppositional scheme becomes a part of officially remembered histories. Thus, an Alexander Lesser might be forgotten, a Leslie White easily remembered. A less obvious problem, but perhaps more important for the development of anthropological thought, is that the presentation of our history in oppositional terms may reproduce or recreate the antinomies, fortifying the appearance of mutually exclusive sets of assumptions and foreclosing the possibility of mediation. For Marshall Sahlins, for example, the opposition, which he expressed as a "conflict between practical activity and constraints of the mind," is seen as "an original, founding contradiction, between the poles of which anthropological theory has oscillated since the nineteenth century" (Sahlins 1976:55). His conclusion that mediation of this conflict is impossible, that one must choose sides and get on with it, is hardly surprising given the way he has set out the terms of discourse.

The problem with the "founding contradiction" view is that it collapses the various oppositions one might distinguish into a single grand opposition. To take the examples used earlier, we could present them on a grid of analogous oppositions.

evolutionism        particularism
science             history
explanation         interpretation
materialism         idealism

On the one side we find the materialists, or those who promote "practical reason"; on the other side we find those who seek a cultural account. The arguments used to criticize one of the poles in one of the pairs can then be used to criticize all of the analogous poles in the other pairs. An argument against evolutionism can be seen as an argument against science, explanation, and materialism because they are all part of a single founding contradiction.

The title of this essay would seem to fit well within such a contradiction, giving us another pair for the list, marxism on the left and culture on the right. That I want to suggest ways of mediating the apparent antinomy, that I want to sketch out the possibility of a marxist understanding of culture and a cultural reading of Marx would seem, for some, to pursue the impossible; others might regard this as a gross form of theoretical pretension. But my goals are more modest: I do not pretend that the personal and idiosyncratic understanding sketched here will become some grand synthesis that will finally destroy all of the antinomies of anthropological thought. Many marxists would find the framework presented here too far from an original vision to be marxist; many cultural theorists would find the concept of culture explored here too social and material to be meaningful. Grand synthesis is neither promised nor possible.

Yet mediation is possible if we reject the analogous positioning of the pairs. Before exploring that possibility, let us introduce a more recent opposition—between political economy and symbolic anthropology. Both are rather loose terms used to categorize heterogeneous movements, but most of us have some general understanding of the sort of work that might be given one label or the other. On the whole, political economists and symbolic anthropologists have some room for dialogue between them, and the level of discourse seems to have improved since the time when charges like "reductive" and "mentalist" were casually thrown around. Some political economists and symbolic anthropologists share certain apparent interests—in history, in the study of particular social groups, in the interpretation of social action and movements. Yet they may understand these terms differently, and their anthropological projects are finally, and fundamentally, different. We can easily point to literature on either side that dismisses the work of the other.

Let us concentrate, however, on a recent criticism of political economy from the interpretive side. In a survey of recent anthropological history, George Marcus and Michael Fischer contend that three internal critiques emerged during the 1960s—interpretive anthropology, critiques of the practice of fieldwork, and critiques of the ahistorical and apolitical nature of anthropological work. The first movement "was the only one . . . that had an early and important impact on changing the practice of anthropologists." The latter two "were mere manifestos and polemics, part of the highly politicized atmosphere of that period" (Marcus and Fischer 1986:33). Of work in political economy, Marcus and Fischer assert that it "tended to isolate itself from cultural anthropology's concurrent development of a more sophisticated ethnographic practice on interpretive lines. It retreated into the typically marxist relegation of culture to an epiphenomenal structure, dismissing much of cultural anthropology itself as idealist" (ibid.:84).

By this view, political economy and symbolic anthropology would fit neatly on the grid outlined above, political economy on the left and symbolic anthropology on the right. We can therefore repeat the grid including the additional pairs of terms:

| | |
|---|---|
| evolutionism | particularism |
| science | history |
| explanation | interpretation |
| materialism | idealism |
| marxism | culture |
| political economy | symbolic anthropology |

Recent works within a loosely conceived political-economic literature, however, suggest a much richer interconnection between the concerns of political economy and those of symbolic anthropology than is recognized by those critics who repeat facile dismissals based on old-fashioned antinomies. Let us briefly consider four rather different and interesting books: Benedict Anderson's *Imagined Communities* (1983), William Sewell's *Work and Revolution in France* (1980), Sidney Mintz's *Sweetness and Power* (1985), and Gerald Sider's *Culture and Class in Anthropology and History* (1986). Only two of the authors are anthropologists, and at least one might well reject a connection with political economy. That is not the point; the point is an intersection of the *concerns* of political economy and symbolic anthropology, where both emphasize meaningful action and recognize that actions are shaped by the meanings people bring to them even as the meanings are also shaped by the actions.

Anderson's book is an attempt to grasp the importance of nationalism in the modern world. It views nationalism as a type of "imagined community" and analyzes its rise in the context of the world-historical demise of other types (e.g., religious communities, monarchical realms). The rise of nationalism is also situated in the emergence of what he calls "print-capitalism," a rather nice welding of a political-economic and a cultural argument. Given this world-historical understanding of nationalism as a general phenomenon, he then examines the emergence of particular kinds of nationalism in their more specific historical contexts; nation building in the nineteenth century Americas, nationalism in dominated regions of nineteenth century European empires, late nineteenth century "official" and reactive nationalism at the centers of the empires themselves (e.g., Prussia), and, more recently, nationalism in postcolonial states.

Sewell's book is a reflection on the origins of the concept of a proletariat in France from the eighteenth century to 1848. He calls upon the cultural anthropology of Clifford Geertz (indeed, the book was written at the Institute for Advanced Study) but deals with a set of issues and a political process of profound interest to political economists. He traces the continuities, from the old regime to revolutionary France, in certain forms of association and the language describing association. Of particular interest were the corporations and confraternities that linked journeymen and workers within a particular trade but maintained rigid divisions between trades, thus hindering class forms of association. Despite such continuities in language and association, the meanings of the terms and associations were extended in fundamentally new directions during the first half of the nineteenth century, so that the image emerged of a union of workers as a class, a confraternity of proletarians despite differences in trade. This fundamental shift in meaning and action is in turn understood in terms of the political movements and events from the French Revolution to the revolution of 1848.

Mintz's book is an important contribution to political economy and social history, linking the transformation of Caribbean islands into a series of plantation economies to the changing diet and increasing sugar consumption in England from the seventeenth to nineteenth centuries. Reflections on relative values placed on certain substances, the changing form and meaning of meals, notions of food and sociality, all fit into an analysis that connects England, empire, and slavery in a particular historical period.

Sider's book considers traditions and forms of interaction in the "traditional" outport fisheries of Newfoundland, especially in the nineteenth century. He combines an analysis of work, merchant capital, and social relations between fishermen and merchants with telling vignettes illuminating the psychological consequences of those social relations as well as the creation of traditions (such as Christmas mumming) that express sociality and isolation. If the connection between Sider's fine-grained analyses and some of his more important cultural arguments (e.g., on hegemony) is not always clear to the reader, the book is nonetheless a moving and important contribution. It vividly illustrates the relationships between practices and cultural meaning.

These books are not, strictly speaking, comparable. They deal with different problems in different historical periods and settings and adopt different strategies. But they also have certain common aspects. All approach the relation of meaning to action in a context of unequal power. That is, they have a political element in which, if power is to a certain extent shaped by meaning, meaning is also shaped, quite profoundly, by power. The books are also deeply historical. They place their observations within precise historical contexts and examine the shaping of meaning and power over time. It should also be noted that none of the books can be made to fit on our grid of founding oppositions in anthropological theory without the loss of all that is special and distinctive about their contributions.

Let us return, then, to the terms in the antinomic grid and sketch a framework for considering marxism and culture that can include the work of Anderson, Sewell, Mintz, and Sider. I do not mean to suggest that any of these authors would agree with such a framework. Indeed, I would expect disagreement. Nonetheless, I think such a framework will allow us to come to an appreciative reading of these works and move beyond the "founding contradiction" view of anthropological theory. We begin by removing the marxism-culture opposition from the list, precisely because their interrelationship is what we are attempting to explore. I also remove the science-history opposition because it is based on a special, and especially narrow, understanding of history and can be understood only in terms of the anthropological oppositions between evolutionism and particularism, and between explanation and interpretation. My approach is historical, but not in the sense implied by a science-history opposition. Rather, it is materialist and simultaneously political economic and symbolic. It rejects both evolutionism and particularism and tries to place itself between the extreme versions of explanatory scientism and interpretive self-absorption.

That is, while rejecting the explanatory-scientific goal of postulating a set of transhistorical laws of history or evolution, it remains resolutely materialist, seeing ideas as social products and understanding social life as itself objective and material. Its approach to public symbols and cultural meanings therefore places these symbols and meanings in social fields characterized by differential access to political and economic power.

I

The materialism called for here is not the sort that comes from a quick reading of Marx's well-known "Preface" to *A Contribution to the Critique of Political Economy:*

> In the social production of their existence, men inevitably enter into definite relations, which are independent of their will, namely relations of production appropriate to a given stage in the development of their material forces of production. The totality of these relations of production constitutes the economic structure of society, the real foundation, on which arises a legal and political superstructure and to which correspond definite forms of social consciousness. The mode of production of material life conditions the general process of social, political and intellectual life. It is not the consciousness of men that determines their existence, but their social existence that determines their consciousness. (Marx 1970:20–21)

This is the classic and most influential statement of Marx's materialism. While most marxists agree with some aspects of it, it has had unfortunate consequences. First, although it seems to begin with people ("men"), it moves quickly to structures: relations of production, economic structure of society, mode of production. These structures then act upon, or "condition," other structures (the political superstructure and consciousness) seen as secondary or derivative. Whether one's approach to the relationship between these structures is mechanical or dialectical, the structural hierarchy remains intact. Later passages of the Preface apply this structural hierarchy to an explanation of the evolutionary shift from one mode of production to another. Thus, a pervasive and tenacious version of marxism, rooted in the words of Marx, would amply justify the inclusion of marxism-culture on the grid of founding contradictions.

In other passages, however, Marx offers a different starting point for his materialism. For example, in *The German Ideology*, a text with its own problems as Sahlins (1976) and others have shown, the basic premise offers more possibilities for an understanding of culture:

> The premises from which we begin are not arbitrary ones, not dogmas, but real premises from which abstraction can only be made in the imagination. They are the real individuals, their activity and the material conditions under which they live, both those which they find already existing and those produced by their activity. . . . This mode of production must not be considered simply as being the production of the physical existence of the individuals. Rather it is a definite form of activity of these individuals, a definite form of expressing their life, a definite *mode of life* on their part. (Marx and Engels 1970:42)

Several aspects of this materialism, as expressed in this passage and later in *The German Ideology*, deserve mention:

First, this materialism starts not with nature or a postulated economic structure, but with a human population; not with matter, but with the social conceived as material.

Second, the materialism is active. People enter into definite relations with themselves and with nature, but simultaneously transform both nature and themselves. Nature and the social world, then, are always socially constructed, historical.

Third, in Marx's conception of activity, the most fundamental activity is that associated with production. But his conception of production was never narrow, for example, merely the production of subsistence. Rather, production is "a definite form of activity of these individuals, a definite form of expressing their life, a definite mode of life."

Fourth, the materialism is historically situated; the forms of activity and modes of life are the products of prior forms of activity and modes of life:

> History is nothing but the succession of the separate generations, each of which exploits the materials, the capital funds, the productive forces handed down to it by all preceding generations, and thus, on the one hand, continues the traditional activity in completely changed circumstances and, on the other, modifies the old circumstances with a completely changed activity. (Ibid.:57)

Only in light of the four previous comments can we now suggest an interpretation of a fifth aspect of this materialism—its approach to consciousness. In *The German Ideology*, Marx and Engels constantly contrast their approach to that of classical German philosophy, and in the starkest possible terms:

> We do not set out from what men say, imagine, conceive, nor from men as narrated, thought of, imagined, conceived, in order to arrive at men in the flesh. We set out from real, active men, and on the basis of their real life-process, we demonstrate the development of the ideological reflexes and echoes of this life-process. (Ibid.:47)

Any materialist must first assert a connection between being and consciousness, but Marx and Engels's conception of this connection has two unfortunate aspects. The first, in the "reflexes and echoes" expression here and elsewhere, places us once again in the realm of hierarchical structures, with primary forces and derivative products. The second, in the description of consciousness as arising *directly* from material activity, is, in part, a consequence of their attempt to tie their statement of premises to an evolutionary speculation, so that consciousness is introduced as part of a discussion of the first supposedly genuine human acts. Yet if we understand material activity in the broader sense suggested above—production as fabrication of a whole way of life, itself part of a historical process—then we need a more historical and less derivative understanding of consciousness.

Two suggestions from Marx's work in other contexts point to his use of this more historical and less derivative understanding. The first comes from the well-known passage in *Capital* in which Marx talks about the specifically human character of productive labor:

> A spider conducts operations which resemble those of the weaver, and a bee would put many a human architect to shame by the construction of its honeycomb cells. But what distinguishes the worst architect from the best of bees is that the architect builds the cell in his mind before he constructs it in wax. At the end of every labour process, a result emerges which had already been conceived by the worker at the beginning, hence already existed ideally. (Marx 1977:284)

At the least, this suggests a simultaneity or unity of activity and consciousness, hand and brain, thus challenging the derivative view expressed in *The German Ideology*. But here consciousness is still tied directly to a material activity or object. For a more historical understanding, we can turn to another well-known passage from yet another work.

At the beginning of *The Eighteenth Brumaire*, Marx makes his famous observation that "Men make their own history, but not of their own free will; not under circumstances they themselves have chosen but under the given and inherited circumstances with which they are directly confronted" (Marx 1974:146). Most people who cite and think about this passage apply it to the relationship between structure and agency, or between historical determination and human activity (to call up some more antinomies). It is seldom noted that Marx's observation introduces a comment on the weight of ideas in a historical process:

> The tradition of the dead generations weighs like a nightmare on the minds of the living. And, just when they appear to be engaged in the revolutionary transformation of themselves and their material surroundings, in the creation of something which does not yet exist, precisely in such epochs of revolutionary crisis they timidly conjure up the spirits of the past to help them; they borrow their names, slogans and costumes so as to stage the new world-historical

scene in this venerable disguise and borrowed language. . . . In the same way, the beginner who has learned a new language always retranslates it into his mother tongue. (Ibid.:146–47)

This text, and the larger work it introduces, are instructive for marxists who would reduce their marxism to a set of formulas, or rules for pedants. The book is an attempt to analyze the political events surrounding the movement in France from a republican revolution in February 1848 to the Bonapartist coup in December 1851. One sees here the engagement of Marx's method with actual political and historical materials, which are not made to fit into some narrow and preconceived scheme—the two great classes of capitalist society give way to a series of competing and combating class fractions. The particularities of the French case—the history and structure of the state, the relative lack of industrial development, the social position of the peasantry, the role of Bonaparte—are all included in Marx's analysis. The epochal or evolutionist materialism of the "Preface" and *The German Ideology* has given way to a historical materialism that starts with "real individuals, their activity and the material conditions under which they live, both those which they find already existing and those produced by their activity."

More to the point, among the material conditions under which they live is included a set, or sets, of ideas, themselves historical products, that serve as material forces. Here we are reminded of Raymond Williams's (1977) telling criticism of the sort of mechanical materialism that might come out of the "Preface," with hierarchical structures of base and superstructure. The problem, he said, is not that this materialism is too materialist but that it is not materialist enough. It fails to see that culture is itself material.

The kind of materialism proposed here, then, is not one that appropriates and subsumes culture and consciousness within an expanding material base but one that starts with a given population and the material circumstances that confront it, and includes culture and consciousness among the material circumstances to be examined. This approach to symbolic analysis is one that most cultural theorists in anthropology would not accept. It seems to grant culture no autonomy and to reduce it to a derivative product of human activity. But the assertion of autonomy can be understood only in terms of a structural hierarchy. In this sense mechanical materialism and a cultural theory that denies the materiality of culture are complementary reflections of each other. Each starts in a structural universe removed from "real individuals, their activity and the material conditions under which they live" and directs questions to relationships (or the presumed lack of relationships) among structural levels.

The "autonomy" of culture, in my view, comes not from its removal from but its connection to the material circumstances of life. As one of many products of prior activity and thought, culture is among the material circumstances that confront real individuals born in a concrete set of circumstances. As some of those circumstances change, and as people attempt to conduct the same sorts of activities under new circumstances, their cultural understandings affect the way they view both their circumstances and their activities. It may imbue those circumstances and activities with an appearance of naturalness or order, so that the utterly new may appear to be a variation on a theme. In this sense, people's activities are conditioned by their cultural under-standings, just as their activities under new circumstances may stretch or change those understandings. Culture's autonomy, and its impor-tance, rest on this dual character: Although meanings are socially pro-duced, they may be extended to situations where a functionalist might say they do not fit, or they may be applied even after the circum-stances and activities that produced them have changed. This is not to call up the old notion of "cultural lag," which would imply that the lack of fit is temporary and that at some point functional correspon-dence will be regained. Here Geertz's (1980) notion of inscription, or the removal of cultural meaning from the *immediate* circumstances of its creation, is especially appropriate. Because action takes place in meaningful contexts—that is, because people come to their actions with prior understandings and act in terms of them—a materialism that saw consciousness arising solely and directly out of activity would be especially impoverished. Culture is at once socially constituted (it is a product of present and past activity) and socially constitutive (it is part of the meaningful context in which activity takes place).

For example, a white boy growing up in a southern city in the 1950s and '60s would be coming of age in a situation of ferment, of changing economic, political, and social circumstances. Yet he might experience these circumstances in the context of a family trying to raise him in a certain way, to reproduce a certain style of life and set of values. He might be learning what it is to be a boy or young man, to be white, to be an American, to be a southerner (or an Arkansan, or a Georgian), to be a Methodist, and so on, at a time when what it means to be all of these things is changing. He would learn these things in changing institutional settings—schools, churches, his family—each of which has developed a particular form of discourse for talking about the world, and each of which is undergoing rapid change. His ideas about race, or sex, or class, or nation would be conditioned by events, but the events would be interpreted in terms of a religious language that emphasizes justice, morality, giving unto Caesar that which is Caesar's, or of a high school civics language that emphasizes ideas about equality, democracy, and freedom. Yet the attempt to talk about new events with old language and meanings stretches the language and develops new meanings.

It should be stressed that this understanding of action and meaning is not akin to Sahlins's (1985) discussion of the "structure of the conjuncture" and the dialectical relation between structure and event. It differs in that (a) its understanding of culture is much less structural and systemic, and (b) it sees this concatenation of structure and event as a constant process, one in which culture is constantly being shaped, produced, reproduced, and transformed by activity, rather than one in which culture encapsulates activity until the structure of culture can no longer hold. Thus the *meaning* of being a southerner would be different for a southern white boy who grew up in the '30s and '40s than for one who grew up in the '50s and '60s, which in turn would be different than for one who grew up in the '70s and '80s. In each case people would be trying, through families and institutions, to reproduce a way of life during a time when local, national, and global events (we could produce a superficial list) were altering the *experience* of life in the South in profound and intimate ways.

But there is, of course, more. The experience of a southern white boy of the '30s or '50s or '70s would be different from that of a southern white girl, or a black boy or girl, or a youngster from the country or the city, or from a sharecropper's or a cotton planter's family. More to the point, some of the experiences of these young people and the events to which they respond would be common (let us say shared), and some would be utterly different.


II


The attempt to understand these commonalities and differences takes us from the experience of persons (though we must return) to the analysis of institutions and structures. It takes us to political economy, first for analysis of social relations based on unequal access to wealth and power. Thus far our discussion of the material nature of ideas and meanings and of the relationship between activity and consciousness has left this dimension out of account. Yet if ideas and meanings are themselves material products and forces, they too are caught up in hierarchical relations based on differential access to wealth and power. Let us return to *The German Ideology* and another well-known and infuriating passage:

> The ideas of the ruling class are in every epoch the ruling ideas, i.e.,
> the class which is the ruling *material* force of society, is at the same
> time its ruling *intellectual* force. The class which has the means of
> material production at its disposal, has control at the same time over
> the means of mental production, so that thereby, generally speak-
> ing, the ideas of those who lack the means of mental production are
> subject to it. The ruling ideas are nothing more than the ideal expres-
> sion of the dominant material relationships, the dominant material
> relationships grasped as ideas; hence of the relationships which
> make the one class the ruling one, therefore, the ideas of its domi-
> nance. The individuals composing the ruling class possess among
> other things consciousness, and therefore think. Insofar, therefore,
> as they rule as a class and determine the extent and compass of an
> epoch, it is self-evident that they do this in its whole range, hence
> among other things rule also as thinkers, as producers of ideas, and

regulate the production and distribution of the ideas of their age: thus their ideas are the ruling ideas of the epoch. (Marx and Engels 1970:64)

This passage is at once suggestive and problematic. Let us begin with one of the suggestive aspects and connect it with Gramsci's (1971) notion of hegemony or Raymond Williams's (1977) concept of dominant culture. The concept refers to a complex set of ideas, meanings, and associations, and a way of talking about or expressing those meanings and associations, that depict circumstances of inequality and domination as if they were ones of equality and reciprocity, and make a product of history appear to be a natural condition. A powerful element in such a dominant culture will be a particular and highly selective version of a people's history, what Williams calls a selective tradition. Such a tradition or history will be taught in schools and expressed in television programs. Thus, differential access to power is crucial in the determination of control over the means of cultural production, the means for the selection and presentation of tradition.

But what makes this hegemony *culture* and not simply ideology is that it appears to connect with the experience and understanding of those people who do not produce it, people who lack access, or have sharply diminished access, to wealth and power. Here, paradoxically, it is important to return to Geertz's notion of inscription, to the removal of meaning from direct experience and activity, not as part of an argument that culture is separate from relations of inequality and domination, but as an essential part of our understanding of its connection to them. In hegemonic processes, events experienced by dominant groups produce traditions, meanings, and forms of discourse that are extended, with apparent success, to groups who could not have experienced those events or who would have experienced them in profoundly different ways. In the process a common set of assumptions and selections from "our" tradition can emerge despite the fact of differentiation. Thus, the Statue of Liberty, which can serve as a meaningful symbol only for a fraction (if sizeable) of the population, is, in the process of official celebration, transformed into a symbol of the nation, a nation in which we "all" were immigrants. Or, as part of the official celebration of Martin Luther King's birthday, his actual activities and the struggles in which he participated disappear from view. He becomes not the black man who struggled for racial justice, who upset the status quo and was murdered, but the Reverend Doctor who died for peace—a kind of midtwentieth-century black Jesus who lived an exemplary life, died for our sins, and can be elevated to a place in our pantheon of civil-religious heroes.

This notion of hegemony is important for any political-economic understanding of culture and requires much more analytical attention than it customarily receives. Here I differ from those marxist and socialist writers who are uncomfortable talking about hegemony because it seems to rule out resistance, or because it seems to suggest a consensual society based on shared values. First, such writers romanticize working-class and other subaltern forms of experience and culture, granting them a heroism that makes it difficult to understand "unheroic decades" (Williams 1979). Second, they make too direct a connection between class and culture, so that the working class is seen to have its own culture, based on its own experience of work and community. Such a view poses two problems. First, it implies much too direct a connection between meaning and experience and ignores the political implications of cultural inscription, the separation of meaning from experience in the context of domination. Second, it ignores the ambiguous and contradictory nature of experience itself, which can produce only a contradictory consciousness. As Gramsci expresses it, the "man-in-the-mass"

> has a practical activity, but has no clear theoretical consciousness of his practical activity, which nonetheless involves understanding the world in so far as it transforms it. His theoretical consciousness can indeed be historically in opposition to his activity. One might almost say that he has two theoretical consciousnesses (or one contradictory consciousness): one which is implicit in his activity and which in reality unites him with all his fellow-workers in the practical transformation of the real world; and one, superficially explicit or verbal, which he has inherited from the past and uncritically absorbed. But this verbal conception is not without consequences. (Gramsci 1971:333)

Nonetheless, simply to describe hegemony or dominant culture as it has thus far been sketched in this presentation would be insufficient, for it grants to culture much too coherent and systemic a quality. To understand its lack of coherence and system, we can return to two passages in the quotation from Marx and Engels on ruling ideas. Let us begin with the sentence "Insofar . . . as they rule as a class and determine the extent and compass of an epoch . . . they do this in its whole range." In their language, Marx and Engels have rendered problematic a relation that many marxists treat as automatic. Elements of a dominant class are split by lines of cleavage and conflict. Such a class is seldom so united or homogeneous as to "determine the extent and compass of an epoch." Even a dominant culture, then, contains elements of tension and contradiction. Aspects of a selected tradition may be rejected or differently valued by different groups among those who control the means of cultural production—witness the conflicts over NEH or NEA funding policies, or over interpretations of the Vietnam War on public television.

Neither, however, should our understanding of hegemony be limited to those who produce dominant culture and ignore those who appear to consume it. To do a slight turn on one of Marx and Engels's phrases, "The individuals composing the subordinate class possess among other things consciousness, and therefore think." If culture is inscribed, if meaning can be removed from direct experience, such inscription and removal can never be total. If some meanings produced by the dominant culture seem to connect with, or at least not contradict, the experience of ordinary people, other meanings may directly conflict with lived experience. That may not matter in normal circumstances, or not matter deeply. In unusual circumstances, such disjunction may be the focal point for the production of new and alternative meanings, new forms of discourse, new selections from tradition, or conflicts and struggles over the meaning of particular elements within tradition. Martin Luther King's birthday again provides an example here: first the struggle over the designation of the day as a holiday, the inclusion of a black man as a national hero; then more recently, and crucially, the struggle over the meaning of his life for "us"—the official attempt to sanitize his life and other attempts to make King a symbol of opposition and struggle. The outcome of these struggles is by no means obvious, and the most important arena will be in public schools, the central forum for the production and modification of a selected tradition. "The line between dominant and subordinate cultures," Jackson Lears notes, "is a permeable membrane, not an impenetrable barrier" (Lears 1985:574).

Let us return to our original example, that of cultural production in the U.S. South. We now have a framework for talking about—but not for reducing to neat formulas—culture and experience in southern United States. It requires, first, the recognition of differential experience, that experience is different for different persons and groups— white and black, male and female, rural and urban, sharecropper and planter, particular generations in particular times and places—and the differences must be understood not only in terms of individuals' lives but also in terms of structures of inequality and domination. Yet it also requires a recognition that across this differential experience, and to a certain extent across time, some common understandings emerge, along with common forms of language and modes of interaction, common sensibilities of place and history. The burden of the discussion of political economy has been to stress that these commonalities are produced through a variety of institutions and means of cultural production (which themselves vary across time)—churches, schools, 4-H clubs, county and state fairs, state celebrations of centennials and sesquicentennials, books, magazines, television, and the like—and that the production or shaping of culture occurs in the context of unequal access to power. But I have also tried to stress that these common understandings and modes of interaction can never encompass all of differential experience. Cultural production is not limited to those who control the means of cultural production. Experience constantly intrudes. Despite the apparent inscription of common understandings and modes of interaction, then, "southern culture" was different in the '30s from what it had become by the '50s or the '70s. And in each of these decades, the *experience* and *meaning* of southern culture was quite different for differently situated individuals. Such discordant experiences had direct effects on events in the South, e.g., on the civil rights movement of the '50s and '60s, which in turn had a profound effect on "southern culture." The attempt to constantly place culture in time, to see a continual interplay between experience and meaning in a context in which both experience and meaning are shaped by inequality and domination, requires a much less structured and systemic understanding of culture than that prescribed by our most prominent cultural theorists.


III

But political economy has another aspect, at least as it has developed in anthropology over the past two decades—its historical aspect, the attempt to understand the emergence of particular peoples at the intersection of local and global histories, to place local populations in the larger currents of world history. Thus the different shapes of southern experience in the '30s, '50s, and '70s would be understood, in part, in terms of the national and global events and movements that had affected that experience. Social relations marked by differential access to wealth and power, then, are understood in world-historical terms. To discuss this aspect of political economy, we must leave behind our consideration of meaning and experience, not because they are irrelevant but because the structure of experience is so much more complex than has thus far been indicated. Just because the word and concept of "culture" are not obviously present in what follows does not mean that the comments are irrelevant to an understanding of culture. The basic framework for talking about culture remains the same, but the more complex structure of experience requires an even more complex approach to the production, shaping, and inscription of meaning.

Historical political economy does not assert simply that particular societies are part of world history. It also asserts that the attempt to draw rigid cultural boundaries around, say, the South, the Navajo, the Ojibwa, the Tsembaga, the Nambiquara, or the Chamula is to reify culture. Because populations are not formed in isolation, their connections with other populations and, perhaps, with the larger currents of world history, require attention. To ignore these connections is to treat societies and cultures like billiard balls, in Eric Wolf's telling phrase (1982: 6).

This political-economic perspective on history, and the connections between apparently distinctive anthropological subjects within that history, dictate our rejection of both extremes of the evolutionism and particularism antipodes. Both took the billiard-ball view of culture as a starting point. Particularists argued that each billiard ball had its own history, understandable on its own terms. Evolutionists placed the billiard balls in an evolutionary game that followed certain rules (laws) by which a scientist could explain the trajectories of the balls themselves. Historical political economy shares the evolutionistic sense that the particular is part of a world-historical process, but differs from evolutionism in key respects.

First, the evolutionists' view is not radical enough to the extent that it still accepts boundaries around particular cultures and seeks generalization by fitting the particular into specific levels on an evolutionary ladder. Such a view ignores the constant shaping of the particular by the evolutionary process itself, the remaking of the "folk" in the civilizational process, the creation of (perhaps egalitarian) peripheries in the process of state formation. Two recent attempts to reinterpret Edmund Leach's analysis in *Political Systems of Highland Burma* (1954) nicely demonstrate this difference between historical political economy and evolutionism. That both reinterpretations are avowedly marxist, and come from two rather different understandings of marxism, makes the example all the more interesting. In 1975, Jonathan Friedman applied his systems theory marxism to an attempt to use Leach's material as a meditation on state formation. Looking at various populations in highland Burma, he tried to view the movement from *gumlao* to *gumsa* to Shan as an example of the process and problem of state formation. In doing so, however, he regarded all the populations as distinct units directly related to an ecosystem, without examining interconnections between the presumed units. More recently, David Nugent (1982; cf. Friedman 1987) tried to interpret the gumlao-gumsa cycle in terms of the incorporation of the Kachin Hills in long-distance trade routes, their apparent relation to the opium trade, colonial attempts to cut the routes or remove the Kachin Hills from them, and so on. That Leach despises both reinterpretations is not very important for the point we are making. We have here two rather different attempts to place the particular in a larger context; one fits the particular into a putative evolutionary scheme, and the other attempts to understand the shaping of the particular by a larger historical process.

Historical political economy would view evolutionism as *too* radical, however, in another sense. From the perspective of historical political economy, we now have world history, and we must understand the particular, at least in part, in terms of that history. But we have not always had world history, which is itself a historical product. Or, rather, we have had a series of world histories, centered in civilization foci, the vast majority of which have not been truly global. If populations generally live in webs of relationships, in complex connection and interconnection with other populations, those webs are not necessarily and have not always been global. Global history comes with the expansion of the world market, which "produced world history for the first time" (Marx and Engels 1970:78), and with the subsequent incorporation of regions within colonial empires or spheres of capitalist investment, a history well sketched by Wolf. The incorporation of local populations within a world market or within empires, and the effect of such incorporation upon these populations, differ (or are "uneven") in space and time. Thus, world history of this sort came to Latin America sooner than to China and is being extended to some other regions (e.g., parts of Melanesia) only in our lifetime. Any attempt to view particular populations in terms of historical political economy, to explore the formation of populations in terms of local and global histories, must take this unevenness into account. As any careful reading of Wolf would indicate, incorporation within the world market, or the introduction of capitalist social relations, does not set a local population en route to an unalterable or predictable series of social or cultural changes.

It should be noted, however, that historical political economy is not without its important anthropological critics, especially in its approach to culture. One widespread view is best expressed, perhaps, in Sherry Ortner's concern that the attempt to write a political economic history reduces other cultural realities to Western experience and Western historicities. Noting various strengths in a political economic perspective, she finds its major weakness in its "capitalism-centered

worldview," its attempt to place a variety of societies and social relations within a capitalist world economy. She writes:

> The problems derived from the capitalism-centered worldview also
> affect the political economists' view of history. History is often
> treated as something that arrives, like a ship, from outside the soci-
> ety in question. Thus we do not get the history *of* that society, but
> the impact of (our) history *on* that society. The accounts produced
> from such a perspective are often quite unsatisfactory in terms of
> traditional anthropological concerns: the actual organization and
> culture of the society in question. . . . The political economists,
> moreover, tend to situate themselves more on the ship of (capitalist)
> history than on the shore. They say in effect that we can never
> know what the other system, in its unique, 'traditional,' aspects,
> really looked like anyway. (Ortner 1984:143)

While Ortner has isolated a genuine problem in political economic (as
well as other) approaches to history, her statement of the problem
precludes a resolution of it. The dilemma for anthropologists is to
view the people we study as *in some way* connected with a wider world
that includes capitalist relations without reducing social and economic
processes within those societies to processes of world history or capital
accumulation. The resolution of that dilemma cannot be to set aside,
even temporarily, the wider world, to reassert the disjunction between
"us" and "them" and claim that "A society, even a village, has its own
structure and history, and this must be as much part of the analysis as
its relations with the larger context" (Ortner 1984:143). If the rejection
of an overly capital-centered and deterministic view leads to the contention that one can isolate a society, a history, or a culture from its
larger context, to understand it "on its own terms" and *then* place it in
context, then one has replaced one simplistic view with its opposite
extreme. Yet this seems to be what Ortner is proposing, and the
evocative imagery of ship and shore supports such a vision. It perpetuates a disjunction between *our* history and *their* history that finally,
regardless of which extreme one starts from, is reductive. And it
returns us to a grid of anthropological antinomies.

But if we consider again the four books mentioned earlier, we see examples of work that is sensitive to the issues we have considered and that render Ortner's objection moot. These books consider the shaping of social meanings in specific historical situations and in the context of relations of power. Each of the specific historical situations is seen in world-historical terms most clearly, but not exclusively, in the work of Mintz and Anderson. Mintz carefully links the creation of Caribbean plantation economies to changing patterns of consumption and sociality in England, while Anderson sees nationalism arising at a particular moment in global history. Yet all four studies are sensitive to the particular, and none attempts to reduce the particular to a variation on a capitalist theme. The way in which they link the global and particular makes the ship-and-shore, us-and-them, our-history-and-their-history imagery used by Ortner especially inappropriate. They point, then, toward an understanding of culture as historical product and historical force, shaped and shaping, socially constituted and socially constitutive.

Like the works considered here, historical political economy is not readily compatible with a scientistic search for transhistorical laws. Nonetheless, the perspective outlined here does have a strong sense of determination. Because its materialism rejects the hierarchy of structures and takes as its starting point real individuals and the conditions in which they live, the determination here adduced is not concerned with the shaping of superstructure by base, even in the putative last instance. Rather, I have in mind a historical determinism, the dependence of action and the consequences of action on the conditions in which that action takes place, conditions that are themselves the consequences of prior activity and thought. Real individuals and groups act in situations conditioned by their relationships with other individuals and groups, their jobs or their access to wealth and property, the power of the state, and their ideas—and the ideas of their fellows—about those relationships. Certain actions, and certain consequences of those actions, are possible, while most other actions and consequences are impossible.

These determinative pressures and limits are quite powerful, especially at present. If we step back from the activity of individuals and consider the formation and action of institutions, we can see a definite shape and direction in the historical process. But the shape and direction of history, and the determinative pressures and limits that give it that shape, are not predictable in a scientist sense. The starting point is always conditioned activity, and even if a large range of actions and consequences is ruled out, a range of actions and consequences remains possible, some of which cannot even be imagined, either by the actors or by those who attempt to understand their action. We need to allow for the creative and sometimes surprising activity of human subjects living conditioned lives and acting in conditioned ways, with results that have a determined and understandable shape. Sometimes, also, under conditions not of the subjects' choosing and with results that cannot be foreseen, they may create something new—whether the concept of a nation or a proletariat, or the practice of Christmas mummery.

## REFERENCES

Anderson, Benedict
  1983    *Imagined Communities*. London: Verso Press.

Friedman, Jonathan
  1975    "Tribes, States and Transformations." In *Marxist Analyses and Social Anthropology,* ed. Maurice Bloch, pp. 161–202. London: Malaby.
  1987    "Generalized Exchange, Theocracy and the Opium Trade." *Critique of Anthropology* VII(1):15–31.

Geertz, Clifford
  1980    "Blurred Genres: The Refiguration of Social Thought." *American Scholar* 49(2): 165–79.

Gramsci, Antonio
  1971    *Selections from the Prison Notebooks*. New York: International Publishers.

Leach, Edmund
  1954    *Political Systems of Highland Burma*. Boston: Beacon Press.

Lears, Jackson
  1985    The Concept of Cultural Hegemony: Problems and Possibilities. *American Historical Review* 90(3): 567–93.

Marcus, George E., and Michael M. J. Fischer
    1986    *Anthropology as Cultural Critique: An Experimental Moment in the Human Sciences*. Chicago: University of Chicago Press.

Marx, Karl
    1970    *A Contribution to the Critique of Political Economy*. New York: International Publishers.
    1974    The Eighteenth Brumaire of Louis Bonaparte. In *Surveys from Exile,* ed. David Fernbach, pp. 143–249. New York: Vintage.
    1977    *Capital,* Vol. 1. New York: Vintage.

Marx, Karl, and Frederick Engels
    1970    *The German Ideology*. New York: International Publishers.

Mintz, Sidney
    1985    *Sweetness and Power*. New York: Viking.

Nugent, David
    1982    Closed Systems and Contradiction: The Kachin in and out of History. *Man* 17(3): 508–27.

Ortner, Sherry
    1984    Theory in Anthropology since the Sixties. *Comparative Studies in Society and History* 26(1): 126–66.

Sahlins, Marshall
    1976    *Culture and Practical Reason*. Chicago: University of Chicago Press.
    1985    *Islands of History*. Chicago: University of Chicago Press.

Sewell, William
    1980    *Work and Revolution in France*. New York: Cambridge University Press.

Sider, Gerald
    1986    *Culture and Class in Anthropology and History: A Newfoundland Example*. New York: Cambridge University Press.

Williams, Raymond
    1977    *Marxism and Literature*. New York: Oxford University Press.
    1979    *Politics and Letters*. New York: Schocken.

Wolf, Eric R.
    1982    *Europe and the People without History*. Berkeley: University of California Press.

# CHAPTER 2

# Willing Freedom

## Law, Culture, and the Manumission of Slaves in North and South Carolina

*David Rosen*

This paper examines the norms and values embedded in the judicial interpretation of the civil law of slavery and especially the laws that controlled the use and disposition of slaves as property. Its specific focus is one issue in the civil law, namely attempts by slave owners to evade prohibitions against the private emancipation of slaves. The cases below show that in this area of the law, and possibly in other areas, the legal system has never been able to develop a coherent view of slavery or the slave system. Although some individual judges did hold clearly articulated views of slavery and its laws, slave law as a whole, at least as it emerged as case law made by judges, contains different and contradictory views of slavery and of the role of law in maintaining the slave system. Indeed, examined as a whole, judge-made law in this area seems less a logical and rational construction than a symbolic system composed of inchoate and fragmented bits of ideology that gave shape and meaning to the actions of judges.

The law, as Clifford Geertz (1983:173) has put it, is a "distinctive manner of imagining the real." It is a normative system in which legal rules, modes of interpretation, facts, evidence, and policies are all socially constructed. A judicial opinion is, from this perspective, a formal symbolic representation in which judges try to make sense of what they do and to convey their understanding to society in a generally comprehensible way. All judicial opinions, especially those at the appellate level, require a judge to provide a complex rationale that weaves together the technical requirements of the civil law and the judicial interpretations of the needs or goals of the larger society.

Many great American jurists have been aware of the complexity of judicial decision making. As Justice Cardozo (1979) put it, "logic, history, custom, utility, are the forces which singly or in combination shape the progress of the law." However, jurists have been loath to examine how social class and status distinctions mar the judicial process. This occupational disability is occasioned by the ideological fact that law is supposed to be universal, to transcend human social distinctions and not be a party to them.

Historians, by contrast, have been less reluctant to examine the legal system as a function of social class. British historians E. P. Thompson (1975) and Douglas Hay (1975) convincingly demonstrated that the law is frequently an instrument of political terror and oppression. The deification of property and enactment of extraordinary capital crime legislation as twin pillars of justice in seventeenth-century Britain comprise but one example. The American historian Edmund Morgan also showed that the contradiction between the reality of class oppression and the liberal ideal of freedom and universal justice created strong ideological tension within the British and American legal systems. Easy recognition of the contradiction between the ideology of freedom and the reality of class oppression in America was masked by the fact that in America the oppressed were not a white working class but an "alien race" of black slaves (Morgan 1975). Nevertheless, the contradiction between freedom and slavery infected judicial decision making and legislative action. Southern jurists could never coherently resolve the problem of reconciling slavery and freedom.

While some scholars have argued that the South as a whole was heading in the direction of a unified worldview of slavery other empirical studies of judicial case materials suggest that judicial opinions regarding the nature of slavery as well as the role of the judiciary in maintaining the slave system were radically different both within and between states (Nash 1979, Morris 1982). The challenge to scholars dealing with the social significance of slave law is to account for these differences in ways that go beyond the ideological idiosyncrasies of individual judges. This is not to deny that certain widespread beliefs about slavery held sway throughout the South. To be sure, most Southerners (indeed most Americans) firmly believed in the inferiority of blacks. Most Southerners believed in slavery and, even if they did not applaud its excesses and injustices, did not perceive it to be immoral or unjust per se. In a world where the racial superiority of white people seemed as natural as the passing of the seasons, it was not hard to find justifications for slavery. But except for a firm commitment to the "peculiar institution" itself, and to notions of racial superiority in general, such justifications could take many different forms, often shaped by local experiences of the slave system. One problem that remained paramount in the eyes of the judiciary was social control of the black population and the effect of state action on the nearly sacred rights of slave owners to control their own slaves.

The existence of slavery continually raised the issue of social control of the black population. Slavery turned much of the South into a "kingdom of fear" in which the specter of race warfare haunted the popular imagination. By the beginning of the nineteenth century, fear of slave revolt permeated the South. Indeed, the possibility of slave revolt was no mere fantasy. Aptheker (1983), for example, found records of about 250 slave revolts since the beginning of slavery in the United States. Moreover, slave revolts grew in intensity at the beginning of the nineteenth century and were especially disturbing in Virginia and North Carolina.

White fear of enslaved blacks was matched only by the fear of free blacks. In fact, throughout the South free blacks were typically regarded as more subversive than slaves to the rule of white society. This fear led to widespread repressive legislation, coupled with the liberal application of capital punishment, to forestall the possibility of slave insurrection. States also tried to control the growth of the free black population by limiting the right of owners to emancipate their slaves.

Throughout the antebellum South, the issue of private emancipation led to conflict between the individual property rights of slave owners and the desire of the state to exercise direct social control over the black population. Legislators in states, such as North Carolina, that felt most threatened by a free black population placed the heaviest legal strictures upon the property rights of slave owners. A fairly compliant judiciary vigorously enforced legislative restrictions on such rights. Elsewhere, in states such as South Carolina, the judiciary fought a strong battle to protect the rights of individual slave owners from legislative interference with the right of emancipation. Needless to say, judges and legislators in both states asserted that preservation of the slave system was their ultimate goal. In the end, as the nation drew nearer to civil war, fear of a free black population dominated the politics of the time, and virtually all southern states made individual emancipation legally impossible.

Despite increasing legislative and judicial curbs on private emancipation, many slaveholders continued to emancipate slaves. They had many reasons. Slaveholders freed slaves because of democratic ideology and/or abolitionist sentiment; for religious reasons; because of long-standing personal ties of loyalty between master and slave; or because they were the kin, often the biological fathers, of slaves. Whatever their reasons, the desire of slave owners to emancipate slaves brought owners into conflict with a legal system that imposed more and more restrictions on their rights.

Slave owners who wished to free slaves had several choices. They could remove their slaves to a free state and emancipate them there; in many states this could be accomplished by writing a will with emancipatory provisions to take effect on a slave owner's death. In many states slave owners also had the option of sending freed slaves to Liberia. While the option of removing slaves to a free state was widely available and legal, by contrast great legal obstacles inhibited freeing slaves within a slave state. State legislatures, increasingly fearful of a free black population within a slave state, created more and more restrictive provisions. Also, many slaves wanted to remain at or near their homes and to maintain ties with their kin. Owners could illegally emancipate their slaves, and in many places in the South local custom permitted such slaves to live as free persons. But this type of freedom did not enjoy the protection of the law and was always subject to challenge. As a result, many slave owners sought novel solutions to the problem of freedom. One solution, the subject of this article, was the legal trust. Through the device of the trust, slave owners sought to quasi-emancipate or give de facto freedom to slaves who could not be legally freed within a slave state.


## THE LAW OF TRUSTS

A trust is a conveyance of property—real or personal—that places one person's property in the hands of another for the benefit of a third person. The conveyor of property is usually called the settlor or grantor, the one who holds the property is called the trustee or grantee, and the person benefited is called the beneficiary. A trust can be created by will or by deed. Those created by will take effect upon the death of the grantor. Those created by deed, termed living, or intervivos, trusts, take effect upon the delivery of the deed instrument to the trustee. When property is given in trust it is accompanied by certain obligations (the "terms" of the trust) which the trustee is bound to fulfill to ensure that the property is managed in the way specified by the grantor.

Once a trust is created, rights to the property are distributed between the trustee and the beneficiaries. So-called legal title is given to the trustee to carry out the terms of the trust and to hold the property for the benefit of the beneficiaries. So-called equitable title is given to the beneficiaries, who from the time the trust is created become the only persons who can enforce the terms of the trust in a legal proceeding.

Slave owners who sought to free slaves through this legal device placed terms and conditions in the trust that would result in de facto freedom for slaves. These "freedom trusts" could include terms permitting slaves to farm land or to hire out their own time, which gave them as much freedom of movement as permitted under the slave regime—allowing slaves to work and support a family. In general, the freedom trust was designed to give a slave as much local and personal autonomy as was practical where true freedom was legally impossible. Needless to say, in order to achieve this goal slaveowner-grantors sought potential trustees who could be counted on to carry out the terms of the trust. These could be reliable friends of the grantor or institutions such as churches (very often Quaker Meetings) that had strong abolitionist sentiments.

Trusts, however, were far from a perfect solution to the problem of manumission. Threats to this arrangement came from two sources: first, state legislators and judges who saw the trust as a means of circumventing antimanumission laws, and second, the kin and heirs of the grantor, who often saw such trusts as depriving them of property. Thus conveyances in trust often set the stage for a major legal battle between the state and the individual and between the trustees of the property and the kin of the grantor. The outcome was freedom or slavery for the slaves held in trust.

The basic rule of law governing the creation of trusts is deceptively simple: A trust exists when a grantor properly manifests an intention to impose enforceable duties on a trustee to deal with property for the benefit of another. Modern trust instruments, usually written by attorneys, are drawn to clearly express this intention. In contrast, most of those involved in the slave cases were home-drawn instruments that courts subjected to strict scrutiny. The courts interpreted the "intent" of the grantor from both the language of the deed or will and the circumstances surrounding the creation of the instrument. So even when the terms "trustee" or "trust" appeared, a court did not necessarily consider them conclusive evidence of the existence of a trust.

Every court faced three major problems in interpreting such instruments. First, it had to determine whether or not the legal instrument created a trust as opposed to a gift or sale of property. Second, it had to decide whether the trust was valid. Third, if the trust was invalid, the court had to fashion an appropriate remedy.

These issues can be illustrated by a few examples. Suppose the terms of a will were as follows: "I hereby give to my husband my slave Joshua and request that he labor for the benefit of our children." Do these words create a gift or a trust? Typically, testators use precatory language—language of hope and expectation—in making devises and bequests in a will. The interpretive issue before the court is whether the language imposes a mandatory enforceable duty upon a trustee or merely expresses a hope or wish not intended to be binding. Its practical implications are that if it is a trust, the trustee holds the property for the benefit of another; if it is a gift, the named individual holds the property for self-enjoyment.

Even clearly intended trusts can fail for other reasons. The reason is frequently a legal technicality, such as the failure to name a beneficiary, but trusts also fail if their nature violates public policy. In addition, trusts designed to abet a criminal or tortious act (such as paying the fine of a beneficiary who commits a crime) or to support a person who lives in adultery with the settlor can also be voided as a matter of law. Courts facing these situations had two broad choices. They could apply either the so-called resulting trust doctrine or the "clean hands doctrine."

If the court determines that the creation of a trust violates public policy, application of the resulting trust doctrine will return the property to the settlor/grantor or, if the latter is deceased, to the estate or heirs at law. Thus the resulting trust doctrine removes the property from the hands of the trustee. If the court decides that the trust was created for a sufficiently illegal purpose, application of the clean hands doctrine means that the court will refuse to grant any relief to either the settlor or the beneficiary. The practical effect of this decision is the exact opposite of the resulting trust doctrine, because by refusing to intervene, the court permits the property to remain in the hands of the trustee.

For the slaves, the way the court characterized an invalid trust meant the difference between slavery and freedom. Ironically, a trust found to be merely a breach of public policy merited judicial intervention and the invocation of the resulting trust doctrine. This meant removal of the slaves from the control of the trustee into the hands of the estate or heirs at law, that is, back into slavery. In contrast, a trust deemed sufficiently illegal to be subject to the clean hands doctrine remained untouched by judicial intervention. Here, by default, the slave remained in the hands of the trustee and in the state of de facto freedom intended by the grantor. The next section of this article shows how the judicial view of the nature of slavery influenced the application of these technical aspects of the law of trusts.

PARADIGMATIC CASES

This section compares the way the court systems of two southern states, North Carolina and South Carolina, applied the law of trusts to slave cases. Although these cases hardly represent the full range of legal opinion in these states, they highlight how judges used contrasting and contradictory legal strategies to handle problems posed by slaves held in trust. As the cases show, North Carolina judges employed a variety of legal devices to prevent the creation of de facto freedom by trust law. North Carolina saw the logic of slavery as requiring the law to recognize nothing but the total subjugation of the slave. In contrast, South Carolina judges, at least until the years immediately preceding the Civil War, did not find the kind of de facto freedom created by trust law to be inconsistent with the slave system and the rights of the slave owner.

*North Carolina and the Doctrine of Resulting Trusts*

The main legal strategy of North Carolina courts was to find freedom trusts invalid and, using the resulting trust doctrine, to return the slaves involved to the condition of slavery. A typical illustration is the case of *Stevens v. Ely* (1830).

*Stevens v. Ely* was a North Carolina case in which a woman named Letitia Gardner conveyed her slaves, a woman and her children, to the defendant Ely for a small sum of money. The terms of the trust were that "Ely, his heirs, etc. shall from time to time, permit . . . [them] and their increase to live together upon his . . . land, and to be industriously employed, and continue to exercise a controlling power over their moral condition and furnish them with the necessities and comforts of life" (*Stevens v. Ely* 1830:497).

The central issue before the court was whether to allow the conveyance to stand or to declare the trust wholly ineffective, which would create a resulting trust. The court could have treated this case in several ways. For example, it could have determined that the conveyance was not a trust but a gift or sale and determined that its wording was merely precatory language of hope and expectation. The practical effect of such analysis would be to leave the slaves in the hands of Ely, presumably enjoying de facto freedom. Instead, the court determined that it was a failed trust, void by virtue of public policy against the emancipation of slaves. Here again, however, the court had to find a remedy that would return the slaves to slavery. Had the court determined that Letitia Gardner's motives in creating the trust were clearly evil, it would have had to refuse to give assistance to her estate and heirs, and the slaves would still have remained in the hands of Ely. Instead, the court had to find a middle ground that would permit judicial intervention. It found such a ground in its nineteenth-century view of the sensibilities of women:

> We cannot say that her hands are unclean and therefore that we cannot aid her [Recall that Letitia Gardner is deceased and that her estate and heirs will be the true beneficiaries of the court's decision]. . . . For sensitive as we are and ought to be as to whatever may interfere with our laws on the question of slaves, and however we may seek to punish those, who, in the most remote manner attempt to weaken the bonds by which we hold them yet these sensibilities are not aroused or acted on against a single female, who from feelings of kindness towards her three or four slaves, or from feelings of conscience, endeavours to better their condition . . . and who . . . did not intend to offend against the law. (*Stevens v. Ely* 1830:500)

Thus the court found the trust invalid, created a resulting trust, and returned the slaves to slavery as the property of Letitia Gardner's heirs.

North Carolina courts applied this strategy to nearly every case where they could find the existence of a trust. Even gifts or outright transfers that the courts imagined would create a condition of de facto freedom were analyzed within the scope of resulting trust doctrine. In *Redmond v. Coffin* (1831) the testator left a will conveying slaves to the Quakers under the following terms:

> I give and bequeath them [the slaves] unto the Society of Friends of the New Monthly Meeting, or their agents and successors. I also give and bequeath all the personal property of my estate to the

above named black people to be sold equally and divided among
them.

Obviously, the court was already suspicious of slaves held by Quakers. But Quakers did possess slaves outright, and it was by no means
illegal for them to do so. In this case, for the court to deny conveyance
to the Quakers it had to find an attempted trust even in the absence of
specific trust language.

The court's analysis here is striking. It essentially invented a trust
in order to invalidate it. Even though no trust language was found, the
fact that the will contained a bequest to slaves (i.e., the personal property of the estate) permitted the court to hypothesize that the testator
meant to create a trust. The court could then invalidate this hypotheti-
cal trust and return the slaves to the heirs at law. In this and many
other cases, resulting trust doctrine was a powerful legal tool that the
courts used to defeat virtually any potential de facto freedom.

## South Carolina and the Discretion of the Slaveholders

In contrast to North Carolina, South Carolina appellate courts did
everything possible to permit slave owners the widest discretion in the
conveyance of slaves. *Carmille v. Carmille* (1842) involved the sale
under a deed of trust of several slaves who were the illegitimate children of the grantor. The lower court in *Carmille* saw the case as an
attempt at illegal emancipation. The choice for the Court of Appeals
was exactly the same as in *Stevens v. Ely* (1830) in North Carolina: (1)
Void the deed as creating an illegal trust and return the property to the
grantor and/or his heirs under the resulting trust theory, or (2) treat
the language of the trust as precatory or as unenforceable limitations
on the grantee's rights of ownership.

The court found two reasons for refusing to create a resulting
trust. First, it tentatively accepted the "clean hands" argument rejected
in *Stevens,* stating that if in fact the act of transfer had been a fraudulent
attempt at emancipation, the plaintiffs, now legally standing in the
shoes of the grantor as his heirs at law, were improperly asking to be
relieved from this fraudulent act. Second, and even more important,

was the court's narrow reading of the legislative acts prohibiting emancipation; the court argued that the legislation did not specifically void deeds purporting to require emancipation, unless emancipation had actually taken place. In the court's view, emancipation could not take place until the grantee actually gave up possession of the slaves. Despite the liberal terms of the trust, the grantee still, in fact, had legal possession of the slaves. De facto freedom was a sham, since an unemancipated slave, i.e., a slave still in the possession of his or her owner, remained a slave. Thus the court allowed the trust to stand, and the slaves were allowed their de facto freedom.

The line of thinking in *Carmille* was further developed in *Broughton v. Telfer* (1851). *Broughton* also involved an attempt at manumission through a trust creating a state of quasi-emancipation. In this case the father of six slave daughters attempted to emancipate them by deed of trust. The deed declared that "being unable to emancipate them, he desired to give them the benefit of their labor, and to suffer them to enjoy, as far as practicable, all the privileges of free persons." Thus, for the sum of five dollars he conveyed them to Telfer and others under the terms that they

> treat them with kindness; protect them in their just rights; exact from them no wages; permit them to go where they please, and to appropriate to their own use the proceeds of their time and labor; and, on further trust, that if any attempt be made to enslave them, to convey them to some non-slave holding state. (*Broughton v. Telfer* 1851:432)

Although the court upheld the legality of the trust, its decision provided an ironic twist. In the court's view, the conveyance of slaves by deed of trust, though valid, practically discharged the grantee from fulfilling the terms of the trust. If the trusts were legal, the beneficiaries were slaves. Because slaves had no legal standing in court, there was no way for them to compel the proper execution of the terms of the trust. If the trusts were illegal, they were void as trusts, but the grantee retained full ownership rights in the slaves under the clean hands doctrine. So the execution of the trust remained entirely dependent upon the benevolence of the trustee. In strong contrast to the North Carolina cases, no resulting trust was created in the South Carolina cases. The actual conveyance remained as intended by the grantor.


## RULES OF LAW AND THE JUDICIAL PERCEPTION OF SLAVE SOCIETY

What accounted for these differing judicial strategies in dealing with freedom trusts? The evidence from the cases suggests that judges, like others in the South, could hold distinctly different views of the nature and purpose of slave society. Here I distinguish differences between the cases on the basis of two broad cultural dimensions: 1) the meaning of slave property, and 2) social control of slave labor.

### The Meaning of Slave Property

*North Carolina: "A Stern Policy"*    In North Carolina, courts found freedom trusts void because the use of the slaves anticipated in the trusts did not conform to judicial concepts of slave property. The judicial concept of emancipation appeared to depend upon using a slave in ways inconsistent with the idea of property.

In *Stevens v. Ely* the court pointed out that it was not important whether the object of the parties was to emancipate the slaves or, in fact, to keep possession of them under the rather liberal terms of the conveyance. The important issue was that the trusts excluded the idea that the trustee hold the slaves as property. Thus the trusts were inconsistent with North Carolina notions about slave property (*Stevens v. Ely* 1830:499).

In other cases courts attempted to determine exactly what was meant by slave property. In *Redmond v. Coffin* the court, in fashioning a compensatory remedy for the owners of slaves held in trust, determined that the illegal trustees owed the rightful owners the profits that could have been exacted from the slaves' labor. It was no defense, in the court's view, to claim that the slaves worked for themselves during the time they were held under the terms of the void trust, since, as a matter of both law and public policy, slaves had no right to work for themselves (*Redmond v. Coffin* 1831:429).

Finally, in *Lemmond v. Peoples* (1848) the court defined the economic rights and duties of the slave owners. In this case the testator conveyed a slave and her child to a free black for the sum of six hundred dollars. The slave and the free black were actually husband and wife. The testator wanted them to be able to remain together after his death and was afraid they would be separated by his heirs. Although the court recognized that "the property" was in the hands of the defendant, the defendant's use of the property was not sufficiently absolute and unconditional to deny the claim of the heirs. A slave, in the court's view, must be held as absolute property, requiring the "exacting of moderate labor from them as humane masters" (*Lemmond v. Peoples* 1848).

*South Carolina: "Kindness to Slaves"*     The view of South Carolina courts was remarkably different from that of North Carolina courts. Instead of focusing on the use to which slave labor was put, they stressed possession as the key issue in determining the rights of the parties. In *Carmille v. Carmille* (1842) the court noted that "to constitute emancipation . . . there must be a 'parting with the possession of the slaves by the owners.' " Here the court asked how it was possible to interpret even the most liberal terms of a trust as creating emancipation. Even a trust permitting slaves to work for their own maintenance, paying the owner just a dollar a year, still involved a "constant recognition of servitude." The object of antiemancipation legislation, in the court's view, was not to deprive owners of the right to do what they please with their slaves so long as they do not confer freedom—the parting with possession (*Carmille v. Carmille* 1842:468).

In South Carolina, possession conferred ownership, regardless of how loosely possession was defined. A trust, having conferred legal title, conferred virtually all the benefits of ownership. Once a title holder was in possession, the courts were loath to regulate the manner in which slaves could be used. How slave property was to be used was a problem that concerned the slave owner or trustee and not the court. Thus, in another case the court could clearly say "the executors have

not forfeited their rights as absolute owners, from their faithfully
fulfilling the wishes of the testator, [but] neither would they have done
so if they had subjected the [slaves] to the severest servitude" (*McLeish
v. Burden* 1847). In contrast to the North Carolina courts, which were
eager to define the nature of slavery as a matter of law and public
policy, the South Carolina courts appeared to be content with allowing slave owners to define the use of slave property as a matter of
individual discretion.

## Social Control of Slave Labor

North Carolina courts also differed from South Carolina courts in
their perception of the problem of control of slave labor. The question
was whether (1) the master–slave relationship should be defined totally
by the master, backed by a stern legal system, or (2) control was an
issue to be resolved between masters and slaves alone.

From the earliest cases North Carolina courts understood quasi-
emancipation to be a dangerous threat to the safety of the Commonwealth. The courts frequently emphasized the necessity of a stern
policy. A free black population was regarded as a threat to the morality
and peace of society, and laws against quasi-emancipation were designed to ensure that slaves were kept under the "dominion and immediate ordering of the master."

Here again the contrast with South Carolina is striking. In
*Carmille* the court, rather than embracing a stern policy toward slaves,
asserted:

> Kindness to slaves is the true policy of slave owners, and its spirit
> should go (as it generally has) into the making of the law, and ought
> to be the ruling principle of its construction. Nothing will more
> assuredly defeat our institution of slavery than harsh legislation
> rigorously enforced. On the other hand, as it hitherto has been with
> all the protections of law and money around it, it has nothing to fear
> from fanaticism abroad or examination at home. If . . . a man dared
> not to make provision to make more comfortable faithful slaves,
> hard indeed would be the condition of slavery. For then, no motive

could be held out for good conduct; and the good and the bad would stand alike. (*Carmille v. Carmille* 1842:470)

This ideological discussion by the court is interesting for its Janus-faced approach; the "kindness to slaves" language and the concern for motivating good behavior in slaves through legal constructions show that slaves were recognized as something more than mere chattel. But the reasons for recognizing slaves as human were not so much humanitarian as practical. "Kindness to slaves" was a good legal policy for the preservation of the social/economic order.

CONCLUSION

These cases show that appellate courts in North and South Carolina held different views of the nature of slavery and that these views were important in determining which rules of law were applied in dealing with the problem of quasi-emancipation. Both court systems were committed to maintaining the slave order. Both were opposed to emancipation per se of slaves.

A cursory reading of the material might suggest that the different judicial approaches amount to nothing more than the difference between applying the carrot or the stick to control the slave population. But underlying the two approaches was the recognition that the humanity of the slave could serve as either a threat to or a source of strength for the slave system.

Courts in North Carolina from the earliest times perceived the presence of free and semifree blacks as a major threat to the social order, and this belief indeed contained some truth. South Carolina courts, at least until approximately 1850, still clung to the notion that slavery required some kind of legally recognized paternalistic or symbiotic relationship between master and slave. By the onset of the Civil War, the South Carolina Court of Appeals, like many lower courts in earlier years, abandoned this philosophy in favor of the North Carolina approach. The ideology of the South Carolina courts finally succumbed to the threat of slave revolt and rebellion. But until the last decade of slavery the judicial imagination was driven by two distinctively different images of the slave system. Moreover, it is hard to imagine that, in a complex social order like the slave South, judges could not bring many other models of slavery into the judicial decision-making process. After all, the day-to-day practical concern of judges was how to make slavery work.

## REFERENCES

Aptheker, Herbert
    1983    *American Negro Slave Revolts*. New York: International Publishers.

*Broughton v. Telfer*
    1851    24 S.C. Eq. (3 Rich Eq.).

Cardozo, Benjamin
    1979    *The Nature of the Judicial Process*. New Haven: Yale University Press.

*Carmille v. Carmille*
    1842    16 S.C. (2 McMullen) 454.

Friedman, Lawrence
    1985    *History of American Law*. New York: Simon & Schuster.

Geertz, Clifford
    1983    *Local Knowledge: Further Essays in Interpretive Anthropology*. New York: Basic Books.

Genovese, Eugene
    1974    *Roll, Jordan Roll*. New York: Vintage Books.

Hay, Douglas
    1975    *Albion's Fatal Tree*. London: Allen Lane.

Johnson, M., and J. Roark
    1986    *Black Masters*. New York: Norton.

*Lemmond v. Peoples*
    1848    41 N.C. (6 Ired. Eq.) 137.

*McLeish v. Burden*
    1847    22 S.C. Eq. (3 Strobe Eq.) 225.

Morgan, Edmund
   1975       *American Slavery, American Freedom.* New York: Norton.

Morris, D.
   1982       As If the Injury Was Affected by the Natural Elements of Air, or
             Fire: Slave Wrongs and the Liability of Masters. *Law and Society
             Review* 16: 569–97.

Nash, A.
   1979       Reason of Slavery: Understanding the Judicial Role in the Pecu-
             liar Institution. *Vanderbilt Law Review* 32: 7–218.

*Redmond v. Coffin*
   1831       17 N.C. (2 Dev. Eq.) 438.

*Stevens v. Ely*
   1830       16 N.C. (1 Dev. Eq.) 497.

Thompson, E. P.
   1975       *Whigs and Hunters.* London: Allen Lane.

Tushnet, M.
   1981       *The American Law of Slavery.* Princeton: Princeton University
             Press.

# CHAPTER 3

# Who Owns the Past?

## History, Cultural Property, and the Logic of Possessive Individualism

*Richard Handler*

e are a nation because we have a culture." So said a Quebec high school student, explaining to an English-Canadian television audience why French Canada considers itself a distinct nation with a distinct identity. We can substitute the word "history" for "culture" in the student's formulation, since people use the same metaphor of possession to depict the relationship between their nation and its past, as in phrases like "the nation's history" or "this nation has a long history." In the present essay I argue that we must take these metaphors of possession seriously. Rather than discount them as trite or lifeless, let us use the powers of cultural analysis to raise them to life, to make us reflexive about certain themes that are central to modern culture but, precisely because of their centrality, are usually overlooked. Pursuing such a tactic, I will show why such expressions as "cultural property" and "who owns the past" must be interpreted in terms of what has been called "possessive individualism" (Macpherson 1962).

Modern Western culture places a high value on the individual. In the explicit cultural wisdom that most modern citizens can recite, individualism entails the equality, freedom, and uniqueness of each person; it also entails opportunity, talent, competition, achievement, just reward, and so on. But certain aspects of modern individualism are less apparent to common sense, and it is these that merit analysis.

First, the modern individual is expected to be a self-sufficient and self-contained monad. Each of us stands, or should stand, on his or her own two feet, as the cliche has it. Each of us is, or has the potential to become, a complete human being. As Montaigne wrote in 1585, at the beginning of the modern era, "Chaque homme porte la forme entière de l'humaine condition" (1962:222), which I translate as "Each man embodies the human condition in its entirety."

To understand the uniqueness and, perhaps, strangeness of these cultural beliefs, we must follow such authors as Tocqueville (1835) and Louis Dumont (1966), who contrasted our individualistic culture to cultures that value social hierarchy. In a culture such as European Christianity during the Middle Ages, it would have been blasphemous to pretend that an individual was complete per se, a monad. To the medieval mind it was obvious that any human person or, indeed, any tree, rock, flower, or angel, was merely a tiny element in God's vast creation, each such element deriving its value from its place in the whole. Moreover, all such places were ranked relative to all others: hence no equality, but all the elements of creation ordered, from the highest to the lowest, according to their distance from God. Such a world sounds alien to us, and perhaps unfair. But we must endeavor to see our own conception—that each separate individual is complete—as equally strange; as creatures who depend on both our physical and social environment, we are obviously not alone, apart, and complete (cf. Bateson 1971).

One further comment on this modern monad: One is not only complete in oneself, one is *completely oneself*. By this I mean that we conceive of the individual person as having, as we say, "an identity." Identity means "oneness," though it is oneness of a special sort. *Webster's New Collegiate Dictionary*, 1980 edition, defines "identity" as "sameness in all that constitutes the objective reality of a thing" (p. 563). In other words, as an individual one is completely and uniquely oneself, through and through, only oneself, nothing but oneself, and, note well, objectively oneself.

The second aspect of modern individualism that I want to bring to awareness is its possessive element. In modern culture an individual is defined by the property he or she possesses. I do not have space to develop this point extensively, but let me suggest Locke's *Second Treatise of Government* (1690) as a key cultural document with regard to this point. In Locke's theory, the origins of society (he called it "civil society") are to be found in natural human acquisitiveness. That is, humans, as Locke depicts them, seek naturally, without the promptings of any cultural teaching, to subdue nature and to transform her bounty into private property. Thus, society, or social rules, are necessary in order to regulate the interrelationships of property-owning individuals and, in particular, to allow individuals to enjoy their property and rights without being molested by other individuals similarly endowed yet always seeking more. For our present purposes, the point is that property is thought to be intimately connected to human individuals, whose most basic instincts compel them to create it. Individuals who do not lust after accumulation, who do not seek to "improve" or conquer nature, were thought in Locke's day to be savages or degenerate specimens of the race. (In the United States, the politics of welfare suggests that this conception still obtains.)

There is a tension or contradiction between individual completeness and individual possessiveness, and this brings me to the third aspect of modern individualism that I want to discuss. The modern individual can never be at ease, can never be satisfied or fulfilled, because modern culture has enshrined endless progress, endless development as a value as potent as simple individualism. Each of us is said to be a complete and worthy human being, but each is also told to become ever more complete and worthy. We must never stop growing, learning, developing, seeking to realize our greatest potential and to fulfill ourselves. "Be all that you can be," says a recent recruitment jingle for the U.S. military. Such instructions hold in the material as well as the spiritual domain, and most of us strive for an ever greater degree of material comfort, or to possess more possessions. As Tocqueville wrote of the American citizen in 1835, "Besides the good things that he possesses, he every instant fancies a thousand others that death will prevent him from trying if he does not try them soon. This thought fills him with anxiety, fear, and regret and keeps his mind in ceaseless trepidation" (1955:145).

The completeness and apartness of the individual, the individual's relationship to property, and the contradiction between completeness and the drive to acquire ever more property—these, then, are three aspects of modern individualism that I want now to apply to the question of who owns the past. To do so, we must make a conceptual jump, to recognize that the individuals pertinent to the present discussion are not single humans but ethnic groups and nations. Louis Dumont (1970) argued persuasively that in modern culture nations (and, I would add, ethnic groups) are imagined as "collective individuals." Each nation or group is imagined to be bounded and apart, and internally homogeneous. This is obvious from a glance at any modern map, which uses dark, unbroken lines to portray the boundaries between nations, and which fills in the interior of each bounded unit with a different color. These cartographic conventions suggest, first, that each nation is unambiguously separated from its neighbors; second, that each nation, colored differently than its neighbors, possesses a unique identity and culture; and third, that each nation, of one and only one color, is internally homogeneous.[1]

Granted that, in the logic of modern culture, groups can be imagined as though they were individuals, we must consider the possessive element of modern individualism as it relates to groups. A group's most prized possessions are said to be its culture and history. Any spokesperson for a nation or ethnic group will tell you what the Québecois high school student said, "We are a nation because we have a culture"—"it is our culture and history, which belong to us alone, which make us what we are, which constitute our identity and assure our survival."

From this perspective, that of self-conscious cultural nationalism, the notion of survival is crucial. It is precisely the ethnic activists' belief that their group's survival, its identity or objective oneness over time, depends upon the secure possession of a culture, that renders debates about who owns the past so passionate. Here let me open a parenthesis in order to explain that "culture" and "history" become nearly synonymous in such debates. This is because a group's history is said to be preserved and embodied in material artifacts, such as buildings, works of art, ceremonial objects, and antiques. All such objects are coming to be known by the term "cultural property," which implies the possessive individualism I am stressing. In other words, a group's existence as a unique individual is believed to rest upon its undisputed possession of property, and that property often comes in the form of historically significant objects. Nations and ethnic groups prove their existence and their worth to the entire world by cherishing their property. It is but a short step from cherishing to "developing"—hence the proliferation of museums and historic-preservation legislation, as well as the competition among nations, including relatively impoverished ones, to demonstrate that they have truly "world-class" cultural monuments and museums.

As an extended example of one type of dispute over ownership of the past and of cultural property, consider a debate that is currently lively in museums and the international art and antiquities market, that between "restitutionists" and "retentionists" (Dummett 1986). The debate concerns cultural treasures from around the world housed in metropolitan museums. Retentionists argue for the right of museums now possessing such treasures to retain them indefinitely, while restitutionists believe that some of those cultural treasures ought to be returned to their places of origin. The restitutionist position (my chief concern in what follows) rests on three arguments, concerning (1) cultural identity, (2) aesthetic integrity, and (3) fair play. Though I favor the restitutionists, I believe that their first and second arguments are of dubious value though for different reasons, to be explained in what follows.

The cultural-identity argument of the restitutionists reproduces the Western ideology of possessive individualism while ostensibly promoting cultural diversity. Restitutionists say that dispossessed nations or ethnic groups have a right to the cultural property stolen from them. They say that the identity and continuity of the plundered cultures depend upon reacquisition of those life-preserving pieces of property. Thus in 1976 a Unesco panel formulated the principle that "cultural property is a basic element of a people's identity," and argued for "the return to their countries of origin of certain items of overriding importance for cultural and historical identity, for the personality and the spiritual values of particular peoples." Two years later a second Unesco panel recommended, in addition to restitution, "the establish-

ment of representative collections in the countries whose cultural heritage has been dispersed" (Robinson 1980:56). The entire argument is
neatly summarized by a Unesco official who described the loss of
cultural treasures as "a deprivation of possession which is a deprivation of being" ("privation d'un avoir qui est une privation d'être,"
Salah Stetie, Chairman [1982] of Unesco's Intergovernmental Committee for the Return or Restitution of Cultural Property, quoted in
Browning 1986:805). In other words, being depends upon having.
One could find no pithier statement of the relevance of possessive
individualism to the international politics of culture.

The problem with these restitutionist arguments is that they
make use of worn-out metaphors—collectivities seen as individuals,
culture seen as property—borrowed from the hegemonic culture that
the restitutionists are attempting to resist. Much of the anthropological literature of the past decade has argued that nations and cultures are
not bounded, continuous over time, or internally homogeneous. It is
no longer useful for anthropologists to imagine cultures as collective
individuals possessed of property and characterized by that "identity"
so central to the individualistic worldview. Rather, it is more fruitful
to think of cultures and groups as being continually reconstructed,
realigned, and reimagined, as various actors negotiate their social
lives. To argue, as the restitutionists do, that artifacts plundered in the
past bear witness to the cultural continuity of the plundered group,
and hence must be restored to that group's possession, is to take a
present-day understanding of one's collective identity and to natural-
ize it as if it were an objectively and continuously existent thing. But
in my opinion, cultures are not things exhibiting this oneness over
time. Today's disputed cultural treasures, at the time they passed into
the hands of Western imperialists, bore witness to human realities that
are only today reconstructed as the "cultures" of victimized non-
Western people. Similarly, to speak of the "countries of origin" of
cultural treasures is to speak anachronistically, since those treasures did
not in most cases "originate" in the present-day sociopolitical entities
we call countries. (I am aware that my argument at this point is similar
to that of the retentionists, who say, for example, that the Greeks who
today wish to reclaim the Elgin marbles ought not to be considered

the descendants of the Athenians who built the Parthenon; I will address this issue below.)

Indeed, the ethnic groups now proclaiming their existence, their boundedness, and their historic continuity are in most, if not all, cases the creations of rather recent events. This holds true for an apparently prototypical nation-state like France (Weber 1976) as well as for groups with less well-validated pedigrees. And the culture that present-day groups claim as belonging to them from time immemorial, embodied in historically particular pieces of cultural property, is likewise the product of a current interpretation and not an objective thing that has possessed a continuous meaning and identity over time. Thus, to constitute "representative collections" is to *invent* a static culture that never existed in the past (cf. Ames 1986: 48–58), though the notion of representativeness implies a truthful portrayal of what is already there (the "what" in this case being a historically existent culture).

In the aesthetic-integrity argument of the restitutionists, cultural treasures are said to be fully understandable only when viewed in their original setting:

> A work of art is the product of a particular time and place, and cannot be fully understood save as being of that time and place. This is . . . especially true of those works that were made to adorn a particular building, or to be used in a particular ceremony: if they have been removed from their intended setting, the viewer has to make a strong imaginative effort if he is to come near seeing them for what they are. (Dummett 1986:809)

"Seeing them for what they are" suggests the logic of identity critiqued above. It is as problematic to speak of the true meaning ("fully understood") or identity ("what they are") of works of art as it is to speak of the essential personality of a culture. I would argue, in either case, that the object (culture or work of art) is constructed in part by the interpretations that viewers, users, and/or participants bring to it. Granted that an artwork or culture can be understood from multiple perspectives, how is it possible to privilege any particular interpretation as conveying the sole or complete truth of the object in question?

Arguing for the return of cultural treasures to their "original" settings, restitutionists apply various criteria to validate their interpretations of the essence or true meaning of such objects. Sometimes they speak of the "natural" setting of an object (Robinson 1980:56), a term whose implicit appeal to "the way things are" can preclude further discussion. Or, as in the passage quoted above, they mention the settings "intended" by the creators of cultural treasures. This second argument poses two problems. First, the meaning of an artwork ought not to be limited by the artist's intentions which, at the most, can supply only one among many clues as to how the work can be interpreted. (Freudian psychology alone suggests how much of the potential meaning of art may be inaccessible to its creators; think also of the Boasian notion of the unconscious patterning of culture.) Second, it is doubtful that a museum in the "country of origin" of a cultural treasure is at all comparable to the setting intended for the treasure at the time of its creation. Indeed, to objectify something as a cultural treasure probably makes it impossible ever to restore it to its original setting, since that setting (assuming it remains in existence) will change or will have to be changed to accommodate the object's new status as treasure, as cultural property.[2] Moreover, artworks and cultural treasures gain new meanings when placed in new settings (cf. Lowenthal 1985:286, 356, footnote 334); to claim that full meaning depends on an original setting seems unnecessarily to limit the potential meaningfulness of human creations.

Having rejected arguments based on cultural identity and aesthetic integrity, I want now to suggest that the retentionists' third argument, concerning fair play, allows us to advocate the return of cultural properties to countries claiming entitlement. I said above that the metaphors of cultural property and the collective individual are "worn out." I believe that they are worn out in the sense of being epistemologically bankrupt, particularly for the purposes of the human sciences. They are not, however, worn out with respect to power; to the contrary, they remain dominant metaphors in the hegemonic discourse of a worldwide postmodern culture. Those who would assert what they see as their rights against the powers-that-be must articulate their claims—in the case discussed here, claims concerning a more equitable division of cultural property—in a language that power understands. Metropolitan museums, whose avowed mission is to display the cultural treasures of humankind's diverse cultures, cannot credibly deny that claimant countries ought to pursue policies to develop their cultural identities and to protect the heritage upon which such identities are thought to depend. As Michael Dummett suggests (1986:809), for retentionists to defend their position by deconstructing the national identity of their opponents— claiming, for example, that modern Greeks are not "true" descendants of ancient Greeks—is fundamentally dishonest, because retentionists are not simultaneously willing to call into question their own nationalistic claims to cultural superiority. In other words, retentionists are quick to condemn the parochial nationalism of their opponents, but rarely question their own more imperial nationalisms, which they mask in the name of internationalism.[3]

In the world of international power relations, then, it is necessary to speak, as restitutionists do, about "heritage" and "identity," the "reapportionment" of cultural property, "art-consuming" and "art-producing" countries, and the "theft" of cultural "treasures." The retentionists and the forces they represent have foisted the logic and language of possessive individualism upon the world. Now let them return the property that logic fetishizes to the collective individuals, or non-Western nation-states, that have sprung up in the wake of Westernization. To do so would make for a good piece of reflexive anthropology whereby we of the West could experience our own rules from the perspective of those without power.

Ironically, even were the retentionists to yield to the restitutionists on every point, the cultural preservation and authenticity so ardently sought would not materialize. Paternalistic retentionists sometimes say they would be willing to return cultural properties were Third World countries endowed with museums and technicians adequate to care for them. Restitutionists often, though not always, agree that the proper setting for cultural property is the museum. But to place one's own property in one's own museum is yet another example of the hegemony of Western culture and the disappearance of alternative modes of living. That putatively diverse national and ethnic groups understand one another well enough to fight about who "owns" the past suggests that all of them have been assimilated into a global culture of the present.

NOTES

1. Elsewhere (Handler 1986, 1988) I have pursued the implications of Dumont's work, arguing that most social science, including anthropology, treats cultures and societies in this individualistic fashion. This is so despite our explicit Durkheimian championing of social rather than individualistic perspectives, and despite our recognition that cultures and societies are not internally homogeneous.

2. With respect to the mutability of setting, consider the following incident: "When our team started work on it [the Bramayani Temple in Panauti, Nepal], we discovered an added hazard: the structure had no foundations. This called for the development of a new technique to float reinforced concrete pads, like large snowshoes, under the main supporting columns. The concept and design were simple enough, but the execution proved difficult, as the chief priest said that we would be threatened with dire consequences should we move the stone divinity" (Sanday 1986:105).

3. As Ekpo Okpo Eyo, head of the Nigerian Federal Department of Antiquities, argues concerning such pretensions to international brotherhood: "In real life the notion appears to be valid *only* as long as art treasures flow in from the 'peripheries of the world' to the 'centre' and not from the 'centre' outwards. Benin bronzes should be seen in museum showcases in New York and London, but it is impossible to contemplate Leonardo's Mona Lisa . . . in Lagos or Accra" (Eyo 1986:203).

REFERENCES

Ames, Michael
    1986    *Museums, the Public and Anthropology: A Study in the Anthropology of Anthropology.* New Delhi: Concept Publishing Company.

Bateson, Gregory
    1971    The Cybernetics of "Self": A Theory of Alcoholism. In *Steps to an Ecology of Mind,* pp. 309–37. New York: Chandler (1972).

Browning, Robert
    1986    The Plundering of Nationhood. *Times Literary Supplement* 4347 (July 25): 805–06.

Dummett, Michael
    1986    The Ethics of Cultural Property. *Times Literary Supplement* 4347 (July 25): 809–10.

Dumont, Louis
    1966    *Homo Hierarchicus: The Caste System and Its Implications.* Chicago: University of Chicago Press (1970).
    1970    Religion, Politics, and Society in the Individualistic Universe. *Proceedings of the Royal Anthropological Institute of Great Britain and Ireland,* pp. 31–41.

Eyo, Ekpo Okpo
    1986    A Threat to National Art Treasures: The Illicit Traffic in Stolen Art. In *The Challenge to Our Cultural Heritage,* ed. Y. R. Isar, pp. 203–12. Washington, D.C.: Smithsonian Institution Press.

Handler, Richard
    1986    Authenticity. *Anthropology Today* 2(1): 2–4, (3): 24.
    1988    *Nationalism and the Politics of Culture in Quebec.* Madison: University of Wisconsin Press.

Lowenthal, David
    1985    *The Past Is a Foreign Country.* Cambridge: Cambridge University Press.

Macpherson, C. B.
    1962    *The Political Theory of Possessive Individualism: Hobbes to Locke.* Oxford: Oxford University Press.

Montaigne, Michel de
    1585    Du Repentir. In *Essais,* Tome II, pp. 222–37. Paris: Garnier (1962).

Robinson, Alma
    1980    The Art Repatriation Dilemma. *Museum News* 58(4): 55–59.

Sanday, John
    1986    Science and Technology in Architectural Conservation: Examples from Nepal and Bangla Desh. In *The Challenge to Our Cultural Heritage,* ed. Y. R. Isar, pp. 99–112. Washington, D.C.: Smithsonian Institution Press.

Tocqueville, Alexis de

1835    *Democracy in America,* Vol. 2, ed. Phillips Bradley. New York: Vintage (1955).

Weber, Eugen

1976    *Peasants into Frenchmen: The Modernization of Rural France, 1870–1914.* Stanford, Calif.: Stanford University Press.

# CHAPTER 4

# Creation Myths and Zoning Boards

## Local Uses of Historic Preservation

*Robert Verrey and Laura Henley*

With the increase in local-level surveys of "cultural resources," archeologists and other historic preservation specialists have become players in the arena of local politics. To be effective cultural resource managers, we must examine historic preservation within the structure and process of local politics. This paper discusses how neighborhoods and local jurisdictions can and do use "history" to achieve ends not related to the preservation of historic resources, to combat perceived threats to the community, and to attempt to maintain the status quo. The preservation process can provide a tool for community manipulation and control at the same time that it supports, exposes, or opposes the mythology of local history. Rather than simply existing within a realm of "truth" and "knowledge," studies of history and prehistory by specialists often compete with residents' concepts of their own local antecedents. In turn, preservation goals can compete with those of other interest groups in a complex, and sometimes volatile, political process of land-use decision making.

Although organized interest in historic preservation predates the environmental movement of the 1970s, it was strongly influenced by these concerns (Fowler 1986). Simply put, historic preservation aims to protect a portion of this country's history for future generations,

to provide continuity between past, present, and future, and to preserve a significant part of the cultural past for future scientific
research.[1]

Management of cultural resources is a decidedly political process,
over and above federal, state and local regulations governing resource
identification and preservation. This arena contains various interest
groups whose opinions often differ as to what constitutes history and
what their respective roles in decisions about history should be. Conflict both within and between groups is not unusual, and potential
adversarial relationships remain a threat, not only to successful preservation but also to a sense of community.

The major groups involved in cultural resource management include: federal, state, and local preservation officials; planners; private
developers; independent professional specialists; and community-based
organizations such as neighborhood coalitions and civic associations.
Given the complexities of the relationships among these groups, it
would be impossible to examine the full politics of historic preservation
in one brief paper. Rather we have chosen to explore two areas of
potential conflict between cultural resource management specialists and
neighborhood community groups: (1) differences of opinion as to what
constitutes "history" and historic resources, and (2) the attempted manipulation of cultural resources for ends that are not solely preservation
oriented. In the first case, a popular narrative of the past sustained by
some neighborhood residents can be at odds with the specialists' interpretation; the popular summary often provides a less detailed, more
straightforward, and often more dramatic picture of the past centered
upon and emphasizing the preservation of neighborhood icons. These
icons are symbols, usually highly visible ones such as historic structures
or their ruins, that come to embody the past to some members of the
community. In the second case, coalitions of residents within neighborhoods use interpretations of history to stop, slow, alter, or otherwise
control proposed changes in their community. These groups can and do
manipulate the interpretation of the past in response to perceived pressures on the current community, as a means to achieve goals not based
on the preservation of historic resources.

PRESERVATION POLITICS

Within the past twenty-five years, cultural resource management has changed considerably in the United States, producing a current emphasis on the identification and preservation of "significant" resources within specifically defined areas. In the 1970s, as cultural resources began to be classed with "other nonrenewable resources . . . in danger of being forever destroyed, hence worthy of protection and conservation" (Fowler 1986:149), preservation advocates recognized an increasing variety of resources as potentially "significant." Cultural resources now address the following:

1. Terrestrial and marine prehistoric, historic, industrial and commercial archeological resources;
2. Formal and vernacular historic buildings or architecture, engineered construction and cultural landscapes;
3. Traditional or cultural "intangible" values . . . and other rural and/or urban folklife traditions and oral history. (Knudson 1986:401)

Guidelines for determining site significance at the federal level are those used by the National Register of Historic Places to evaluate nominated resources.[2] States and many local jurisdictions enacted laws and ordinances similar to the federal statutes and guidelines in order to recognize and preserve their cultural heritage, particularly resources that might not be considered eligible for the National Register. The process of nominating resources, particularly at the local level, included representatives of community groups as well as preservation specialists. Both groups can exert influence by nominating sites, retrieving and organizing the necessary documentation, and testifying for or against the inclusion of specific sites. Moreover, decisions concerning preservation or destruction of historic resources by privately funded projects on private land are often left in the hands of local jurisdictions where the concept of "significance" is just one of many forces shaping the preservation process.

Federal and local preservation laws are not applied in an environment in which history or preservation of the "significant" past is the sole consideration. Preservation legislation and policy cannot be divorced from their current and future impact on economic development, for example. Preservation laws do not exist in a vacuum, but in a world of persons and groups who can avoid the laws altogether or opt to use the legislation for ends not directly related to saving the past. As an example, we can briefly compare two small communities that have chosen divergent paths. One elected preservation through historic site designation, while the second avoided this course of action because it would severely restrict what owners could do with their property. These owners recognized that historic site designation could usurp some of their entitlement to control and modify their property. One could argue that the residents of this second community cared little about preserving tangible evidence of their cultural past or that as preservation specialists we had failed to adequately articulate the potential importance of these resources. While this may be so, such explanations grossly oversimplify the issues involved.

Ideological support for preservation need not always be consistent with the practice of preserving cultural resources on one's own property. Preservation goals are frequently weighed against nonpreservation issues deemed of equal if not greater importance; for example, the "right" to alter one's house as one sees fit to fulfill family necessities. In some communities the cost of historic preservation may be judged too high, demanding that owners relinquish what they may view as a significant degree of control over at least a portion of their environment. Our failure to recognize this hidden agenda, the adverse reactions to the manner in which these laws impinge on the sanctity of private property, and the ways in which professional research may disrupt a local popular historical narrative or "mythology" of the past can seriously undermine our effectiveness. As Fowler notes:

> Archeologists, and many others, take a broader view, centering on the concept that *all* cultural traditions, all pasts, have equal validity. . . . But most people and most politicians regard themselves as members of a specific ethnic group, or social class. *Their* past is *their* roots. Others' pasts are interesting, curious, and possibly fascinating

but not something to abrogate the sacredness of private property for, nor even necessarily a reason to obey laws protecting cultural resources for and of all the people on public lands. (1986:152; emphasis in the original)

## NEIGHBORHOOD CREATION MYTHS AND ICONS

Another area of potential conflict among groups involved in preservation concerns the creation of popular local histories and symbols of the past as part of the definition of historic resources. To be sure, the historic preservation process, culminating in National Register designation, creates powerful and influential icons of past cultures, the meaning and impact of which deserve a separate examination. Neighborhood groups, however, create their own popular history, reinforced by physical remains, sometimes even getting these tangible symbols nominated to the National Register or adding additional meaning to sites already on the Register. In a manner similar to rationalizing the present by rewriting the past, neighborhoods can formulate what we have termed "neighborhood creation myths," complete with the physical icons that symbolize the myths. For some members of these communities the myths provide a sense of the beginning of the neighborhood, a link to the past, placing the modern world into a continuous historic fabric, while at the same time reaffirming the uniqueness of each individual neighborhood.[3]

Sometimes the process of creating these myths overemphasizes one or two aspects, leaving much of the area's history unexplored or unstated. Some of this creation is clearly linked to the popular portrayal of history as normative or iconographic—a procession of famous people and major events—not as processes of cultural change. This normative approach makes it easy to "know" history—just memorize the names and dates. But the creation myths seem to be more than a simplified normative approach to local history; they may fulfill a perceived need for a sense of the beginning of the community grounded in a specific and knowable time, with events and people unquestionably related to the present.

The potential for conflict between the research generated by cultural resource management specialists and the local portrayal of history is apparent. Community residents most intrigued with local history can be the same individuals who most ardently support the myths. The popular histories can be useful to the historic preservation process in that they interest neighborhood residents in their own history, foster a concern about the preservation of cultural resources, and focus attention on one or two important historical individuals, events, or topics. We suggest that historic preservation can be most successful where the identified cultural resources reinforce a sense of history already present within a community.

The dilemma we face as cultural resource management specialists is complex and far-reaching. In situations where historic and prehistoric resources have failed to become incorporated into a community's historic myth, the "worth" of these resources declines when worth is translated as value or influence in land-use decisions. On the other hand, concepts of neighborhood history can lead to the creation of histories and the establishment of icons different from those of preservation specialists. Here the cultural resource manager must be cautious. When professionally written history attacks neighborhood myths, or attempts to undermine the meaning of an icon, we run the risk of losing support or having our research devalued by the community. An assault on a particular group's myth, therefore, is often not the most prudent course of action. The time and place of disagreement must be carefully considered, for understanding the origin and maintenance of the myth can be as informative about the dynamics of the present and past community as any other source, and could well expose omissions on our part. Sometimes the local myth does not diverge radically from the picture of the past produced by specialists and can be easily incorporated into that history without overemphasizing minor differences.

In cases where the neighborhood myth is grossly in error, for example, by omitting the contributions of one ethnic group, or deviates significantly from research grounded in a comprehensive review of primary and secondary sources, it must be confronted directly. Even then, however, the approach of the specialist is of critical importance. If we are antagonistic, condescending, and/or pompous in our confrontation, we run the risk of alienating neighborhood residents and strengthening their resolve to maintain their own version of history.

CASE STUDIES: BACKGROUND AND DISCUSSION

The recognition of these dilemmas resulted from our participation on three projects during 1986 and 1987. Our first two examples, Deanwood and Brookland, are urban communities located in the northeast sector of the District of Columbia⁴ where no one had conducted a comprehensive cultural resource management study prior to our research.⁵ Research in these communities was not stimulated by impending large-scale urban development projects; rather the D.C. Historic Preservation Division had targeted this sector for survey in part because of previous neglect.

During the 1970s it became apparent that cultural resource management projects need not be directed solely by the immediacy of development, a circumstance that often resulted in markedly uneven coverage of the historic resources of an area. The lack of a comprehensive historical context for all areas of a city or state can bias decisions about cultural or historical significance, thereby inhibiting successful planning. To combat this problem, the Interior Department instituted a program of matching grants-in-aid for survey and planning projects, to stimulate research by individual states and jurisdictions in areas not immediately threatened by development (but with the potential for future development) and to provide the context necessary to improve assessments of significance. This kind of grant supported reconnaissance surveys in both of these District of Columbia communities.

The third example, from Arlington County, Virginia, focuses on a local conflict over preservation of the Civil War site of Fort C. F. Smith. This example is particularly appropriate for this discussion because, unlike the other two cases, it illustrates important aspects of the political process of historic site designation. Since much of this process was public, it offered a valuable opportunity to better develop many of the concepts presented here.

*Deanwood*

Located east of the Anacostia River, Deanwood is a working- to middle-class, predominantly Afro-American neighborhood. About 1790 much of the area surveyed comprised the 330-acre farm of William and Nancy Benning. Two years after Benning's death in 1831, his heirs sold the property to Levi Sheriff, who became one of the largest landowners in this part of Washington County[6] during the nineteenth century. Sheriff and his descendants owned and/or resided on at least a portion of the Deanwood survey area until early in the twentieth century (Overbeck et al. 1987).

Not long after his purchase of this property, Levi Sheriff retired from his mercantile enterprise in Bladensburg, Maryland, and relocated to his land in Washington County. Like other landowners in Washington County, Sheriff's agricultural productivity depended on slave labor. In 1840, however, a small number of free blacks also resided in this neighborhood, one of whom was listed in the Sheriff household in that year (Overbeck et al. 1987). Therefore, both slaves and free blacks had then inhabited the survey area itself and/or the surrounding region, a critical point in understanding the popular local history of Deanwood. At Sheriff's death, his land was divided among his three daughters—Margaret Lowrie (widow), Emeline Sheriff (unmarried), and Mary Cornelia Dean, wife of John T. W. Dean (Overbeck et al. 1987).

The Civil War stimulated dramatic changes in the District of Columbia, not just in its social and economic aspects but also in its physical character. From nearby forts, Union soldiers felled trees in large numbers to provide, among other things, building and maintenance materials for the fortifications and to remove obstructions to their observation of the surrounding countryside. Levi Sheriff's son-in-law, John Dean, gave some of this wood to a congregation of black Methodists for the construction of their chapel south of the project area (Overbeck et al. 1987). After the District of Columbia emancipated its slaves in 1862, some of the new freedmen remained in Deanwood, but after 1870 most of them disappeared from the documentary history of the community (Overbeck et al. 1987). The war also fostered a significant growth of Washington City, and, not unexpectedly, by the late nineteenth century city developers and others had recognized the suburban potential of the agricultural land in Washington County. Like others, the descendants of Levi Sheriff seized the opportunity to create a small suburban development, called "Whittingham," on the western portion of their land, but this venture was much less successful than hoped in attracting potential suburbanites (Overbeck et al. 1987).

By 1888 the use of the place named "Deanwood" had become common, apparently initiated by Dr. Julian W. Dean, grandson of Levi Sheriff.[7] Dr. Dean bankrupted his part of the family through heavy investments in a company manufacturing perpetual motion machines (Overbeck et al. 1987)—a fascinating story in its own right. This financial collapse necessitated the sale of 57 acres with approximately 30 buildings, "including at least three Sheriff-Lowrie-Dean family dwellings"(Overbeck et al. 1987:17).

During the late nineteenth century, the land-use pattern in the project area gradually changed from rural to suburban. By 1900 Deanwood's population was quite diverse, consisting of "white and black homeowners as well as white and black renters . . . [and] included the old farm families as well as both black and white newly arrived residents" (Overbeck et al. 1987:17). Deanwood's ethnic heterogeneity persisted through the first twenty years of the century as the older farming families continued to subdivide and sell their land (Overbeck et al. 1987).

By the close of the 1920s, Deanwood had become "a sizeable, stable, family-oriented black community. Still in many ways it remained almost rural through World War II" (Overbeck et al. 1987:21). Some streets lacked pavement, small farms persisted, and indoor plumbing remained a luxury for many. This scarcity of typical urban amenities did not diminish the strong sense of mutual assistance evident in the community. Deanwood's black residents helped each other find jobs and build and repair their homes, exemplifying the theme of black self-help and "a twentieth century community whose black residents took control of their own destiny" (Overbeck et al. 1987:22).

Our research in this community relied on such primary documents as deeds, tax and assessment records, oral interviews, wills and inventories, and census data, which were amassed, reviewed, and organized by the project social and architectural historian, archeologists, and oral historian. This research indicates that blacks *and* whites occupied the surveyed area from possibly as early as the eighteenth century. In contrast, Deanwood's "neighborhood creation myth" holds that the community is now and always has been an Afro-American enclave, founded by blacks and black-owned even prior to the Civil War. According to the popular local history, the mythical founders of the community were "men of color," one named "Dean," who are perceived as the original Colonial landowners of Deanwood and, on the basis of their description, black. While an original land grant in the vicinity was called "Little Dean," it encompassed none of the surveyed area, and the "Dean" of this grant, a man of color, appears unrelated to the Deans descended from Levi Sheriff.

Deanwood's popular history, like Brookland's, is grounded in certain selected primary historical material. In this case, however, large temporal gaps exist between the primary sources retrieved to "confirm" the myth. This fact, coupled with the community's relative latitude in interpreting the source materials, underlies a major difference between our outline of the past and the popular version of history.

The former use of the place name "Deanwood" only complicates resolution of the conflict between these competing versions of history. During our research, we discovered that the term "Deanwood" once referred to a much larger geographic district than the present survey area. The use of the name "Deanwood, D.C." in building permits and other sources of the late nineteenth and early twentieth centuries "afforded one of the first confirmations of the oral tradition that Deanwood covered a geographic area larger than that covered by the present survey area boundaries" (Overbeck et al. 1987:16). Quite possibly, then, a small pre-Civil War free black enclave existed within the larger region once considered Deanwood. As yet, however, no primary sources directly associate this or any other free black enclave with the "men of color" who owned "Little Dean" in the Colonial era.

The popular neighborhood history, the local "myth," transforms the fact of early twentieth-century black residence in Deanwood into a portrayal of the ethnic composition and geography of the modern community as extending unchanged and continuous into the past. In this case, the local myth uses the supposed first landowners, Colonial "men of color," to justify and reaffirm the ethnic continuity between the modern era and the distant past. Furthermore, the known existence of pre-Civil War free blacks within the bounds of the much larger geographic district once considered Deanwood may contribute to the myth, reinforcing the link between the supposed Colonial black presence and the twentieth-century community. To a large extent, events, people, and processes bridging the gap between the Colonial and modern eras have been neglected, or their ethnicity questioned, in order to force congruence with the myth. The neighborhood myth, then, extracts only selected parts of the historical record to explain the formation of the modern community.

Recognizing this, how do historic preservation specialists respond to the inherent conflicts between neighborhood or popular history and their own research? While this will be dealt with more fully after presentation of the background of the Brookland survey, we note here that we must be extremely cautious in our treatment of these competing histories. One of the greatest dangers we face is to repeat the unverified myth in its whole cloth, for this only perpetuates oversimplification while reinforcing the power and "truth" of the myth.

*Brookland*

Brookland is a multiethnic urban neighborhood of detached, predominantly owner-occupied houses on rather spacious lots. Apartment buildings are few and small by Washington, D.C., standards. For the most part, the Brookland community has escaped major alteration resulting from private or government-sponsored urban development projects. Suburban development of the survey area began in 1887, and by 1910 most of what is now considered "Brookland" had been subdivided. The first subdivision, approximately 134 acres, was the largest section of Brookland and the one from which the community derives its name. Descendants of Jehiel Brooks, who died in 1886 after residing on this property for over forty years, sold this land for development immediately following his death. It is the Brooks family for which this first subdivision and the community itself are named. Built about 1840, the residence of Jehiel Brooks, once named "Belair," still stands and was placed on the National Register in the 1970s.

Like Deanwood's, Brookland's history began in the late seventeenth century with two original land patents—the "Inclosure," sometimes referred to as "Beall's Inclosure," and "Cuckhold's Delight." Although it is not certain when the first Europeans settled in the area, primary evidence places the date prior to 1780. As in Deanwood and the surrounding area, Brookland's late eighteenth-century landowners grew tobacco as their major cash crop and relied on slave labor (Verrey et al. 1987).

With each economic depression of the eighteenth century, a few more planters abandoned tobacco as their primary cash crop (Kulikoff 1986). This gradual trend away from the primacy of tobacco toward more diverse agricultural production continued through the century. After 1800, slowly increasing market demands of the newly established District of Columbia probably further encouraged this trend, so that by 1850 all vestiges of tobacco production within the survey area had disappeared (Mitchell and Muller 1979; Verrey et al. 1987).

Even though tobacco lost its prominence at the expense of more variable crop production, many landowners continued to rely on slave labor. We have verified that most of the landowners in what was to become the Brookland survey area held slaves until emancipation, but historical documentation concerning the pre-Civil War Afro-American population is only scanty at best. This is unfortunate when one considers that Afro-Americans played a significant role in the evolution of the cultural landscape of Washington County, as well as of Brookland, making knowledge about this ethnic group essential to understanding the socioeconomic dynamics of this community and the region.[8]

In the 1830s the children of one Nicholas L. Queen, a member of an early Maryland Catholic family, inherited the land that became the heart of modern Brookland. Jehiel Brooks, who was not as significant a historical personage in this community as the mythology would suggest, gained a share in this land only through his marriage to Ann Queen, daughter of Nicholas L. Queen. Jehiel Brooks appears to have envisioned himself as a "gentleman planter" with all the trappings of that position—land, slaves, political influence, and a substantial residence to symbolize his stature. Except for one of these perquisites, Brooks achieved only the image not the substance of the position. He owned no land outright, but rather gained access to property through his wife and her siblings. Also, although the documents are not definitive on the point, recurrent financial difficulties appear to have deprived him of ownership of or access to slave labor (Verrey et al. 1987). No evidence indicates that Brooks ever wielded significant political influence. On the contrary, his attempts to acquire political appointment were largely rebuffed, particularly following the onset of legal problems stemming from his questionable activities as an Indian Agent in Louisiana. However, he did build a suitably symbolic dwelling with a formal garden. As a component of the cultural landscape of the time, this building, now known as the "Brooks *Mansion*," embodied all that Brooks aspired to but never quite attained.

As in Deanwood, events associated with and processes encouraged by the Civil War led to far-reaching changes in the Brookland survey area. With the emancipation of slaves, many families who held substantial properties became "land poor," finding it difficult to attract and maintain the wage labor necessary to operate their large farms. During this transition from slave to wage labor, the land could be sold or leased to meet economic needs. For example, in the 1870s Brooks's in-laws, the Queens, sold all the remaining portion of their father's old farm located north of, but adjacent to, the survey area. With his in-laws, Brooks tried to maintain the Brookland property intact, even though it seems to have been economically disadvantageous for him to do so. Not surprisingly, shortly after Brooks's death, his heirs sold most of the old family estate, divesting themselves of what we believe had probably become a serious economic burden (Verrey et al. 1987).

In 1887, with the first subdivision of the area, modern Brookland began to take form. Initially considered a suburb of Washington City, the community gradually became more fully incorporated into the urban sphere in the early twentieth century owing to some degree to factors such as the extension of the streetcar lines, the founding and expansion of the adjacent Catholic University of America and associated Catholic institutions, and the overall growth of the population of the District of Columbia. In particular, "it was only when the city grew out to meet it and considerable numbers of federal workers ventured to the suburbs in the 1910s and 1920s that Brookland began to function in part as an urban neighborhood" (McDaniel et al. 1982:3). Early twentieth-century development did not immediately or completely eradicate Brookland's former character for it retained an attractive small-town flavor that probably enticed many of its early residents.

According to the creation myth of Brookland, the date of the community's genesis was 1887. Strongly associated with Jehiel Brooks, the myth portrays the neighborhood progenitor as a "benevolent Victorian gentleman" rather than an aspiring early nineteenth-century gentleman planter. The creation myth and our version of Brookland's history agree that the sale of the Brooks/Queen property signaled the beginning of the modern urban community, but the myth omits precedent historical details and processes. While stressing the post-1887 era, the myth treats earlier history in a particularistic fashion. This has the effect of deemphasizing complex pre-Civil War interrelationships and dynamics, including the extensive role of Afro-Americans in the evolution of the local economy. By selecting 1887 as the mythological beginning of the neighborhood, however, the myth renders the question of slavery merely tangential to its history.

Brookland's popular history converted Jehiel Brooks into a Victorian gentleman and his residence into the central icon of the community myth. The visibility of this structure and its role in the community preservation movement (see below) have given it an importance not justified by its history and architecture. The perception of Brooks and his home as Victorian places them in the era just preceding creation of the modern urban community. Brookland derived its name from Brooks through his children, and some of his descendants and relatives continued to reside in the community until well after 1887. In addition, modern descendants of Brooks donated an extensive collection of the family papers to the Catholic University of America Archives, the only old farming family in the area to do so. The availability of this primary documentation has also emphasized the singular importance of the Brooks/Queen family to neighborhood history. We would argue that these several factors, in combination, encouraged the perception of Brooks as the progenitor of the community. It is to him that the Brookland community traces its roots, and from him that Brookland receives its historical continuity. The popular history does not ignore other early farming families who were Brooks's neighbors; rather the question is one of emphasis. The other families are represented only in the primary documents and have left no visible material symbol as a perpetual reminder of their earlier presence.

CONFLICTS AND ALTERNATIVE RESPONSES

The real question of neighborhood myths, then, is how preservation specialists respond to conflicts between their findings and some residents' concepts of local history (or relevant history). There are no easy answers, but we recognized several possible responses, each with its own limitations and advantages. One we have termed the "Jack Webb" response—report "just the facts" of the survey without addressing conflicts with popular history. In a sense, this is the unstated position of too many survey and contract projects in historic preservation. Cultural resource management reports are too frequently circulated only to a very limited professional audience. By simply providing inventories of sites and artifacts, for example, while avoiding the interpretations of the historical record, we perpetuate neighborhood historic myths by the sin of omission. Survey results are not made public and either are not communicated to the neighborhood involved or reach it in limited form, passing through the filter of the popular portrayal.

In our work, we decided to take a different approach: facing the communities directly by presenting our survey results and their implications to a public audience.[9] An opportunity to do so arose when the community sponsored a series of public discussions to celebrate the centennial of the formation of modern Brookland. In our presentation to the community, we discussed our interpretations of its history, trying to avoid displaying either antagonism or condescension toward the audience lest we alienate the very individuals who had been most supportive of our work. In fact, our fears never materialized; those

most interested in neighborhood history welcomed the additional information and were not as committed to the local myth as we had
anticipated. This group, however, represented only a small fraction of
the community, and we are still concerned that our survey results have
failed to reach the community at large.

Other problems may be encountered when confronting local creation myths. Despite prior compromise of its integrity, archeological
testing of the grounds surrounding Brooks Mansion was essential to
evaluate its significance relative to the National Register status of the
building. Unfortunately, other cultural resources such as an eighteenth-
century plantation, which if intact would have been at least as important
for historical and/or archeological interpretations as the Brooks Mansion, had already been adversely affected by modern construction and
development (Verrey et al. 1987). Archeological testing served to perpetuate the importance of Brooks Mansion as an already existing historic resource. Brooks Mansion's perceived significance had led to its
preservation; its survival in turn demanded reconnaissance-level archeological testing, and the testing then strengthened the importance of the
structure as an icon. The use of the building in the neighborhood's
struggle against outside development (see below), and the building's
singular survival, age, and association with the family whose name
graces the community have all contributed to its establishment as the
symbolic center of Brookland—an icon of a particular place and a specific time in the past. In our public presentation of the survey results,
while we discussed the importance of historical process and emphasized
pre-1887 history, it was the archeology of Brooks Mansion that most
captivated the audience, putting the frosting on the cake of popular
neighborhood history.

In Brookland, the competing versions of "history" evidenced
more agreement and less conflict than anticipated; such was not the
case in Deanwood. A well-known, respected, and long-resident member of Deanwood retrieved the information underpinning the local
popular history. With perseverance and commitment, he contended
with disinterested bureaucrats and scholars unconcerned with black
history, compiling sufficient data to "confirm" to his own satisfaction
a continuity in ethnic composition between old and modern Dean-

wood. Therefore, any attempt to replace the neighborhood myth with our own portrayal of the past now carries with it a greater potential for conflict, the magnitude of which could entirely jeopardize the preservation process in this community. As yet we have not had the opportunity to directly confront this issue.[10]

Throughout this discussion we have avoided defining what, after all, constitutes historical reality. While our survey did add more "names and dates" to the existing histories of these two neighborhoods, we also added interpretations and discussions of the process of cultural change that are, in a sense, only a more sophisticated creation myth. The neighborhood version is pleasing in its directness and informality, and gains potency through its association with community-based material icons. Such popular portrayals can help unify disparate components of the modern community while linking it to a knowable past continuous with the present. Our version is more complex, since it includes not only the mundane aspects of history but also large socioeconomic issues of the eighteenth and nineteenth centuries and interrelationships between Washington City and County and rural Maryland. It is still, however, *our* reading of the past, not simply "just the facts" of history.

The irony of this for Brookland is that the post-1887 history we collected is very much one of urban development—precisely what modern residents wish to slow, or at least control. For a Brookland community to exist, development had to radically alter the nineteenth-century land-use pattern. Subsequently, however, the new residents of the development wished to control the forces that might change their neighborhood and made use of the perceived history of the people they replaced as one tool in achieving their objective.

HISTORIC PRESERVATION AS PART OF
NEIGHBORHOOD PRESERVATION

*Brookland*

Of the two communities we studied, only Brookland has taken advantage of historic preservation to protect itself from radical and unwanted change. Preservation of Brooks Mansion, the icon of the historic myth, became a rallying point to oppose two projects that would have split or seriously encroached on the fabric of Brookland. We cannot measure the pervasiveness of the Brookland myth or the symbolic force of Brooks Mansion as icon prior to these projects. We argue that the success of the neighborhood's opposition, however, has served to reinforce the myth and guarantee the Mansion's symbolic status.

In the early 1970s, Brookland was seriously threatened by a proposed extension of Interstate Route 95, and later by the anticipated detrimental effect of construction of the Metro rapid transit system. The Washington Metropolitan Area Transit Authority (WMATA) had purchased several lots, among them the parcel containing Brooks Mansion, which it intended to demolish. Civic groups, other community organizations, and residents mobilized and through various strategies modified or prevented the most undesirable proposals. The main group interested in Brookland's history, the Brookland Tour Committee, traces its beginning to this time. Also at this time, Brooks Mansion achieved National Register status; consequently, while WMATA constructed station facilities nearby to the west, the building itself was preserved. Concern for the historic value of the structure undoubtedly stimulated support for its preservation, but this process also became a means through which the neighborhood restricted encroachment and defended itself against outside pressures. The success of these struggles further enhanced the status of Brooks Mansion as an icon of Brookland, and of history in general.

As indicated above, several of those most active in these struggles also participate in the Brookland Tour Committee, the community group with which we had the most contact. This organization sponsors an annual tour of points of local historical interest within the community, and its members have zealously helped to collect the oral and documentary history of Brookland. Clearly, these neighborhood residents feel strongly about preserving their community history. In fact, the Brookland neighborhood has long valued its past. In the 1960s, the community held festivities honoring individuals and families who had lived there for fifty years or more, producing a brochure that included the names of those honored and brief descriptions of local points of historical interest. As might be expected, however, the named sites and individuals related only to the post-1887 history of this community.

The Brookland Tour Committee has recently incorporated in order to nominate local structures and/or areas to the D.C. Historic Preservation Review Board. The committee is also working closely with the D.C. Historic Preservation Division to protect a twentieth-century landmark—the Newton Theater—and to achieve landmark status for a commercial corridor within the community. By the autumn of 1987, Tour Committee members and others in the neighborhood had become fearful that the commercial strip, owned by absentee landlords and located near the Brookland Metro rapid transit station, had become a prime target for development.

These concerns are not unfounded, as was demonstrated during the struggles of the 1970s, which probably sensitized many of the Tour Committee members and other neighborhood residents to the dangers of unbridled development. Also, they have witnessed dramatic changes in other areas in and around the District of Columbia and Maryland, stimulated by the presence of Metro rapid transit stations. Finally, recent discussion of the establishment of "enterprise zones," areas of economic development particularly in sections of northeast Washington, has likely also contributed to a perception of impending threat. Some Brookland residents recognize that major development along their neighborhood's commercial corridor could transform the community, damaging both material and nonmaterial elements that make this a "neighborhood." The considerable support we received for our research stemmed mainly from their interest in local history *and* their awareness that our data could be invaluable in neighborhood preservation efforts.

*Local Preservation Politics*

The example of Brookland makes it clear that historic preservation is not simply a matter of saving significant material elements of the past. The struggle also involves maintaining the status quo or, at least, retaining some degree of control over a way of life against perceived external encroachment. A community is many things; for one, it is composed of people, material elements, and the relationship between them. Some would argue that residential property ownership within a community entitles the owner, within legal limits, to control and manipulate a tangible entity—the land and associated structures. But buying a house also means buying a stake in the quality of a community, a share of interest in what the community is and becomes. Preservation laws offer one way to restrain or better direct development at the community level. As one Washington resident has noted, " 'Historic District' means that you get a chance to say something before they try and tear it down" (Wheeler 1986). Not only has a tangible material element of the past been saved, but, as importantly, individuals retain some power through the collective voice of their neighborhood. It is impossible to say which is more important to a community, but we must recognize the relatedness of these perspectives.

The majority of Brookland's residents probably do not view development as intrinsically either detrimental or beneficial. As in the resolution of other complex problems, there is a trade-off, a weighing of advantages and disadvantages in each case. Certainly there are various degrees of development—a quarter-block townhouse complex will not have the same impact on the community as a superhighway. Generally, however, with large-scale development projects the real question is one of control. Residents view some projects as threats that require them to relinquish too much individual and collective control over the quality of life in their community. The preservation laws have become part of the tactical arsenal available to residents as they struggle to retain a modicum of control over the character of their neighborhoods.

In political situations of this kind, adversarial relationships can easily develop. Support is rarely unanimous for historic district nominations:

> strong convictions and short tempers are often on display when Washington neighborhoods are considered for historic designation . . . [as] proceedings tend to highlight the racial and economic conflicts that are part of every city neighborhood. (Wheeler 1986)

Opponents of historic district designation have argued, for example, that preservation leads to a dramatic increase in real estate values, resulting in the displacement of minority and low-income renters. Although formal studies are few (Wheeler 1986), some suggest that the causal factors were in place well before preservation became an issue. Interestingly, if we follow this argument we see that while preservation maintains the architectural and material status quo by restricting gross alteration of the built environment, it could actually contribute to the transformation of other community elements of equal importance in defining the character of the neighborhood.

Questions that pit individual rights against community rights have no easy solutions. Central to such conflict is the question of restricting basic entitlement of ownership by an outside entity. When a community accepts preservation, its members relinquish some control over their own property. On the one hand, homeowners will generally fight any proposals that take from them what they perceive as an "inalienable right" to modify their property. On the other hand, when the threat to the survival of the community as a whole is believed to be great enough, individuals may voluntarily surrender some of their rights to help preserve the neighborhood. This is an important issue in the historic designation process—to what degree will owners surrender their individual rights in order to preserve control over all or part of the greater community? We would argue that unless residents perceive a force that could detrimentally alter the structure of the community, it is unlikely that they will wholeheartedly endorse historic designation, no matter how benign. Conversely, when historic designation is viewed as the lesser of two evils, as a way to preserve a threatened neighborhood at the cost of some individual control, then the likelihood of acceptance increases. Between groups in opposition, however, protection of the community by historic designation may still exact too high a price when weighed against individual sacrifice. According to one New York City minister, whose church is located within a historic district,

> Belligerent designation of religious property as a landmark is an impermissible usurpation by government of religious assets for an

inferior secular purpose [while] landmark regulations have demanded that religious congregations direct their first energy and
their resources to the maintenance of mortar and not to the church's
mission and ministry. (Swallow 1986)

## Rezoning in Arlington

This third and final example specifically examines the rezoning procedure for a proposed residential development in Arlington County,
Virginia. It differs from the previous examples in that we observed
much of the politics of historic site designation as an ongoing process
encompassing both the conflict and its resolution in connection with
the preservation of the Civil War site of Fort C. F. Smith.[11] As in the
other examples, however, it is apparent that communities involved in
preservation use history as a means to protect other valued aspects of
their lives. This case again demonstrates the important role of icons in
this process, but also shows that disagreements can arise over the
precise definition of the material symbol.

Owned and maintained by the same family since the turn of the
century, the property in question possessed still visible physical remains of Fort C. F. Smith, including earthworks, storage and bomb-
proof features, and the identifiable location of the well. Built in 1863,
the fort is located on high ground just west of the Potomac River
crossing at Rosslyn, Virginia, where it helped close gaps in the system
of fortifications, thereby strengthening Washington's defense on the
Virginia side of the river. Garrisoned throughout the remainder of the
conflict, the fort was decommissioned, dismantled, and sold for sal-
vage at the close of the war. It never faced attack, nor did any of the
troops stationed there engage in battle with hostile forces (Barnard
1871; Cooling 1975; Crowell et al. 1987).

Prior to our involvement in the Fort Smith controversy, the local
history board had begun systematically to identify Civil War fort sites
and assess the extent of their survival. This procedure identified Fort
Smith as a resource worthy of preservation in the eyes of all parties
involved in the subsequent political process and helped establish its
status as an icon. Its significance resulted from its "accident of preserva-

tion" as the last surviving Civil War fort in which a substantial portion of the above-ground features remained within the boundaries of Arlington County. Many natives of the Commonwealth of Virginia still consider the Civil War as *the* major historical event in this vicinity. People from other parts of the country are often surprised to discover the strong feelings that persist in portions of the "Old South" about the "War of Northern Aggression." The linkage of a historic resource to the Civil War greatly increases its importance in the eyes of native residents, and identifying a resource as "the last . . . of the Civil War" in the particular jurisdiction provides a strong justification for preservation. In a sense, the developer who purchased the tract of land faced problems, not for proposing destruction of a Civil War fort, but for planning the obliteration of all vestiges of the *last remaining* fort. Fort Smith, then, became the last visible symbol of all activity and history associated with the Civil War fortifications within Arlington, a historic icon representing the county's last physical link to what some perceive as the most important historical event in Northern Virginia.

The question of preservation surfaced when the developer of the Fort Smith tract presented a proposed plat to the Zoning Board. The developer wished to create more lots on the tract than allowed "by right" under current zoning and therefore sought approval of the Zoning Board and final approval of the County Board. Willing to donate to the county what he identified as the remains of Fort Smith, the developer expected in return a favorable decision concerning the number of lots permitted.

In addition to the developer and the County Board, the following interest groups emerged: (1) a natural resources conservation group; (2) historians and other specialists involved in preservation; (3) avocational historians, especially those keenly interested in the Civil War era; and (4) the neighborhood civic association. While most of these groups sought to use preservation as a means, their ends differed markedly. In addition, while all paid at least lip service to the desirability of preserving Fort Smith, serious differences arose concerning the intrinsic historic value of the different components of the fort's cultural resources.

Fortunately, in this case, the developer remained committed to the quality of his project and interested in preserving the historic resources of Fort Smith. It would be too cynical and simplistic to view his interest in history as an opportunistic use of the fort as a bargaining chip in negotiations to obtain a greater density of development over the rest of the tract. As later events revealed, he became more sensitive to the preservation of Fort Smith during the course of historical research and archeological testing.

The previous owner of the tract had been an avocational horticulturalist, and the large, partly wooded property retained a decidedly rural flavor, with a view of the Potomac River and some lovely typespecimens of a variety of trees. The group that strongly advocated conservation of the natural resources also supported historic preservation, especially where the preservation of archeological resources coincided with conservation of important floral specimens. Yet in formal negotiations, this group consistently maintained its distance from historic preservation issues, preferring instead to fight a separate battle. Presumably this strategy ensured the integrity of its issue as a separate and distinct consideration, not bound to the success or failure of historic preservation or limiting preservation solely to a consideration of historic resources.

Those involved specifically in preserving the fort's historic resources fell into two camps—the local historic preservation board and the local historical society. The historic preservation board, whose members volunteered their time and expertise, included historians, architects, and an archeologist. An avocational historian with a great interest in the Civil War represented the historical society. The distinctions between these two camps became apparent as the need arose to determine the fort's historic resources of greatest "value" to the community. The historical society's respresentative strongly advocated protection of visible remains and the fort's vista, or "fields of fire," to add the appropriate "feel" to the preserved fort. In contrast, the board's historian and archeologist supported protection of what they perceived as the most scientifically valuable resources, especially the buried remains of troop activities and support structures. The conflict between these two positions found spatial expression in the fact that the archeological resources located in the eastern part of the fort were in direct opposition to the "fields of fire" off the fort's western side. Since the entire fort could not be protected, the spatial opposition clearly divided the two camps as each promoted its favored resources to the county as the appropriate choice.

The well-organized civic association from the neighborhood adjacent to the Fort Smith property participated actively in this political process. While this group's representative publicly supported historic preservation, it became clear that the unstated position of the community opposed any kind of development on this tract. Instead, they advocated preservation as a means to maintain the status quo, and only as long as it remained expedient to do so. If their position required compromise, they sought one that would result in the least development, meaning the fewest new houses constructed.

In the early stages of the controversy, the developer proposed a plan that would maximize the number of lots and protect only the immediate area of the surviving earthworks of Fort Smith. In response to this proposal, the historic preservation board nominated the entire property as a county historic district, a plan that would give it the authority to decide the appropriateness of any development proposal. The County Board rejected both plans and instead appointed a task force, composed of individuals representing each of the concerned groups, to resolve the conflicts. Placed under the aegis of a former chairman of the County Board, himself knowledgeable about local history and preservation issues, the task force negotiated a compromise solution granting the developer more lots than current zoning allowed, but fewer than he had requested. In turn, the developer donated to the county the part of the property that included the physical remains of the fort and a portion of the fields of fire. The county also agreed to purchase several lots from the developer to protect more of the fort's vista to the west and a portion of the area to the east. With funding from the developer, the county further agreed to conduct a Phase I archeological survey, to be followed by mitigation, if required, of the area threatened by development but with the potential for archeological significance.

Within local jurisdictions, officials make particular land-use decisions for a variety of political reasons, often influenced by pressure brought to bear on the decision-making authority by individuals or groups. Different interest groups may use history or their concept of history to further their different positions or causes. In these situations, one finds the importance of history or historic preservation downplayed or ignored if it weakens a political stance. The compromise reached concerning Fort Smith represented a logical solution to a complicated problem. The actual process of achieving this resolution, though arduous and cumbersome, clearly demonstrated the political use of local history.

This particular case offers two illustrations of the manner in which local groups can manipulate history. The first concerns the neighborhood civic association whose representative initially backed the efforts of the historic preservation board to gain decision-making authority over the development plan. Such support did not derive from a simple belief in the importance of historic preservation. At every juncture the civic association placed obstacles in the path of the developer, perhaps in an attempt to induce him to abandon the project altogether. The developer's unwavering commitment to the project, coupled with task force intentions to authorize a greater density of housing in exchange for the preservation of Fort Smith's historic resources, provoked the civic association to abandon historic preservation. The association's primary goal, then, had been to use any and all legal means at its disposal to restrict development as much as possible—a goal that took precedence over the likely destruction of at least part of the fort's historic resources. We would argue that this does not necessarily indicate that history is unimportant to this neighborhood group. Rather, protecting "their" community from what they see as an unwanted, permanent, and community-transforming intrusion has a higher priority and greater immediacy in this case.

The second illustration concerns the difference of opinion as to the relative value of specific cultural resources. When the historical society's advocate recognized that the compromise would preserve only a portion of the area outside the fort, he dramatically broke with the historic preservation board, stressing his belief in the importance of protecting the fields-of-fire vista. Since this representative endorsed reconstruction of the fort, preservation of the vista and the fort's visible physical remains outweighed the importance of protecting "invisible" archeological resources. In other words, to this individual, who is undoubtedly not alone in his perspective, the visible, material symbol of the Civil War in Arlington, that is, the icon—the physical remains of the fort and as much of its setting as possible—constituted the most meaningful aspect of history, even if some of that "history"—the archeological resources—had to be sacrificed.

In the end, the compromise solution protected the icon—the fort and its fields of fire—without ignoring the need for a survey and mitigation of buried archeological resources—the "invisible" history. None of the groups involved, however, found the compromise completely satisfactory, but it represented an acceptable accommodation for all. The decision by the county to purchase additional lots, primarily in the fields of fire, also mollified the local community since it reduced the total number of new houses planned. Throughout the process, however, "history" was just one of many issues. Those who recognized the advantage of having "history" as an ally, for example, the developer who used it to gain more lots and the neighborhood civic group that used it to slow or restrict development, advocated preservation. In contrast, once "history" lost its usefulness or even obstructed desired goals, its importance to an individual or interest group diminished markedly. The presence of an icon—the visible remains of the *last* surviving Civil War fort in the county—greatly aided the historians' cause, but emphasis on this material symbol competed with the need to preserve other equally important cultural resources.

CONCLUSION

We have tried to demonstrate some of the ways people can manipulate "history" to support and create popular myths and symbols of the past, and achieve ends not grounded exclusively in a commitment to preserve that past. As archeologists and cultural resource managers, we would be naive to ignore other, sometimes powerful, goals, interests, motives, and issues that compete with preservation. As social scientists, we have only begun to explore the cultural impacts of preservation, an area that we suggest demands more attention than it has received. Exposing some of the potential for conflict and compromise within and between groups reveals not only the politicizing of historical issues, but also some of the inherent complexities in real communities.

We would argue that most communities weigh preservation against other strongly held and deeply rooted goals and values. We do not intend to suggest that communities are homogeneous, composed of individuals whose attitudes, values, and goals are in perfect harmony. We recognize that communities can exhibit deep internal divisions reflecting social, political, economic, and/or ethnic differences. The point here is that preservation may have a low priority for many residents of a community relative to the significance assigned to other values and goals.

In ranking priorities, issues, causes, and goals, to say that the cost of historic preservation is too high relative to other aims does not necessarily imply that "history" is unimportant to communities. As we have shown, we would often be wrong to assume that members of a neighborhood either fail to grasp or ignore the value of history. This means that as cultural resource managers our emphasis on public education is insufficient to stimulate a commitment to a "conservation ethic" (Fowler 1986). Some suggest that we must find a way to raise the stature of preservation in terms of other significant values and goals: "Historic preservationists have been successful only when they can demonstrate or develop legal tools to allow preservation to become a matter of economic gain" (Fowler 1986:153). Again, however, this may be too simplistic an approach, for it neglects an evaluation of the local effects and repercussions of preservation as strategy and as process.

Even in communities that support historic preservation, as we have seen, the motivation for this support may not derive exclusively from a strong belief in the conservation ethic. When threatened by real or perceived transformation imposed from without, community groups can and do respond with a number of strategies, including the use of preservation statutes. We must recognize that community support for preservation can evaporate when its usefulness in achieving other more significant individual or neighborhood goals falters.

Imbedded within and complicating these issues is the neighborhood mythology or popular history, and historic icons. Conflict between competing pasts, and between popular local history and that collected and interpreted by specialists, can have deleterious effects on preservation procedure and process. These conflicts can erode cooperation and support within the local community being studied and lead to disagreements over what constitutes historically valuable resources. Should historic preservation actively embrace identified "icons" in order to gain local support and interest, or should the icons be challenged if historical research fails to reinforce their perceived importance? The quandary has no one simple solution, but we have suggested that a willingness of cultural resource managers to present their findings to the local community, and to participate on local commissions or boards, can foster channels of communication among all groups involved and retard the development of some of the more damaging aspects of this conflict.

Certainly we have addressed only limited aspects of the complexity of this issue. As has been noted, the "real," more "objective" neighborhood history we produce is itself a kind of "creation myth," and National Register status can establish icons or reaffirm their symbolic historical importance. As we attempt to control the historical record by selecting sites to preserve, and protect, like the local communities we are adding meaning to the past, even if our procedures are more organized, explicit, and clearly defined.

If cultures can be viewed as "collective phenomena" composed of "symbols and meanings as public and shared . . . [and] knowledge as *distributed* and *controlled*" (Keesing 1987:161; emphasis added), then it would be of value for us to explore the "anthropology of preservation." As cultural resource managers, we are committed to the conservation of historically and archeologically significant sites for present and future generations. Yet this goal is not separate and distinct from others, but is part of a sociopolitical milieu that must be examined and understood if we are to be successful.

NOTES

1. The history of preservation in the United States and the current status of historic preservation legislation, particularly as it pertains to archeological sites, have been summarized elsewhere (e.g., Knudson 1986; Fowler 1982, 1986; King and Lyneis 1978) and will not be repeated here.

2. For more in-depth discussion of the "significance" concept and its application to the historic preservation process, see Butler 1987; Dunnell 1984; Tainter and Lucas 1983; Raab and Klinger 1977; and Glassow 1977, for example.

3. We have used the term "myth" to describe fictionalized accounts of the past at least somewhat grounded in fact and incorporated within a local value system. While the term "legend" might be more appropriate, we used "myth" because of the associations of these stories with community values and perceptions of the community's past, and also as a link to the concept of "creation myth." We have called these accounts of the founding of modern communities "creation myths," even though they do not have the strong religious/belief connotations usually associated with the term. They do, however, help to place members of the communities in time and historic space by establishing the beginning point for the community in which they live.

4. Our survey work in Brookland and Deanwood was conducted under two matching grants-in-aid sponsored by the National Park Service and the D.C. Department of Consumer and Regulatory Affairs, D.C. Historic Preservation Division. These grants supported research from September 1986 to September 1987.

5. Prior to our research, George McDaniel et al. (1982) published an excellent summary of Brookland history. Although their work was invaluable to our research, it cannot be considered comprehensive as defined by our grant since it failed to address the pre-1887 history of this neighborhood, included no archeological survey, and only sampled the variety of Brookland's built environment.

6. When the federal city of Washington was established, only a portion of the new District of Columbia was platted into streets and city blocks. In the northeast quadrant of the District of Columbia, this was the area west of the Anacostia River (or Eastern Branch) and south of Boundary Street (Florida Avenue). The remainder of the District of Columbia, known as Washington County, remained agricultural and rural through most of the nineteenth century, with pockets of small farms persisting even to the twentieth century.

Most published material concerning the history of Washington, D.C., focuses almost exclusively on Washington City and Georgetown.

7. As will be seen with Brookland, the surname of the male—"Dean" of Deanwood and "Brooks" of Brookland—who married into the landed family, the Sheriffs and Queens, respectively, was used to designate the later suburban community.

8. Although Washington County had many slaveholders, not all farmers relied on slave labor, nor were slaves evenly distributed among those who did. For example, in the Deanwood area in 1850 Levi Sheriff owned nineteen "hands," or slaves, while another prominent landowner of the survey area, James Fowler, possessed only two (Overbeck et al. 1987). In Brookland in 1860 the large landowners possessed a total of fifty-six slaves, while it appears that one small farmer/gardener owned none. In addition, in 1860 Brookland slaves were not the only source of labor, for free blacks and white laborers and servants worked in the same households (Verrey et al. 1987).

9. Within the D.C. Historic Preservation Division, recipients of survey and planning grants are encouraged to notify community groups of their research and present their findings at public forums within the community.

10. In Deanwood, unfortunately, although a similar presentation was planned, discussed, and prepared by the cultural resource specialists involved in the project, it never materialized owing to administrative problems encountered within the agency that received the grant.

11. After all parties involved reached a compromise solution on the preservation of this site, and after the completion of this paper, we learned that the landowner subsequently refused to finalize the sale to the developer. In an out-of-court settlement, the landowner paid the developer to regain possession of the property containing Fort C. F. Smith. Since the preservation compromise depended on the plat of lots provided by the developer, it is now nullified, and the historic preservation status of the property is unresolved.

REFERENCES

Barnard, J. G.
1871    A Report on the Defenses of Washington, to the Chief of Engineers, U.S. Army. *Professional Papers of the Corps of Engineers, No. 20.* Washington, D.C.: Government Printing Office.

Butler, William B.
    1987    Significance and Other Frustrations in the CRM Process. *American Antiquity* 52: 820–29.

Cooling, Franklin B.
    1975    *Symbol, Sword and Shield.* Hamden, Conn.: Archon Books.

Crowell, Elizabeth, Dennis Knepper, and Marsha Miller
    1987    *Archeological Investigations at Fort C. F. Smith.* Report completed by Engineering Sciences for the Arlington County Division of Community Improvement.

Dunnell, R. C.
    1984    The Ethics of Archeological Significance Decisions. In *Ethics and Values in Archeology,* ed. M. B. Schiffer, pp. 62–74. New York: The Free Press.

Fowler, Don D.
    1982    Cultural Resource Management. In *Advances in Archeological Method and Theory,* ed. M. B. Schiffer, Vol. 5, pp. 1–50. New York: Academic Press.
    1986    Conserving American Archeological Resources. In *American Archeology, Past and Future,* ed. David Meltzer, Don D. Fowler, and Jeremy A. Sabloff, pp. 135–62. Washington, D.C.: Smithsonian Institution Press.

Glassow, M.
    1977    Issues in Evaluating the Significance of Archeological Resources. *American Antiquity* 42: 413–20.

Keesing, Roger M.
    1987    Anthropology as Interpretive Quest. *Current Anthropology* 28(2): 161–76.

King, T. F., and M. M. Lyneis
    1978    Preservation: A Developing Focus of American Archeology. *American Anthropologist* 80: 873–93.

Knudson, Ruthann
    1986    Contemporary Culture Resource Management. In *American Archeology, Past and Future,* ed. David Meltzer, Don Fowler, and Jeremy Sabloff, pp. 395–414. Washington, D.C.: Smithsonian Institution Press.

Kulikoff, Allan J.
    1986    *Tobacco and Slaves: The Development of Southern Culture in the*

*Chesapeake, 1680–1800.* Chapel Hill: University of North Carolina Press.

McDaniel, George, John Pearce, and Martin Aurand
1982    *Images of Brookland: The History and Architecture of a Washington Suburb.* George Washington University, Center for Washington Area Studies No. 10.

Mitchell, R. D., and Edward K. Muller
1979    Interpreting Maryland's Past: Praxis and Desiderata. In *Geographic Perspectives on Maryland's Past,* ed. R. Mitchell and E. Muller. The University of Maryland, Occasional Papers in Geography No. 4.

Overbeck, Ruth Ann, et al.
1987    *Final Report of Historical and Building Investigation of the Northeast Washington, D.C. Community of Deanwood, Phase I.* For the D.C. Department of Consumer and Regulatory Affairs, Historic Preservation Division, and the National Park Service.

Raab, L. M., and T. C. Klinger
1977    A Critical Appraisal of "Significance" in Contract Archeology. *American Antiquity* 42: 629–34.
1979    A Reply to Sharrock and Grayson on Archeological Significance. *American Antiquity* 44: 328–29.

Sharrock, F. W., and D. K. Grayson
1979    "Significance" in Contract Archeology. *American Antiquity* 44: 327–28.

Swallow, Wendy
1986    Restrictions on Historic Churches May Get Court Test. *Washington Post,* September 27, Section E1.

Tainter, J. A., and G. J. Lucas
1983    Epistemology of the Significance Concept. *American Antiquity* 48: 707–19.

Verrey, Robert, Laura Henley, William Gardner, and Judith Capen
1987    *Report of Results of the Brookland Community/Catholic University Historic Resources Survey in Northeast Washington, D.C.* For the National Park Service and the D.C. Department of Consumer and Regulatory Affairs, Historic Preservation Division.

Wheeler, Linda
1986    Split on Historic Districts. *Washington Post* (August 1): B1.

# CHAPTER 5

# Good Guys and Bad Toys

## The Paradoxical World of Children's Cartoons

*Brett Williams*

This chapter[1] explores the complicated, contradictory world that many American children inhabited in the 1980s. I examine the syndicated cartoons produced by toy companies and backed up by arrays of dolls and equipment. I am interested in the politics of producing, distributing, and managing culture for children, and in the implications of children's contrary uses of mass media.

Three dilemmas underlie this study. First, how can ethnographers in the United States unravel the many cultures this society contains? Second, how can students of popular culture move beyond a privileged reading of cultural texts to capture the interaction between those texts and an active audience? Finally, how can one balance a critical cultural perspective of seemingly commoditized play against a respect for children's views of what they do, and ethnographic authority against the ethical and methodological problems of studying children?[2]

To explain how I have tried to ground this reading of popular culture in time, place, and a social group, I must offer considerable background. I stumbled upon this world of children's play while writing an ethnography about adults living in a Washington neighborhood I called Elm Valley. Elm Valley had developed in the late nineteenth century as a streetcar suburb for commuting government workers. In the 1950s and '60s many of its white residents had left, and black Americans, mostly from North and South Carolina, settled there and built a community rich in shared southern traditions. Its lovely row-house architecture, scenic streetscapes, and convenient proximity to downtown Washington, D.C., made it attractive to gentrifying whites in the late 1970s. However, the high interest rates, faltering housing industry, and general economic hard times of the early 1980s stalled what probably would have been a harsh and rapid displacement of both renters and older owners. For several years Elm Valley experienced a precarious, intriguing kind of integration that was both rich in cultural character and rare in the contemporary United States. Its 5,000 residents included longer-term black residents, newer and more affluent whites, and an increasing number of refugees and immigrants from Central America, Southeast Asia, East Africa, and parts of the Caribbean.

Elm Valley proved to be an unusually interesting place to study different kinds of culture at work. Residents shared the same physical space but contributed the resources and traditions of varied backgrounds. The various residents therefore saw and used their place very differently, making it both lively and conflicted, illuminating both the promise and the problems of integrated cities. In *Upscaling Downtown* (Williams 1988) I wrote about the folk-cultural traditions that black residents preserved from the Carolinas in their alley gardens and family feasts; about different cultural and national traditions that undergirded multiethnic apartment building life; about different class-cultural values that inspired more middle-class residents to look outward and less affluent ones to root more deeply into the neighborhood. I also tried to examine public culture because I thought it might be a source of shared vocabulary and vision, and I was especially interested in television.

I was inspired in part by the work of Todd Gitlin (1981, 1987) who, along with scholars such as Muriel Cantor (1987, 1989), has done important research on how the organization of production shapes television content. Their work represents a worthwhile advance over popular culture research that merely offers one scholar's idiosyncratic reading of the layered meanings of a text. Nonetheless, some of Gitlin's arguments troubled me: How, for example, do we know, as he claims, that television brings us the familiar, the cultural mainstream, a kind of common-denominator culture? How do we know what real viewers see?

While doing research, I began to watch and talk about television with various residents of Elm Valley. I discovered class and cultural differences in the use of television and in the choice of programs to watch. While white middle-class viewers were drawn to such programs as "Hill Street Blues," "St. Elsewhere," and "L.A. Law," less affluent black viewers often enjoyed watching and discussing shows that treated the wealthy: "Dallas," "Dynasty," or "Knot's Landing." I was surprised to discover that a supposedly mass medium is divisive and even damaging, presenting members of one social class to those of another and often framing encounters between neighbors of different classes (Williams 1988).

I also performed many other kinds of research during ten years of living and working in Elm Valley. I variously lived in a large apartment building and in rented row houses on two different streets. I visited churches, schools, day-care centers, shops, and social agencies, and interviewed workers there. I attended many neighborhood and political meetings and festive events. I talked to longer- and shorter-term residents of many different backgrounds about their houses, their gardens, their families, and their feelings about the neighborhood. And I participated daily in Elm Valley's public life.

I was interested in adults and how they responded to the possibility of integration, but I also talked to many children in a variety of settings. However, I did not pay particular attention to their television viewing or to their play. Toward the end of my study, however, this changed for two reasons. First, I began to notice that young children's play in Elm Valley's parks and alleys, streets and sidewalks was quietly, easily integrated. If the slant of this paper seems romantic and the children unwitting heroes, it is because this integrated play contrasted with a backdrop of teenage and adult life usually divided along lines of class and race. This children's world offered a rare place where neighbors came together across the sharp boundaries that separated adults.

Second, I began to work with other residents on a series of programs highlighting folk traditions rooted in different stages of the life cycle. Our plan was to celebrate both commonality and diversity by demonstrating what people might share because they were the same age and yet how they varied by virtue of being from different cultural groups. These programs explored hair art, gardening, cooking, healing, dance, and play. My task was to visit Elm Valley's nursery schools and day-care centers in search of such folk-play traditions as Mexican clapping games, Salvadoran tops and marbles, double Dutch and Vietnamese jump rope. These games were there. However, when I asked children to talk about what they liked to play, and especially when I sat in a corner and just watched them, I was struck by what they actually liked to do when given the choice: They took on identities and performed acts borrowed from syndicated cartoons (Mergen 1982).

When they were at home, children supplemented their play with action figures, action-fashion figures, and an array of other props. Black American children joined middle-class white children from gentrifying families, as well as refugee children from El Salvador, Guatemala, Ethiopia, Jamaica, Laos, Cambodia, and Vietnam, in watching, sharing, and "knowing" a cartoon and toy world aimed at children younger than six. Was this folk play? It was rooted in a commercial medium, yet brought children together as a group distinct from social groups of different ages. Although I largely set this phenomenon aside to complete my ethnography, I continued to observe and talk to children about it. The toys and cartoons that once seemed so powerful and omnipresent have now disappeared from public culture.[3] Yet I continue to believe that this phenomenon opens up intriguing theoretical questions, which I explore in some detail below.

This paper has five parts. I begin with a short discussion of the political and economic forces that shape the production of the cartoons. I turn to the cartoons as texts and then link those texts to several layers of consumer culture. I next explore processes of viewing and sharing, through which children tried to separate themselves from adult gatekeepers and built ties (perhaps accidental or illusory) to one another across boundaries of ethnicity, race, gender, and class. I conclude with observations on the children's construction of a liberating generational identity out of the odious offerings of the mass media.

THE PRODUCTION OF CULTURE

Children's cartoons clearly intersect recent political, economic, and technological history in the United States. Cartoons of the mid-1980s reflect the widespread deregulation and some of the dominant cultural themes of the Reagan years. Cartoons that many adults find stultifying and repetitive grew out of daring, original experimentation by toy companies and attracted masses of diverse child viewers and consumers. The roots of the cartoons' commercial success lie in the phenomenon of character licensing.

Character licensing began modestly with the appropriation of Buster Brown to market Brown shoes in 1904. In the 1930s Walt Disney pioneered more ambitious links among toys, motifs, and film when he introduced Mickey Mouse, followed by a legion of other characters. Early in that decade he began to offer merchandisers the use of his animals for school writing tablets. By 1934 he drew international royalties from the use of Disney characters in return for 5 percent of all profits on the items sold. Consumer tie-ins flourished during the 1930s, and Disney's strategies were widely imitated. Later, toy manufacturers capitalized on a variety of cultural fashions and fads: space and military toys for boys and sexy Barbie dolls for girls; Howdy Doody, the Flying Nun, and Vietnam's G.I. Joe (later miniaturized and linked to a syndicated cartoon). The 1970s established a firm pattern of marketing both fads and persons whose fame came from movies or television. By the late 1970s Hanna Barbera boasted that their characters appeared on 4,500 different products. During these years manufacturers paid for the rights to use already established characters to sell their products (Engelhardt 1987; Mergen 1982; Williams 1986).

Federal Communications Commission (FCC) deregulation of children's programming in 1982 encouraged the networks to abandon such programming in favor of more profitable shows for adults. The additional financial crunch suffered by public broadcasting left a weekday vacuum in television for children. Creative entrepreneurs in the greeting card and toy business filled the hole in novel ways. Beginning with such characters as "Strawberry Shortcake" and "He-Man," these entrepreneurs quickly discovered the advantage of creating the character first then constructing a backstory for it. Companies sold the backstories to independent stations for syndication, saved the character-licensing fees they had once paid networks, and gathered much higher profits for themselves.

Their success was made possible because the FCC had dropped both its insistence on educational, alternative programs and its regulation limiting commercial minutes per show. Thus an entire program could be a commercial. By the mid-1980s the most important producers of syndicated children's television programs were Coleco, Hasbro, and Mattel, with the help of inexpensive overseas labor. They sold programs offering recyclable episodic plots, featuring animation many adults found shoddy, with computer-generated, static, posed figures, paradoxically forced and stilted action streamlined of all incidental and naturalist movement, and minimalist, awkward writing. They also created characters whose replicas children could buy in toy stores. So many more shows and toys appeared in seemingly endless proliferation that the market, as well as television time, was soon saturated. However, for several years an elaborate network of manufacturers, advertisers, distributors, and television producers dramatized modern connections between the mass media and play, with perhaps unprecedented cultural power over American children's lives (Engelhardt 1987).

## "SHE HAS THAT LONG HAIR AND THAT SWORD"

Three kinds of cartoons dominated syndicated programs. One aimed at little girls and included groups of characters joined by relational values. "Rainbow Brite" had a set of multicolored friends; both friends and kin surrounded "My Little Pony"; each of the "Care Bears" stood for one emotion; and each of the "Smurfs" represented one human idiosyncrasy (for example, "Brainy's" strangeness lay in being smart and therefore wearing glasses, "Smurfette's" in being female and wearing high heels). "Strawberry Shortcake" presided over a group, mostly little girls, named after such things to eat as

"Plum Pudding" and "Lemon Tart." The community included two little boys, one lazy, the other smart and therefore wearing glasses. These groups worked cooperatively and easily expressed feelings for each other. They did not fight but did live under perpetual threat. Strawberry Shortcake and her friends, for example, felt menaced by the "Purple Pieman," who minced around in purple tights and appeared to represent a homosexual child molester.

At the other extreme lay programs the toy companies intended for boys, which also displayed striking similarities. All presented heroes on teams, as opposed to other kinds of groups united by kinship, religion, community, ethnicity, or work. Teammates had no common ties or work other than those involving fighting. Each good team faced an evil team that chased, attacked, captured, and deceived them. Some teams had forceful leaders, such as "He-Man," the "Phantom" (on "Defenders of the Earth"), and "Duke" (on "G.I. Joe"). Most teams, however, featured many players with particularized, but important, roles.[4]

Good teams and their corresponding "bad guys" included: "Mask Invaders," whose members Hurricane, Vampire, Thunderhawk, Rhino, and Condor battled the forces of Venom; G.I. Joe, a code name for a group of American soldiers who "defended the peace" against the terrorist forces of Cobra; the "Transformers," which pitted Autobots (such as Megasupreme and Optimus Prime) against the Decepticons; the "Thundercats" (including Cheetara, Liono, Tigra, and Wileycat), who fought the forces of Mumra; "Silverhawks"; and Defenders of the Earth. All offered children a vision of good, strong, competent characters who with their colleagues do battle in perpetuity.

Perhaps because the cartoons were all so similar, new teams frequently emerged, each offering a special twist. Many transformed from one state of being to another, ranging from the animal-human Thundercats to the entirely machined Transformers and "Voltrons." He-Man hid out as the cowardly Prince Adam. For the most part, the characters were grown-ups, although childlike team members occasionally appeared who were important mostly because they knew the secrets of transformation. The action figures had animal friends such as He-Man's Battlecat/Cringer and an array of more sophisticated vehicles, weapons, castles, and fortresses. In fact, for the Mask team, vehicles were seemingly more important than their human operators, as they bore names, identifiable qualities, and diverse skills at transformation and illusion.

Each team seemed to represent an "imagined community," in Benedict Anderson's evocative description of nationalism as a sense of affective horizontal ties to strangers (for whom one would kill) operating simultaneously in empty homogeneous time (Anderson 1983). G.I. Joe captured a variety of folk Americanisms in its integrated cast, which included black soldiers such as Iceberg, an Indian named Quick Kick, an Asian American called Gung Ho, and a host of others who symbolized bedrock working-class masculine associations that sometimes celebrated the compound word: Seahawk, Shipwreck, Dialtone, Scrapiron, Flint, Stormshadow, Lady J, Bazooka, and Barbecue. Their opponents (Cobra) represented citizens of an ill-defined other nation led by the Baronness. Enemies often bore the names of snakes or women.

Defenders of the Earth featured an unusual cast of children who did battle on behalf of and through the medium of the earth's computers. Their leader was a Texan with the inappropriate name of Bluegrass. Otherwise these imagined communities were strikingly up- and unrooted, especially in contrast to such 1950s characters as Yogi Bear, who lived in "Jellystone National Park." Their nations were imaginary but deeply nationalist in spirit. Utterly outside time and space, they offered the illusion of culture, through complicated linguistic codes, theme songs, biological or mechanical similarities, and through the firm boundaries that separated them from the teams of evil. He-Man's "Eternia" had a national anthem and a national origin myth; others experienced episodic repetitions of a legendary past. For example, a female Skyband occasionally reinvaded the Defenders of the Earth. The Defenders could not kill these women, but lived under an ancient curse because Phantom's grandfather had once mistakenly killed the women's leader.

These national teams took their identity most powerfully from their perpetual battle with other teams who looked different. The

Thundercats battled the Mutants, human bodies bearing animal heads. He-Man and his friends fought Skeletor and the dead. Cartoons incorporated a world of differences and recombinations, bringing them all into unambiguous membership on teams and seemingly claiming that it takes two to make a nation.

These nations existed in a world without history. Cartoons recombined historical motifs, logos, costumes, architectural styles, vehicles, and weapons. Kings, queens, and princes lived in medieval castles and jetted around on airborne motorcycles. Swords, the weapons of choice, met force fields. One episode of Thundercats featured leader Liono's Lilliputian capture by the Micrants, angered that his team was trampling their homes. While Liono was tied up, the Mutants infiltrated his castle and reprogrammed his robots. Cartoons relied deeply on the illusion of history while turning it upside down.

These cartoons offered little children an arrogantly gendered world for the 1980s, featuring perpetual battles for boys and banal interpersonal relationships for girls. From the first, He-Man, although an unnaturally muscular, nearly naked blonde, seemed to offer a milder alternative, reflected in his refusal to "harm a living thing." I believe that producers intended He-Man as transitional for little boys, who were expected to graduate from the more banal and relational programs to the more military ones. Little girls were intended to stick with such shows as Rainbow Brite. While many little girls enjoyed girls' programming, many also strained to find a place for themselves in the world of heroes and teams. Girls referred to themselves as "He-Girl" or took on the identity of his friend Tila. Responding to research showing that 30 percent of those tuned into He-Man were girls, Mattel introduced his sister She-Ra, a "fashion-action figure" (Engelhardt 1987).[5]

The large bat Hordac had captured She-Ra when she was an infant, but her brother He-Man rediscovered her when they were young adults. While in captivity, she had managed to build a sort of Herlandian utopia called Etheria, composed almost entirely of other women with names like Mermist, Angella, and Perfuma (who wore a backpack that squirted perfume at her enemies). The jealous green-eyed beauty Catra, whose main liability was her long tail, harassed

Etheria through her power to create such noxious things as weeds and
sea monsters. Catra's teammates Frosta, Castaspella, and Double Trou-
ble helped her menace the women of Etheria.

Taking her place alongside her brother He-Man, She-Ra mediated
the violent and banal worlds of children's cartoons. She was almost
instantly popular among little girls, who articulated her doubleness.
One four-year-old girl from a Vietnamese family said of She-Ra: "I like
her because she's a woman. She has that long hair and that sword."
"What does she do?" I asked. "She fights." "Who does she fight?"
"Hordac." "Why?" "Because he's bad." "How do you know?" "He
looks bad." Other girls commented: "I like her because she's strong."
"She has that long hair and those boots." "She has that sword." She-Ra
lasted in syndication in Washington for only about two years and disappeared from toy stores quickly after leaving television.

## "I DIDN'T GET ANY BAD TOYS"

Todd Gitlin (1987) argues that television offers an amoral ode to the
blessings of a consumer society, and Brian Sutton-Smith writes with
particular power of the ways that television mediates the toy market
through repeated advertising and magnetic programs. Sutton-Smith
worries that television's power to control play may make modern play
a kind of consumer training, especially since television addicts children
to novelty (Sutton-Smith 1986:169). Certainly, syndicated cartoons
glorified consumption. Many children could recognize commercials
and reproduce them in meticulous detail. The culture of consumption
represented in syndicated cartoon/toys had several layers, beginning
with the celebration of collections, moving through the transformation of children's social relationships and rites of passage (which I call
the commoditization of celebrations), and most problematically influencing children's sense of consuming as "knowing."

Beginning in 1982, toy companies simultaneously produced programs and dolls, or "action figures," that reproduced the cast of each
show. Children enthusiastically collected and shared a wide range of
dolls, usually beginning with Superfriends or creatures such as Beast-

man, Ramman, Fisto, Skeletor, Mossman, Man E Faces, and the like from He-Man. As they grew older, they moved on to G.I. Joe, Mask, and eventually Transformers. Children also bought animal and vehicle carriers for their dolls—Swift Wind or Glimmer for She-Ra, Gambolfish or Snowcat for G.I. Joe. They bought special weapon packs, castles, and fortresses. These toys were advertised during the programs, displayed prominently in toy, variety, drug, and grocery stores, and promoted through word of mouth by children themselves. Children's enthusiasm for classifying, organizing, and collecting action figures seemed to verify Stewart's (1984) sense that collecting represents a paradise of consumption, where the labor of the consumer is the labor of total magic.

The toy brand names took on a life of their own, as they legitimized other objects, from sandpails through bedsheets, underwear, pajamas, dishes, watches, luggage sets, vitamins, toothbrushes, bathing suits, belts, backpacks, slippers, kites, comic books, sleeping bags, cake pans, raincoats, windsocks, lunchboxes, bicycles, and even Halloween costumes and birthday cakes. Girls received special marketing attention through dolls' fashion items and a large repertoire of animals with long manes, tailpieces and other hairy attachments, and clothes, including My Little Pony, Furrever Friends, Fluppie Puppies, and a whole host of other insipid creatures who "make affection seem unhealthy" (Bull 1987:B2).

The toys contributed to the transformation of the rites of passage in children's lives into passages of style, as many children's birthday parties had Smurf, Rainbow Brite, Superfriends, or Transformer themes, with logos from these programs adorning invitations, lootbags, napkins, plates, cups, and cake. Children often demanded such brand-name legitimizing for many objects and events in their lives; some parents found that every purchase became a negotiation about their children's participation in this world. Particular brand names, and television toys in general, were important sources of status. After visiting a new friend's home, children often returned to list the "bad" toys that child possessed. I once watched a group of children gather around a woman and her son parking their car. As the little boy emerged with a brand new Castle Greyskull, the children murmured both enthusiastically and regretfully, "What a nice Mama," and "I wish I had a Mama like that." After a large festive birthday barbecue in the park, another boy remarked, "I didn't get much toys for my birthday." In response to his mother's incredulous reply (the back of their car was filled with gifts), he explained, "I didn't get any *bad* toys."[6]

Beyond presenting children with toys they must own, legitimizing their possessions and celebrations, and offering them status in the world of other children, child consumer culture is disturbing on a deeper and more complicated level. Jean Agnew discusses the confusion in consumer culture between acquiring things and knowing. Consuming, he argues, often reflects "a passion for the code," a need to navigate the "forest of symbols" through which advertisers attach clusters of attributes to products. Because business introduces so many new products each year, advertisers must reshuffle the symbolic qualities (sex appeal, down-home ethnicity) they have attached to other products (mouthwash, toothpaste, lemonade, or pizza). As travelers in consumer culture, we need to be vigilant about recontextualizing these weightless attributes, yet each reorientation is ultimately another dislocation (Agnew 1983:65–100).

Agnew examines how advertisers pose these problems of knowledge, not how people actually behave. Yet Elm Valley's children almost exaggerate his claim that as members of a consumer society we learn to treat consumption as knowledge. They learned dozens of compound names such as Sy-Klone, Psykill, Mekaneck, Two Bad, Spikor, Stinkor, Evil-Lyn, Jitsu, Clawfull, Merman, Mantenna, Modulok, Rokkon, Scare Glow, Rio Blast, Snout Mouth, Grizzlor, Clamp Champ, Snout Spout, Man E Faces, Stridor, Zoar, Dragon Walker, Road Ripper, Battle Ram, Attak Trak, Wind Raider, Night Stalker, Roton, and Spydor. They learned to attach unrealistically narrow skills to varied characters who specialized in particular destructive capabilities. They learned about illusory cultures and the vocabularies that knit them together: Thunderanium, Thunderillium, Thundera, and the Thunder-Thunder-Thunder-ThunderCATS. They frequently exchanged information, sharing knowledge as they listed names, traced genealogies and relationships, detailed qualities, and debated who could beat whom. They knew the theme songs and battlecries and how to attach them to programs and characters. On one summer evening in 1986, for example, my neighbors and I were serenaded by a rock band composed of musicians under the age of six, with parents from Ireland, Egypt, North Carolina, and Peru, who, with badminton rackets for guitars, sang twenty-minute medleys of cartoon theme songs! Mergen (1982) writes that children may learn from movies as much about how to tell a story as they do about the content of a particular film. Perhaps one clue to how children's lore seems to survive the standardizing influence of the mass media is that cartoons and toys help them learn about and practice the idea of shared, known childlore.

A glossy insert inside each Mask Invaders box linked that toy to the whole world of connected toys. It also featured a test, including vehicle acrostics, fill-in-the-blanks, matching, multiple choice, and true or false questions about Mask toys. Children who passed the test could help to rescue the Secretary General of the United Nations, kidnapped by the forces of Venom. Appropriately titled "Illusion is the Ultimate Weapon," it fused in a powerful way themes of buying, owning, knowing, acting, and being.

The acquisition of such knowledge seemed to be an integral part of child culture and was disturbing because it was both meaningless and at the same time deeply meaningful: Children learned to celebrate and honor consumption in a universal language that knitted them together in an ever-transportable and recreated kind of local and national community.

## "WE CAN PLAY BROTHER AND SISTER"

If this were the end of the story, I could conclude, dismally, that our children are easily brainwashed by a powerful combination of messages about war and consumption from corporations trafficking in the business of culture. However, I feel somewhat encouraged by what children actually *did* with what they saw. As Mergen writes: "Although toys are presented to them heavy with the missions of the culture or the toymakers, children do nevertheless exact from within those constraints some small pieces of their own destiny" (Mergen 1982:213).[7]

Children in this Washington neighborhood enjoyed many opportunities for integrated play, in their apartment buildings, in alleys and parks, and in an array of multicultural nursery schools and day-care centers. Much more than the adults did in their lives, the children participated in an integrated community. They invented and played many kinds of games, ranging from folk games, learned in nursery school and from each other, to the spontaneous imaginary play so important to urban life, to games inspired by playground equipment. They "went camping," built clubhouses, jumped rope, played freeze tag and "Old Lady Witch," and improvised games with toy cars and stuffed animals. Yet their most widely shared and inspired play emerged from television.

Homogeneous syndicated programs relentlessly entered many homes in the neighborhood during the vulnerable hours of 7–9 A.M. and 3–6 P.M., to be greeted by a variety of household routines, resources, and webs of approval, indifference, and condemnation. Even adults who refused to buy TV sets or to allow their children to watch found that their children took part. Unlike programs such as the Cosby Show, which tried to attract whole families, the syndicated cartoons set up cultural boundaries between children and adults, who served mostly as gatekeepers to shows and toys.

Children often took a perverse pleasure in these boundaries, smuggling toys to school, concocting terms such as "bad toys," and staging melodramatic toy-store scenes and negotiations. In Washington toy stores at least, one could often see irritated adults trying to draw their children away from the bad toys on display. Other bemused but ignorant grown-ups pondered which bad toys to buy, tried to decode the complicated information that helped children know which ones were appropriate, or sought advice from other child consumers in buying gifts for their own. No matter which interactional style adults chose on a particular day, they were likely to dramatize the boundaries that separated them from children in this world.[8]

Many parents tolerated the programs and the toys because, in spite of their militaristic character, they sometimes spoke to values parents shared. Some parents felt that the toys gave their sons the excuse to "play with dolls," or helped their daughters develop mechanical skills. Almost all the programs featured some competent, fighting female characters, a clever strategy for retailing feminism while still offering toys with hairpieces because "little girls like to comb and brush" (Bull 1987:B1). Most good human teams in the programs featured black characters. He-Man was purposefully nonviolent, never really harming a living thing and concluding each program with a pat moral. Each episode of Silverhawks ended with a brief science lesson. One progressive mother defended She-Ra as the leader of a never-quite-successful rebellion against an unjust and oppressive regime, unlike many of the other teams that fought to defend the status quo.

Parents at times debated these values. Some were more concerned than others. Many in this harried neighborhood simply did not have time to do battle with television for their children's attention. Although some of the new white families forbade their children to watch these programs or to watch television at all, this injunction rarely limited their children's participation in this hallmark of child culture in Elm Valley.

Children's commodities were unlike many that adults come to know and consume because they were deeply communal and participatory. They linked children across boundaries that divide adults. I have watched children transport bad toys, talk, and play to other cities and states with ease. Children from Central America and Southeast Asia talked about programs, exchanged evaluations of different characters, compared notes on possessions, formed teams, and invented their own games. They tied towels around their necks, swung from trees and monkey bars, built caverns and castles, and recreated themes from their favorite shows. They showed dolls to one another (sometimes as smuggled contraband at school recess), lined them up, inspected and manipulated them, placed them in vehicles, took them into the bathtub and into bed, dressed and talked to them, and asked them to talk to each other. I have often wondered if teams of women and men figures equipped with such tools as ice axes, trapezes, and guitars might not have served these children's purposes just as well as teams of soldiers.

I once watched a group of children improvise an intricate web of yarn for G.I. Joe figures to slide gracefully from tree bush to railing, in contrast to toy advertisements, which unfailingly showed children carefully recreating the perpetual wars of the TV shows. Parents who refused to buy the toys were sometimes distraught to see their children playing easily with garbage-can covers for shields and sticks for swords atop the jungle gym as Castle Greyskull. Parents who thought the toys would make their children more aggressive or patriotic were sometimes surprised to see the gentle uses to which the toys could be put. As one little boy wrote in a first grade essay: "I like G.I. Joe vehicles a lot. Some fly and some ride on the ground or water." One afternoon I watched a little girl and boy play house, a game that commenced with the girl's exclamation: "Oh, good, you have Battle Armor He-Man. I have Starburst She-Ra. We can play brother and sister!" Program-length commercials, character licensing, and even family rules could not control how children perceived and reinterpreted their toys. In some sense they seemed to transform popular culture into folk culture as they built new shared identities and made it their own.

Although children's television culture seemed communal, both gender and class influenced children's participation in contradictory ways. For example, both Barbie and action-figure dolls like She-Ra, intended for girls, had elaborate costumes, hairpieces, and glitz. And as little girls and boys became five or six, they seemed to turn to more gender-segregated TV programs. For example, during the rock band episode described above, several older boys hooted when little boys joined the girl musicians in singing songs from My Little Pony and Rainbow Brite. In 1987 Washington's local station substituted Flintstones reruns for She-Ra in its apical afternoon position; G.I. Joe at the same time removed the popular character Lady J. The two coinciding events made a number of little girls in Washington feel dislocated and confused. Commented one, "I guess it was too hard to make two shows." As these little girls turned back to Barbie, the boys of their age found Nintendo, to be described below.

Class seemed to become important even earlier. For example, middle-class children even while very young were more likely to live in houses and have easier access to the outdoors. Children whose parents or servants could cook and clean while the children played outside were less dependent on the syndicated programs. As children aged, class-related differences in participation became more pronounced. Those with middle-class parents began to range farther outside the neighborhood to attend private or more prestigious public schools, to take soccer, music, or swimming lessons, and to participate less in integrated neighborhood life. Those who learned to read and to value reading sometimes found that books helped to free them from the syndicated cartoons. Thus, parents' strategies for seeking cosmopolitan breadth for their older children removed such children from the world of cartoons, leaving it more segregated.[9]

In late 1987 Japanese and U.S. companies moved into the elite and privileged arenas that include home computer software and videos, more available to families with greater resources. The Japanese company Nintendo overwhelmed the U.S. market for boys older than six, enticing the more affluent with an array of vibrant interactive video games that miniaturize the heavens, the underworld, the Middle Ages, and the Space Age. These games once again gave high status to white male characters while featuring white women and people of color in more stereotypical roles. Nintendo systems seem perfectly designed for the cohort of little boys graduating from the action-figure syndicated cartoon stage. The game rewards complicated visual skills, precision, and concentration; little boys soon began to build collections and complicated social systems for swapping games, tricks, and secrets. Little girls once again try to find a place for themselves in this all-male world (cf. Mergen 1982; Sutton-Smith 1986).

As these phenomena blend television and toys in ever more sophisticated ways, we can see more clearly the extraordinary mix of national cultural processes, community demographics, and household resources and strategies for living that helps to shape the world of children's commoditized play. Cartoons invaded and disrupted community routines and household agendas through flexible syndicated scheduling, rescheduling, and even recycling previously discarded texts. As children and their families responded to this invasion and to each other's responses they also wrestled with central conflicts between autonomy and powerlessness in American culture.

Those who want to understand how children take part in American culture face a dilemma. How do we listen to children's voices, honor their authority to interpret their own acts, understand and respect what they know and do, and yet criticize the media that seem to taunt and betray them? How can we interpret a web of connections that look like vital boundary-crossing folk traditions but take root in shallow, fleeting, empty commercial offerings and tired but dominant Western values? How can we respond to what appears to be a generation's false consciousness without yielding to the very commercial processes that separate children from adults? How should we react to children's celebration of that separation?

I have been tempted to see Elm Valley's children heroically resisting hegemony, attaching their own meanings to cartoons and building folk-cultural bridges across the barriers that separate adults. I would like to argue that children collectively liberated themselves from both the noxious themes of television cartoons and the weight of race, class, and gender in the lives of their parents. I would also like to argue that the world the children built could not transcend the limits of its origins. Both portraits offer partial truth, I believe, reflecting perhaps the partialness of folk culture itself, as it both takes part in the dominant ideology and expresses its contradictions, paradoxically recreating both autonomy and constraints (Denning 1987; Radway 1984; Sider 1986).

The children of Elm Valley acted out powerful fictional identities rooted in ahistorical worlds created by toy manufacturers especially for them. They took joy in these disjointed, fantastic worlds, planted their own meanings, delighted in manipulating memory and detail, separated themselves from the visible adults in their lives, and yet ultimately connected themselves to adults with far more cultural power than their teachers and parents. These adults have developed powerful, profitable media for reaching various children and offering them the means to play and talk together through some of the most horrifyingly violent, sexist, militaristic, nationalistic, tasteless, and ephemeral means imaginable. In many cities children learned to invent communities out of these commodities and to make them their own. Yet children may have learned to replace community with consumption, as more and more American adults have learned to do. Children may also have learned that consuming is empowering, that people come in teams, that the good guys always win, that history does not matter but bad toys *do*.

## NOTES

1. I presented an earlier version of this paper at the meetings of the American Ethnological Society in 1987. I am grateful for comments there from Margaret Goldberg, Karen Ito, William Leap, Norma Linton, John Lucey, Roger Sanjek, Ted Schwartz, and Carol Stack, and for extensive comments afterward by Richard Handler and Bernard Mergen. I presented a second version at George Mason University's Second Annual Feminist Roundtable in 1988 and appreciate the advice I received there from Tracey Boisseau, Muriel Cantor, Barbara Melosh, Kathy Peiss, and Leslie Prosterman.

2. Mergen (1982) expresses some of the difficulties faced by adults who study childhood, which he compares to a larval stage to which adult butterflies cannot quite return. Fine offers helpful advice for studying children's groups ethically and nonintrusively in his (1987) book on Little League. Other scholars today take an interest in examining popular culture more interactively. These include Michael Denning (1987), who studied the production of dime novels and their contradictory meanings to working-class people. Denning writes that the history of popular culture is best read as the history of social relations among industries producing cheap commodities, symbolic forms raised by working-class culture, and attempts by the dominant culture to reform and police the working class. Janice Radway (1984) cautions eloquently against treating a literary text as complex but fixed, comprising several layers of meaning that a scholar can translate in order to lay bare the ideological content through which it controls readers. Such a conception, argues Radway, reifies commodities, precludes resistance, and portrays readers as passive consumers of meaning. She sees them instead as contributing to the making of meaning, in both combative and compensatory, conservative and oppositional ways.

3. Most readers anywhere in the United States, especially if they knew children, will probably remember these toys. Despite my romantic notion of

how children played, I do respect the cautions of Sutton-Smith and Kelly-Byrne (1984), who worry that adults increasingly laud play as voluntary, egalitarian, and positive, and overlook its cruel and unseemly qualities. I have tried to balance the need to criticize the cartoons against a desire to respect the children.

4. An exception was the "Bionic Six," a family. The word "team" appears to have passed temporarily into everyday conversation to stand for such phenomena as "friends," "groups," or short-term alliances. Kindergarten and first-grade children at Elm Valley's elementary school would sometimes detail the division of their classroom into such groups as "Cheryl's team." One could sometimes overhear such remarks as "Kevin won't let me ride his bike just because I'm on Joey's team," in reference to a passing neighborhood schism. One boy remarked to his mother during a dispute about bedtime, "I'm not speaking to you because you're on Daddy's team."

5. Barbara Melosh (personal communication 1988) notes that it would be interesting to know more about why little girls prefer She-Ra: Do they already sense that relational values are devalued in American culture, or do they learn that from the cartoons? What are the multiple sources of their consciousness? How dependent are the texts on the larger society? To what extent do the problems of meaning lie far outside the cartoons themselves?

6. Engelhardt (1987) reports that the sale of non-name dolls had dropped 30 percent in the early 1980s! Children of course *did* question the messages of advertisers. One little girl commented, surveying her new Crystal Castle: "It doesn't look like it does on TV."

Sutton-Smith (1986) writes persuasively about several paradoxes that surround the consumption of toys. For example, 60% of all toys are purchased for Christmas, when love is shown through a virtual festival of consumption, and when gifts signify both the bonds and the control of the family. Sutton-Smith believes that children are especially vulnerable to the culture of consumption during their first five years, after which "the larger community exacts its own sanities" (Sutton-Smith 1986:214). Ironically, I found that toys and cartoons, in a sense, *constituted* the community's own sanities. Mergen describes the overall paradox well:

> "Toys are central in rituals of family and community. They are bought and used to mark important moments in the life cycle, to commemorate seasonal changes and yearly ceremonies. That they are also ephemeral, that they are used to fill otherwise empty time, does not lessen their symbolic importance in the social structure" (Mergen 1982:120).

7. Janice Radway looks at the irony of a women's community of romance readers whose private, isolating reading is mediated by mass production and capitalism, so that the women join forces only in a symbolic way. See also Fine (1987), who argues that children construct a social community and common culture that survive and flourish even under such formalized adult control as Little League baseball.

I recall here the interesting debate over fairy tales by psychoanalyst Bruno Bettelheim (1976), literary critic Roger Sales (1978), and critical folklorist Jack Zipes (1979; 1983). Bettelheim stressed their mythic, archetypal qualities linked to the needs inspired by children's psychosexual development. Little Red Riding Hood, for example, kills the bad daddy in order to have a healthier, postmenarche relationship with the good one. Sales sought an intersection between the tales' historical emergence and their value as literary texts. Zipes argued persuasively that we "break the magic spell" and connect the fairy tales to emerging bourgeois concerns during a time of profound social change. In such a context, Charles Perrault transformed Little Red Riding Hood from a plucky, resourceful peasant girl into a silly snippet who received a Victorian punishment.

I agree with Zipes that we need to root texts in history, as Engelhardt (1987) does in illuminating the cartoons' overarching messages about nuclear anxiety. Roger Sanjek (personal communication 1987) notes that we also need to be critical of violent, militaristic themes that seem to reemerge in other cultural arenas such as mascotry, in youth groups like the "death rockers," and in the proliferation of teenage suicides. In addition to rooting both the texts and the children in history, I argue that we need to focus some attention on how children themselves reinterpret cultural productions.

8. Adults, who often find it hard to appreciate what children know when they're superficially wrong, seemed to choose special mystification relative to the cartoons and the toys. Linguists and students of metaphor have begun to appreciate the creativity and productivity of children who cling to such deeply correct expressions as "yesternight," "out of balance," and "baby suits" and refuse to agree with Piaget that the same mass in a different shape is not somehow bigger. We need to find ways to honor the astonishing knowledge that children build and share, based on their world of cartoons and toys, and also to find ways to listen to their explanations.

9. One interesting, and contradictory, development, however, was the appearance of He-Man and G.I. Joe on the upscale television program "L.A. Law." As a divorced lawyer tried to befriend another divorced lawyer's son before they left on a date, he commented approvingly on the child's pajamas: "Oh, you have 'He-Man.' My little boy likes 'G.I. Joe.' " This message might

indicate a move toward more upscale tolerance of children's mass cultural images.

## REFERENCES

Agnew, Jean-Christophe
    1983    The Consuming Vision of Henry James. In *The Culture of Consumption,* ed. Richard Fox and Jackson Lears, pp. 65–100. New York: Pantheon.

Anderson, Benedict
    1983    *Imagined Communities.* London: Verso.

Bettelheim, Bruno
    1976    *The Uses of Enchantment.* New York: Knopf.

Bull, Bart
    1987    Toys '87: Fast and Furry. *Washington Post* (February 10): B1, B2.

Cantor, Muriel
    1987    *The Hollywood TV Producer: His Work and His Audience.* New Brunswick, N.J.: Transaction Books.
    1989    Women in Popular Fiction: Content and Control. In *Women: A Social Science Perspective,* ed. B. Hess and M. Ferree. Beverly Hills, Calif.: Sage Publications.

Dawson, Victoria
    1986    He-Mania: The Heroes' Welcome. *Washington Post* (February 27): C1, C3.

Denning, Michael
    1987    *Mechanic Accents.* London and New York: Verso.

Engelhardt, Tom
    1987    The Shortcake Strategy. In *Watching Television,* ed. Todd Gitlin, pp. 137–61. New York: Pantheon.

Fine, Gary Alan
    1987    *With the Boys.* Chicago: University of Chicago Press.

Fox, Richard Wightman and T. J. Jackson Lears
    1983    *The Culture of Consumption.* New York: Pantheon.

Gitlin, Todd
    1981    *Inside Prime Time.* New York: Pantheon.
    1987    *Watching Television.* New York: Pantheon.

Mergen, Bernard
    1982    *Play and Playthings*. Westport: Greenwood.

Radway, Janice
    1984    *Reading the Romance*. Chapel Hill: University of North Carolina Press.

Sales, Roger
    1978    *Fairy Tales and After*. Cambridge: Harvard University Press.

Sider, Gerald
    1986    *Class and Culture in Anthropology and History*. New York: Cambridge University Press.

Smith, Michael
    1983    Selling the Moon: The U.S. Manned Space Program and the Triumph of Commodity Scientism. In *The Culture of Consumption,* ed. Richard Fox and Jackson Lears, pp. 175–210. New York: Pantheon.

Smith, Peter K.
    1984    *Play in Animals and Humans*. New York and Oxford: Basil Blackwell.

Stewart, Susan
    1984    *On Longing*. Baltimore: Johns Hopkins University Press.

Sutton-Smith, Brian
    1986    *Toys as Culture*. New York: Gardner Press.

Sutton-Smith, Brian and Diana Kelly-Byrne
    1984    The Idealization of Play. In *Play in Animals and Humans,* ed. Peter K. Smith, pp. 305–22. New York and Oxford: Basil Blackwell.

Williams, Brett
    1986    1930s Animals as Hard Times Heroes in American Children's Books. *Central Issues in Anthropology* 6(2): 43–51.
    1988    *Upscaling Downtown*. Ithaca: Cornell University Press.

Zipes, Jack
    1979    *Breaking the Magic Spell*. Austin: University of Texas Press.
    1983    *The Trials and Tribulations of Little Red Riding Hood*. South Hadley, Mass.: Bergin and Garvey.

# CHAPTER 6

# African-American Folk Medicine in the Southeast Lowlands of the United States

*Arvilla C. Payne-Price*

This paper is based on an ongoing study of folk medicine and popular health care practices in the Southeast Lowlands begun by two medical anthropologists from Howard University in 1978.[1] It addresses the question of why folk medicine persists at a time of burgeoning scientific discovery and widening availability of modern medical resources to the general population. The three sections deal with: (1) the sociocultural and historical aspects of African-American folk medicine, (2) findings about current usage, and (3) the powerful persistence of folk medicine.

The primary objectives of the initial research were to explore the validity and parameters of the African-American folk medical system and: (1) to find and identify types of users and practitioners, for example, herbalists, "root doctors," midwives, and ancillary medical personnel involved in local health care; (2) to compile information about folk materia medica; (3) to collect samples of medications such as herbs (both cultivated and wild) and biologicals; and (4) to interview practitioners about their philosophy, motivation, and individual systems of diagnosis and treatment.

The African-American folk medical system continues to be a vital component in health care delivery, despite the advances and availability of modern scientific medicine. Watson (1984:53) states that:

> The widespread development and persistence of traditional medicine among Afro-Americans and their corresponding underutilization of modern medical practitioners are largely traceable to the economic poverty of the Black masses and the social history of racial discrimination and oppression that has assured perpetuation of their poverty, ignorance and poor health.

Modern medical facilities and health care benefits have been limited for the African-American population. When treatment and facilities were available their quality was inadequate and administration discriminatory. Consequently, many African Americans, primarily those of the working class and who live in rural or depressed urban areas, continue to rely on old "tried and true" home remedies. Folk practitioners treat not only physical ailments but also mental, interpersonal, and spiritual disorders (cf. Watson 1984:1).

## SOCIOCULTURAL AND HISTORICAL ASPECTS OF AFRICAN-AMERICAN FOLK MEDICINE

Today's African-American folk medical system has identifiable characteristics with a unified core of perceptions and practices including both pharmaceutical and ideational components. Snow (1974:83) defines the African-American folk medical system as:

> a composite of classical medicine of an earlier day, European folklore regarding the natural world, rare African traits, and selected beliefs derived from modern scientific medicine. The whole is inextricably blended with the tenets of fundamentalist Christianity, elements of the Voodoo religion of the West Indies, and the added spice of sympathetic magic. It is a coherent system and not a ragtag collection of isolated superstition.

The concepts underlying early African-American health practices derived from similar concepts shared by the cultures of European colonists, Africans, and American Indians, which facilitated the mixing of the multiple health care systems from the three major populations (Kiev 1968; Mitchell 1978; Watson 1984). At times the intermingling of cultures brought about the combining of medicinal herbs and new ways of using them (Mitchell 1978; Watson 1984).

Colonial English settlers introduced such therapeutic concepts as bloodletting, trepanning, and blistering and transplanted familiar herbs and simples from their homeland, most of which flourished in the New World environment. European and African Americans also adopted native American-Indian botanicals (Vogel 1970; Hamel and Chiltoskey 1975; Mitchell 1978). The various American-Indian groups had their own ideas and practices, including the cleansing steam bath and massage. African contributions are described by Berlin (1980:56):

> The transplanted African's intimate knowledge of the subtropical lowland environment—especially when compared to the Englishman's dense ignorance—magnified white dependence on blacks. . . . Since the geography, climate, and topography of the low-country more closely resembled the West African than the English countryside, African not European technology and agronomy often guided lowland development. From the first, whites depended on blacks to identify useful flora and fauna and to define the appropriate methods of production . . . In short, transplanted Englishmen learned as much or more from transplanted Africans as did the former African from them . . . both whites and blacks incorporated much of West African culture into their new way of life.

During slavery, "the Africans' new environment presented new health problems. The incidence of respiratory diseases, tuberculosis, hypertension, lactose intolerance and many infectious diseases . . . was probably facilitated by new dietary habits and cramped living conditions" (Deas-Moore 1987:476). Plantation owners and overseers were the primary caretakers (Otto 1984:114–15). Physicians, on retainer, generally attended the needs of the slaves only during times of epidemics or acute illnesses.

Medical practitioners in the eighteenth and nineteenth centuries, besides the copious use of drugs, resorted almost entirely to bleeding and blistering, measures which weakened the patient or aggravated his suffering. Emetics, purgatives, opiates and barks formed the materia medica and could be dispensed by anyone, along with home remedies from herbs and tonics, whiskey and brandy (Anderson 1985:106).

Rosengarten (1986:187) describes the medical relations on plantations as "relations of force":

The threat of calling the doctor was enough to drive some hands out of the sickhouse and into the fields, because they feared the doctor would find nothing wrong with them or because they feared his treatment. Blacks tried first to cure themselves, with teas, powders, and salves made from local plants and animals; with charms, prayer, and conjuration—magic. Drugs alone, they believed, could not restore good health. Only by conciliating an evil spirit loosed by an enemy, living or dead, could a person overcome illness. If herbal remedies and magic failed, the patient's condition might be desperate by the time the master was notified. Once seen by the doctor, the patient had to be closely watched if he or she was to follow the doctor's instruction. Planters wanted to think of their slaves as unwilling children who had to be made to take their castor oil. The slaves wanted to control their own bodies and souls. Their attitude suggests the existence of an alternative theory of disease. But whites in general showed no interest in the blacks' ideas of causation, which Chaplin typically dismissed as "foolishness."

Savitt (1978:173–74) also describes the medical practices of slaves in antebellum times. Select slaves dispensed "white" remedies and participated in obstetrics, bloodletting, extracting teeth, administering medicine, and caring for the sick. They also used their own medicines. Conjure doctors, who stemmed directly from the African tradition, were the main source of ideas of magically induced troubles, including illness, and had become well versed in herbal and root medicines on the plantation. Plantation owners, on the whole, condemned the "hoodoo," "voodoo" witchcraft and forbade its practice.

Mitchell (1978:13, 15) points out that from an early period "Afro-Americans were involved in health-related activities . . . slaves maintained their own medical practices especially to cure everyday illnesses" because of the neglect of owners and overseers. (See also Deas-Moore, this volume.)

Throughout slavery and to the present day, various perceptions of illnesses and injuries have been culturally patterned. Causes and cures are divided into two basic categories: natural and unnatural (Foster 1976; Mitchell 1978; Watson 1984; Deas-Moore 1987). The perception of natural illness explains "illness in impersonal systemic terms. Disease is thought to stem . . . from such *natural forces or conditions* as cold, heat, winds, dampness, and above all, by an upset in the balance of the basic body elements" (Foster 1976:775). Unnatural illnesses are either occult—caused by evil spirits or the sorcery of "root doctors" or "conjurers," (Mitchell 1978; Watson 1984) or spiritual—a penalty for sins. Occult and spiritual illnesses can affect both physical, emotional, and spiritual health.

These perceptions of the causes of illness and injury are echoes of age-old beliefs found in the ancestral homelands of the slaves. Raboteau (1986) explains how religion, including worldview, magic, and medicine, affected the health and pathology of the slaves. He underscores interactions within the sociocultural dynamics of family and community and with the natural surroundings. Sociocultural disharmony or conflict with the natural environment resulted in illness. Treatment not only called for natural herbal remedies but also invoked a need for religious rituals and magical charms.

Religion and magic continued to play a central role in folk medical health care during slavery. Christian "shouting churches" or charismatic worship offered a satisfactory alternative to the African precedent of spirit possession; the ecstasy of possession by the Holy Spirit replaced the possession by ancestors and other spirits in African religions. Being possessed conveyed status and prestige to worshippers and their community (Raboteau 1986:541–5).

The magical ingredients in African religious curing ceremonies and rituals were transformed into "conjuring" or African-American "magical medicine." Conjuring attributed illnesses to sociocultural causes, that is, inimical projections from hostile persons. Also

> for a largely powerless people, conjuring functioned as a symbolic assertion of power. Story after story of black folklore celebrated the ability of conjurers to manipulate whites as well as blacks. . . . The contention that the white doctor's medicine was useless against the charms of the black conjurers represented a subtle but effective rejection of white supremacy in matters medical and magical. And the sight of white clients patiently waiting upon the skills of black conjurers proved the same point. (Raboteau 1986:550; cf. Hyatt 1970–78)

Midwives or "granny midwives" constituted another category of health personnel. From the days of slavery to recent times they commanded great respect from the community. Midwives not only helped deliver babies but were "also responsible for other medical practices on the plantation. The day-to-day health care of slaves was entrusted to these black ladies, who effectively combined their bitter herb and root teas with the medicines left by the physician or dispensed by the mistress" (Deas-Moore 1987:482).

Most slave families or plantations had one or more slaves knowledgeable about medicinal herbs and their uses. In the event of illness, the herbalists were the first health care resource outside the family. If an illness lingered, and herbal cures were ineffective, a conjurer offered alternative therapy. Only after these two avenues proved fruitless did the plantation doctor come on the scene.

The same scheme for explaining and coping with illness continued following emancipation. It exists today, despite the changes in socioeconomic status.

After slavery, the tobacco, cotton, and rice agricultural complexes "utilized the common forms of southern tenure—owner, tenants, and sharecroppers. . . . The elements of paternalism that developed during slavery persisted and increasingly crossed the color line" (Daniel

1985:*xii*). Legislation of racially divisive labor and "Jim Crow" laws also adversely affected access to and the quality of health care. African and European Americans were served by separate medical facilities.

Secular social organizations and special church activities and church organizations such as sodalities helped meet the medical needs of African Americans. Family members, friends, and church members came to the aid of families during a time of illness. Fraternal orders such as The Independent Order of Saint Luke, headed by Maggie Walker in Richmond, Virginia, offered sickness and death benefits to African Americans (Marlowe 1987). Herbalists, midwives, and conjurers still served the community, augmented by itinerant religious healers and by men and women who sold a variety of herbal and patent medicines from medicine wagons.

Mistrust of white personnel in positions of authority and social control extended beyond politicians and police to health care professionals, heightened by the dramatic contrast between the available medical facilities. The pejorative attitudes of white health care personnel were far from reassuring. The mistrust is reflected in a 1979 statement by Abraham Jenkins, a descendant of the Sea Islands slaves: "How could I develop an attitude of respect for someone who is supposed to be a professional and who has no respect for me?" (Jenkins 1979:11).

The decline of the old culture based on tobacco, cotton, and rice, brought on by the depression of the 1930s and the industrialization and mechanization of agriculture in the 1950s and 1960s, resulted in large migrations of African Americans to urban areas. Access to medical facilities was better than in rural areas, but lingering mistrust of health care personnel and excessive costs discouraged a rapid popular usage of the modern health care system.

As education and economic status have improved so has the use of modern medicine. Today, mostly poor African Americans use folk medicine as the dependable alternate health resource (Mitchell 1978; Snow 1981; Watson 1984).

The present-day network of African-American healers serving urban and rural communities is a continuation of the older system of traditional folk medical practitioners. Its base is the immediate family and community elders who are still the first resource in case of illness or emergency.

If an illness is "natural," the sufferer may consult an herbalist. The herbalists are part-time specialists who have a fund of information about symptoms and remedies. They diagnose ailments, prepare medications, and when necessary assume the role of "folk psychiatrist." Their therapies include both botanicals and other biological materia medica (e.g., cobwebs and dirt-dauber nests), which may be accompanied by rituals. Some herbalists are paid in cash, some with gifts, but others are forbidden by religious beliefs from accepting any rewards.

Until recently, midwives also treated childhood ailments and injuries, often combining midwifery with herbal cultivation and the collection and preparation of natural materia medica. Licensing of midwives began during the 1940s, primarily for the purpose of teaching hygiene (cf. Deas-Moore 1987). They usually learned their profession through apprenticeship to doctors or other midwives. They were sometimes paid with money but more frequently "in kind" with produce or animals. Lay midwives are no longer trained.

If an illness is "unnatural," the sufferer may go to either a "root doctor" or a faith healer. Root doctors, or "conjurers,"[2] are practitioners who, for a fee, allegedly use their powers to poison as well as heal, who supply aphrodisiacs, and who "fix" or "put roots" on people, animals, and things.

Faith healers, either denominational or "store front," are practitioners who call on supernatural forces and use prayer and the "laying on of hands" to effect cures for illnesses thought to be of a "spiritual" nature, that is, caused by God or Satan. They also offer services for everyday problems, depression, worry, and general complaints. Payment is expected or required (cf. Mitchell 1978; Primack 1984). Hall and Bourne (1973) also describe the work of "neighborhood prophets" in Atlanta, who treat and diagnose emotional and other personal problems, relying on prayer, divine intervention, dreams, and déjà vu.

Three other types of supernatural religious healers are highly specialized: they "talk out fire," "talk out bleeding," and "talk off warts." Blood-stoppers use a verbal ritual, repeating Ezekiel 16:6, to invoke individual supernatural powers. Warts are removed by prayer and a prescribed pattern of movements using a piece of animal bone. Healers who talk out fire, or burns, pray and perform ritual acts such as blowing over the burned area.

Watson (1984:54, 56–57) also points out the importance of neighborhood druggists in the folk medical system:

> Elderly Afro-Americans use a variety of herbs and over-the-counter preparations that appear to be unique to their ethnic group. [They also] showed a marked preference for and belief in the efficacy of remedies recommended by local druggists with little or no reference made to the comparative utility of modern medical doctors.

Hall and Bourne (1973) found "magic vendors" in Atlanta who sell magic and operate from, or in association with, herbal shops. They specialize in health aids, achievement of domestic harmony, improvement of sex life, making more money, and changing to a more desirable destiny. Nearly all use patent medicines, drugs, health and beauty aids, and magical religious objects to achieve their ends. They request fees for their services.

Today, economically marginal rural and urban African Americans in need of medical services may resort to the alternative health care systems because they are more accessible and less costly than modern medicine, more interpersonal, and more compatible with their perceptions of disease etiology and treatment.

FINDINGS ABOUT CURRENT USAGE

This preliminary investigation of the African-American folk medical system in the coastal Southeast Lowlands began in Washington, D.C., with informal interviews with friends. It then led to networks of contacts in Virginia, North Carolina, South Carolina, and Georgia and resulted in 155 hours of taped interviews with ninety-one informants. A map (Figure 6.1) shows interview sites. Data from sixty-seven of the informants form the basis of this report.[3] Sixty-one percent of the interviewees lived in rural settings or small towns and had either

FIGURE 6.1  Map indicates primary interview locations.

gardens or access to woods surrounding their homes. Thirty-nine percent lived in urban areas or the suburbs; many had close ties with relatives who lived in the country. Seventeen of the sixty-seven informants were folk practitioners of various types: herbalists, granny midwives, home care aides, and root doctors.

The beginning of the interviews met with a general tendency to deny the effectiveness of "those old time remedies" and to belittle them as things old people used. To counteract this disparaging attitude, the interviewers spoke of the "scientific specificity" and "active ingredients" in many of the old time remedies, for example, alcohol in onion and aspirin in willow bark. They also pointed out that the empirical validation of the old time remedies was impressive, that much of today's pharmacopoeia originated from substances they contained, and that scientists now investigate them for overlooked benefits. After this explanation, the informants usually dropped the pretense of not knowing much about the subject and actively contributed to the list of traditional remedies.

The informants ranged in educational background from the minimally schooled to established physicians. Economic status also varied widely; several were landowners of considerable wealth, some were welfare recipients, and one middle-aged dependent lived on family property in a broken-down trailer. Personalities ranged from bold to shy and from almost frightened reluctance to enthusiastic participation. Various idiosyncrasies, experiences, biases, and beliefs emerged. Only one refused to cooperate, a woman who had been interviewed two months earlier for a television special on old home remedies. As a member of her family explained, "They made the people look like fools!"

Geographical and ecological factors sometimes accounted for variations in responses or emphasis on certain medicines; for example, inland informants tended to use hog jaw marrow for the mumps, while the prevalent coastal remedy was sardine oil. Also, social and regional differences were evident in linguistic variations; for example, informants from different areas referred to rabbit tobacco (*Gnaphalium obtusioflium*) by different related names such as "life everlasting," "leaf of life," and "life of molasses." On the whole, however, the homogeneity of responses was remarkable so that, despite the small number of the selected sample, patterns emerged that could be analyzed. The similarities and differences are indicated in the following presentation of data.

The research findings can be classified in six categories: (1) How often do people use traditional therapy? (2) Who taught the informants (both practitioners and users) about the old home remedies? (3) Why do people rely on old home remedies? (4) What cures did the informants

know? (5) What are the perceptions of the general system for diagnos-
ing illnesses? (6) What are the perceptions of supernatural healing?

*How Often Do People Use Traditional Therapy?*

Four factors signaled or determined frequency of use: (1) whether the
informant was an active practitioner; (2) whether past or present tense
was used in discussing remedies, for example, the "old people used to"
versus "I use"; (3) whether an informant was then undergoing treatment and whether or not remedies were on hand; and (4) reference to
the degree of use during the interview itself.

In general, age, class, and location of residence correlate with and
influence the use of old home remedies. Although data were not systematically collected from informants under thirty-five years of age,
conversations with younger members of informants' families indicated that they knew very little about the old home remedies.

All urban middle-class informants seldom used medicinal herbs.
Working-class informants in general, whether rural or urban, were the
most frequent users of old home remedies. Table 6.1 summarizes the
frequency-of-use data on the sixty-seven informants according to social class and residence location.

TABLE 6.1

*Number of Informants Using Old Home Remedies*
*Relative to Residence and Social Class[a]*

| Frequency of use | Frequent | | Moderate | | Occasional | | Rare | |
|---|---|---|---|---|---|---|---|---|
| | Number of respondents | | | | | | | |
| Residence | MC | WC | MC | WC | MC | WC | MC | WC |
| Urban | 0 | 7 | 2 | 5 | 7 | 1 | 4 | 0 |
| Small town | 1 | 4 | | | | | | |
| Rural | 3 | 17 | 7 | 2 | 2 | 5 | | |
| Totals | 4 | 28 | 9 | 7 | 9 | 6 | 4 | 0 |

[a]*MC* = middle class; *WC* = working class.

*Who Taught the Informants about the Old Home Remedies?*

Responses to the question, "How did you learn to use plants as medicine?" confirmed the passing of information from generation to generation. Both practitioners and users most frequently mentioned learning about the remedies from mothers, fathers, or both. Knowledgeable elders and "granny midwives" in the communities were the second most cited source.

Several practitioners said their powers and abilities were a "gift from God." One midwife told about being "ritually marked" shortly after her birth by her midwife grandmother, who designated the grandchild as the one to follow in her footsteps. Some practitioners, as well as users, also referred to "medicine books" such as *Back to Eden* (Kloss 1975) as additional sources.

*Why Do People Rely on Old Home Remedies?*

The older informants said that "in the old days, there were no doctors close by," and the people had to rely on local resources. A doctor, if and when available, cost too much and was often the last resort.

A general distrust of modern drugs and physicians, persisting since plantation days and nourished by recent exploitations, was also evident. Several common refrains were: "Why pay money for medicine from a drug store that costs a whole lot of money and don't do no good?"; "Maybe it [doctor's medicine] helps one thing like the pain of 'arthuritis' but the doctor don't tell you it bad for you heart"; and "When all you have to do is step out you back door and you can pick a plant for nothing."

Two other frequent comments were: "The Lord put something here for everything, all we have to do is find it," and "Every plant is good for something, you have to know what for."

*What Cures Did the Informants Know?*

Table 6.2 correlates the informants' age and frequency of use with the number of illnesses for which informants knew old home remedies.

TABLE 6.2

*Number of Reported Illnesses Treated with Old Home Remedies*

| Informant age group | | Frequent | Moderate | Occasional | Rare | Group average |
|---|---|---|---|---|---|---|
| 90 | $A^a$ | 25 | 39 | 22 | | 28.7 |
| | $N^b$ | 5 | 1 | 1 | | |
| 80 | A | 45.4 | 44 | 22 | | 37.1 |
| | N | 5 | 3 | 1 | | |
| 70 | A | 37.2 | 30.8 | 22.7 | | 30.2 |
| | N | 12 | 5 | 3 | | |
| 60 | A | 51 | 45.7 | 25 | 22.5 | 36.1 |
| | N | 7 | 3 | 2 | 2 | |
| 50 | A | 32 | 46.8 | 43 | | 40.6 |
| | N | 3 | 4 | 4 | | |
| 40 | A | | | 37.3 | | 37.3 |
| | N | | | 3 | | |
| 30 | A | | | 37.3 | | 37.3 |
| | N | | | 2 | | |
| 20 | A | | | | 6.5 | 6.5 |
| | N | | | | 2 | |

[a]$A$ = average number of illnesses known per informant.
[b]$N$ = number of informants.

The numbers give only an indication of the general knowledge. The interviewing process was varied to cope with responses that were incomplete for various reasons. For example, several older informants could not "remember" specific remedies even though they knew "something" had been used. Older informants also tended to tire quickly, so remaining questions were not asked. Earlier interview forms contained fewer questions than later versions. Some practitioner informants were retired or semiretired or, as in the case of the first root doctor, were specialists. In general, however, the averages for frequent, moderate, and occasional users in Table 6.2 showed a consis-

tent level of knowledge for all ages. Even occasional users were familiar with a substantial number of remedies.

Samples of over ninety-two medicinal plants were collected.[4] The
repertory of cures reported by informants extended far beyond our
botanical samples (see next chapter, by Lee and Payne-Price). Responses also described separate uses of different parts of the same
plant. For example, the root of pokeweed (*Phytolacca americana*) was
considered poisonous, but its berries could be used for making wine,
its fresh green shoots in spring made a health-giving salad, and various
infusions, decoctions, and alcoholic tinctures of the roots were prescribed as "useful" for different ailments. Ailments themselves were
diagnosed ambiguously, for example, "swellings" and "misery." Pana-
ceas such as sarsaparilla (*Menispermum canadense*) and sassafras (*Sassafras albidum*) were frequently mentioned. The bark, root, and/or leaves
of sassafras are used as "plain tea" or "medicine."

*What Are the Perceptions of the General Diagnostic System of Illness?*

The data revealed that one characteristic of African-American folk
medicine is partly based on a remnant of the early European and
colonial belief in body "humors," such as blood, phlegm, and bile.
Blood is the primary diagnostic index of health, and phlegm and bile
are secondary. Blood is the primary health regulator and must be
maintained in "balance." The conditions and binary qualities associated with blood are: purity (good/bad), circulation (fast/slow),
quantity/location (high/low), temperature (hot/cold), and viscosity
(thick/thin). (See next chapter, by Lee and Payne-Price.) Folk practitioners may also adopt elements of modern medicine, for example, recognizing the existence of red and white blood cells, but assigning functions to them based on an interpretation of the humoral system.

In parts of the Southeast Lowlands, dreams, omens, and the signs
of the zodiac, phases of the moon, and other meteorologic information from the *Farmer's Almanac* are used to determine a person's state
of health, treatments for ailments, times for operations, diet, and
behavioral modifications (cf. Snow 1977; Lee and Payne-Price, this
volume).

The dual etiology of "natural" and "unnatural" causes of illnesses and their cures emerged from the data as discussed above.

*What Are the Perceptions of Supernatural Healing?*

Informants' wary reactions to questions about supernatural healing sharply contrasted with the respect they showed herbalists, midwives, and practical nurses. They were often reluctant at first to talk about the bona fides of ethnopractitioners but were easily persuaded to do so. Not so with questions about "root doctors," "conjurers," and "fixers." Ambivalence was especially evident with regard to root doctors because their powers were both beneficial and destructive. Questions about religious practices, such as laying on of hands and healing by "tarrying when the spirit hits" evoked mixed responses, including some derogation apparently related to class and status; believers were looked down upon as "poor and ignorant." However, ambivalence or even disdain regarding some practices carried overtones of caution about dealing with the "unknown." For example, "Those root doctors are nothing but quacks after money, but you better be careful around them."

THE POWERFUL PERSISTENCE OF FOLK MEDICINE

Even though African and other Americans in general now accept the basic tenets of modern medicine and therapy, many continue to use folk medicine because it meets psychological as well as physiological needs within their sociocultural setting. Ironically, a renewal of interest in the validity of alternate folk medical systems coincides with the enactment of federal and state legislation outlawing nonlicensed dispensing of medicine, which includes herbal remedies.

Many herbalists have been forced out of business, but not all have given up. A case in point is the widely publicized story of the well-known herbalist Alfredo Bowman (Dr. Sebi) of New York City who faced civil and criminal charges because he refused to close his herb shop as ordered after advertising a cure for AIDS. The lengthy civil trial ended in an agreement with the Attorney General of New York State allowing Mr. Bowman to continue his business but not to make claims for his products. The criminal trial follows pro forma. Due to the interest aroused by the case, a major medical school is testing the remedy.

The mass media carry hundreds of medical releases and human interest stories popularizing health subjects, which fosters self-diagnosis and treatment. This in turn influences people's choices of health care personnel they believe to be appropriate for a given health problem. Interestingly, adherents of folk medicine have become more selective and now tend to choose physicians for physical ailments and folk medical practitioners for psychiatric and social problems (de Albuquerque 1979).

Financially disadvantaged people in both towns and rural areas, lacking the latitude of options enjoyed by the more affluent, take advantage of the availability of a relatively inexpensive health care system offering various types of folk medicine, such as nonprescription herbs and patent medicines that can be purchased from herbal shops and drug stores. Folk medicine also provides the personal element that scientific medicine tends to overlook. While folk medicine is used predominantly by old, poor, and working-class African Americans, a new clientele is developing among the young and middle class in both rural and urban areas. This is the result, in part, of the perceived inadequacy of scientific medicine (de Albuquerque 1979:38).

The question posed at the outset was why folk medicine persists today. The pervasive preference for old traditional folk medicine as opposed to scientifically advanced medical care is a matter of personal choice that supersedes economic concerns. People find more comfort in traditions compatible with their cultural perceptions and experiences than in the unfamiliar and depersonalized practices of modern medicine. The personal element is more evident in the interpersonal network of recommendations and referrals in folk medicine than in the detached professional referral system of conventional medical practice, and the folk method inspires significantly more trust. The economic factor is a second powerful determinant in the selection of medical treatment.

Raboteau (1986:555) aptly describes the reasons that folk medicine became and continues to be so pervasive in the African-American community:

> Given the poverty of many black Americans and the high cost of medical care, given the cultural distance between black communities and predominantly white medical facilities, given the lack of rapport between black patients and white medical professionals, it is not surprising that alternate forms of healing became important for African Americans.

The links between health, culture, and the choice and use of health services interact with medical politics in influencing the allocation of funds for research and medical facilities and the control of developing programs. Scientific medicine has, on the whole, shut out alternate traditional health care systems in favor of the more established and socially and legally approved forms of health care, contributing to the alienation between physicians and folk medical adherents. Until modern medical practitioners and lawmakers become more aware of, sympathetic to, and less contemptuous of the numerous health care alternatives, differing medical philosophies are likely to encounter continuing disparagement. This would be regrettable because both sectors have benefits to offer, and combining forces might bring about more dynamic and effective health care programs.

NOTES

1. This work was made possible in part by support from the faculty research program in the Social Sciences, Humanities and Education at Howard University from the Office of the Vice President of Academic Affairs, 1979–80. This initial research was undertaken with Dr. Jane Philips, my colleague at Howard University. On subsequent field trips students were given the opportunity of field work training for credit.

2. One informant explained the difference between "root doctors" and "conjurers" as follows:

> A conjure man and a root doctor are almost the same thing. It works kind a together. . . . The way I see it, a conjurer, they mostly jus'

put it down for you, an' you be sick if you step over it. . . . A root doctor, he jus' fix up medicine for you . . . maybe in bottles, or put it in little sacks for you and things like potions or charms, an' name it, causin' you to hurt.

3. Omitted interviews include those with non–African-American informants, some elderly informants who did not complete questionnaires, and courthouse, hospital, and clinic personnel. The interviewers asked sets of questions, some specific and some open-ended, as well as some general leading questions during tours of farms and herb gardens and visits to homes and health institutions. Interviews called for demographic information from each informant whenever possible: age, sex, nativity, and locus of socialization. Not uniformly available was information concerning known illnesses and injuries of family members and neighbors and the therapy used. Following are examples of questions designed to evoke specific information about botanicals and other biologicals used, diseases treated, and types of practitioners:

(1) Did you ever use ginseng root?
(2) What did you do for the measles?
(3) Did you use hog-jaw marrow for anything?
(4) Did you ever know anyone who could "talk out fire"?

4. Identification and classification of herbs was made primarily by Dr. James Duke, Economic Botany, U.S. Department of Agriculture.

## REFERENCES

Anderson, Jean
   1985    *Piedmont Plantation: The Bennehan-Cameron Family and Lands in North Carolina*. Durham, N.C.: The Historic Preservation Society of Durham.

Berlin, Ira
   1980    Time, Space, and the Evolution of Afro-American Society on British Mainland North America. *American Historical Review* 85(1): 44–78.

Daniel, Pete
   1985    *Breaking the Land*. Chicago: University of Illinois Press.

de Albuquerque, Klaus
   1979    Non-Institutional Medicine on the Sea Islands. In *Proceedings of a Symposium on Culture and Health: Implications for Health Policy in*

*Rural South Carolina,* ed. M. Varner and A. McCandless, pp. 33–78. Charleston, S.C.: Center for Metropolitan Affairs and Public Policy, College of Charleston.

Deas-Moore, Vennie
1987    Medical Adaptations of a Culture Relocated from Africa to the Sea Islands of South Carolina. *The World and I* 2(1): 474–85.

Foster, George
1976    Disease Etiologies in Northwestern Medical Systems. *American Anthropology* 78: 771–82.

Hall, Arthur L., and Peter Bourne
1973    Indigenous Therapists in a Southern Black Urban Community. *Archives of General Psychiatry* 1(2): 137–42.

Hamel, Paul, and Mary Chiltoskey
1975    *Cherokee Plants and Their Uses: A 400 Year History.* Sylvia, N.C.: Herald Publishing Company.

Hyatt, Harry M.
1970–78 *Memoirs of the Alma Egan Hyatt Foundation: Hoodoo, Conjuration, Witchcraft, Rootwork,* 5 vols. Cambridge, Mass.: Western Publishing Company.

Jenkins, Abraham
1979    An Insider's History of the Sea Islands and Efforts to Bring Health Care to the Islanders. In *Proceedings of a Symposium on Culture and Health: Implications for Health Policy in Rural South Carolina,* ed. M. Varner and A. McCandless, pp. 5–15. Charleston, S.C.: Center for Metropolitan Affairs and Public Policy, College of Charleston.

Kiev, Ari
1968    *Curanderismo: Mexican-American Folk Psychiatry.* New York: Free Press.

Kloss, Jethro
1975    *Back to Eden.* Santa Barbara, Calif.: Woodbridge Press.

Marlowe, Gertrude
1987    Maggie Lena Walker: African American Women, Business and Community Development. Paper presented at Berkshire Conference on the History of Women, Wellesley, Mass., June 21.

Mitchell, Faith
1978    *Hoodoo Medicine: Sea Islands Herbal Remedies.* Berkeley, Calif.: Reed, Cannon, and Johnson.

Otto, John
1984    *Cannon's Point Plantation, 1794–1860: Living Conditions and Status Patterns in the Old South.* New York: Academic Press.

Primack, Aaron
1984    The Gospel According to the Voice of Experience. In *Field Training in Applied Anthropology,* ed. L. Cohen and T. Ready, Vol. 3, pp. 55–75. Department of Anthropology, Catholic University of America.

Raboteau, Albert
1986    The Afro-American Traditions. In *Caring and Curing: Health and Medicine in the Western Religious Traditions,* ed. R. Numbers and D. Amundsen, pp. 539–62. New York: Macmillan.

Rosengarten, Theodore
1986    *Tombee: Portrait of a Cotton Planter with the Journal of Thomas B. Chaplin (1822–1890).* New York: William Morrow.

Savitt, Todd
1978    *Medicine and Slavery: The Diseases and Health Care of Blacks in Antebellum Virginia.* Chicago: University of Illinois Press.

Snow, Loudell
1974    Folk Medical Beliefs and Their Implications for Care of Patients. *Annals of Internal Medicine* 81(1): 82–96.
1977    Popular Medicine in a Black Neighborhood. In *Ethnic Medicine in the Southwest,* ed. E. Spicer, pp. 19–95. Tucson: University of Arizona Press.
1981    Folk Medical Beliefs and Their Implications for the Care of Patients: A Review Based on Studies Among Black Americans. In *Transcultural Health Care,* ed. G. Henderson and M. Primeaus, pp. 78–101. London: Addison-Wesley.

Vogel, Virgil
1970    *American Indian Medicine.* Norman: University of Oklahoma Press.

Watson, Wilbur
1984    *Black Folk Medicine: The Therapeutic Significance of Faith and Trust.* New Brunswick, N.J.: Transaction Books.

# CHAPTER 7

# John Lee

## An African-American Folk Healer

### John Lee and Arvilla C. Payne-Price

A study of African-American folk medicine in the Southeast Lowlands of the United States brought together the two authors of this paper. African-American folk medicine is a topic of ongoing interest at the Department of Sociology/ Anthropology at Howard University. Two members of the anthropology section went on a research field trip in 1978.[1] A friend working at the Moncure Community Health Center in Moncure, North Carolina, recommended Mr. Lee as a "famous healer" who used ethnobotanicals and who had won the respect and interest of members of the conventional medical profession. The researchers went to his farm and were warmly welcomed. Mr. Lee started with a walk around his farm and cultivated herb garden and told of other medicinal plants to be found in the woods and countryside. The walk was followed by a full interview.

Dr. Payne-Price made many extended visits to Moncure during the following ten years. Mr. Lee was an outstanding informant, not only knowledgeable but extremely cooperative. He wanted to record his experiences and skills and was enthusiastic in support of this research.

## RESEARCH METHOD

More than fifty hours of interviews were tape-recorded, augmented by informal discussions with members of the family and some patients during prolonged visits to the Lee farm. Collected data were also supplemented by handwritten notes about observations. Over seventy-five of Mr. Lee's medicinal plants were collected and photographed.[2] Dr. James Duke, of Economic Botany, U.S. Department of Agriculture, generously identified and classified the plants. A list of the more frequently used ethnobotanicals, their usages, and the local system of classification are given in the appendix.

Mr. Lee is an African-American herbalist who is a healer in the best sense of the word and the leading member of a family of healers that has served their community for at least three generations. He is a recognized and respected practitioner. His system is typical of the practice of scores of folk healers across the southern United States.

He is himself thoroughly and sincerely persuaded of the efficacy and validity of folk medicine. He has studied the local flora and fauna and is well informed about the empirical folklore of medicinal plants.

Mr. Lee's knowledge of botany, however, is not limited to local plants. He is also familiar with the relevant general literature, such as *Back to Eden* and the scientific works of James Duke, and refers to numerous resource books such as *The Herbalist,* by Joseph Meyer, *Growing and Using the Healing Herbs,* by Gaea and Shandar Weiss, *The Herb Book,* by John Lust, and *Magic and Medicine of Plants,* published by Reader's Digest. Information on Lee's professional development described in this paper is based on his notes and is accessible on tapes.[3]

## BECOMING AN HERBALIST

Mr. Lee recounts that as a child he collected herbs for his mother and accompanied her on her calls. He became aware of the community health care system consisting of networks of family support units. If anyone were ill or incapacitated for a period of time, people in the community would come to the aid of the family without expecting compensation. People who were helpers would do farm chores, cleaning, cooking, washing, or whatever else was required. They might come for a day, a few days, or longer. Illnesses were treated primarily with "old home remedies." A doctor was called in only when the afflicted seemed to be "going backwards." For example, someone with a high fever would be given a hot bath and treated with a poultice wrapped in red flannel that had been warmed over a fire. If the fever did not break or the temperature begin to go down, or if sweating stopped, then the doctor was called.

The foundation of Mr. Lee's practice came from his family, long known for its healers. He and his brothers and sisters learned their basic botany and medical practice chiefly from their mother, Eliza Jane Seymour, a woman of mixed descent: American Indian (Lumbo-Cherokee), British-Irish, and African. He said his mother was the local midwife and had learned her healing arts from her mother, who was of Indian descent. She helped to deliver black, white, and Indian children in Chatham and Lee counties and was frequently called upon to treat childhood and adult diseases. The education she gave him included not only folk health practices but also ideals and ethics. John, the youngest of nine children, frequently accompanied his mother on her calls and was taught to collect botanicals and in some cases to prepare the medicines. The children also learned about some herbs and treatments from their father, Thomas Lee, who was not only an herbalist but also famous for his ability to "talk out fire" and "talk out bleeding."[4]

In general, the interviewers established the fact that Mr. Lee is thoroughly acquainted with plants. He knows over 100 medical botanicals, prepares medicines meticulously, is very cautious about prescribing them, and gives explicit instructions for their use. These characteristics of accuracy and his concern for the maximum benefit of his patients are evident in the way he searches for, collects, and processes plant material.

While practical training in ethnobotany came primarily from his mother and family, he was also considered to have been born with a special gift. At birth he had a "veil" (caul) over his face, which, according to local folklore, bestows an ability to see and hear things other people cannot. In the case of healers, it is said to help them diagnose difficult and perplexing problems.

Mr. Lee describes how he continued his practice after his mother's death. When she died in 1928, people continued to come to the Lees for help. His older brother, Tom, and he continued serving the community. Tom worked for a time in the coal mines of West Virginia where he learned new health practices from mountaineers. In the following years the brothers collected and prepared plants and built up their herbal practice. Mr. Lee's sister Maude followed her mother's midwifery practice. The nearest doctor was over twelve miles away, and people could reach him only on foot or by mule.

After Mr. Lee married, his job took him out of the community during the work week. When he retired about 1970, people started coming to him again on a regular basis. After his retirement his wife, Hattie Mae, also became fully involved as a partner in his work.

In the beginning Hattie Mae used herbs only to prepare remedies for their own children. For example, she administered catnip (*Nepeta cataria*) tea to help settle their stomachs. She did not really "believe in" the plant medicine. Her attitude changed, however, after her husband cured her of a bad case of poison ivy by using the crushed leaves and berries of nightshade (*Solanum nigrum*). Hattie Mae told how it happened:

> I went down to the river to fish. I stood there awhile until I started to get tired. Someone had chopped out a place, so I sat down, not thinking about anything bothering me. When I got back home, the back of my legs and the bends of my knees were all red. I had broken out in poison ivy. At that time my husband was working away from home at the saw mill. When he came home, I was walking kind of stiff-legged. He said, "What is wrong with you?" I said, "I went fishing and got poison ivy." He got some nightshade and told me to bruise the leaves and berries and put them in a piece of cloth and then put it in milk and bathe the back of my legs. In a day or two I could hardly tell I had it. So then I began to pay a little more attention.

Since then, Hattie Mae has taken a serious interest in the work and over the years has become a committed practitioner. Her main function is preparing the herbal remedies, but she also frequently talks to women having "female problems" and consults with Mr. Lee about appropriate treatment.

> Lee's knowledge of herbs is a gift from God to help and to serve people. After I see I have helped people, I feel justified in getting these herbs for them, because I have the feeling of helping them. It's good to have knowledge and if you don't use what you have, you might as well bury it. The Lord helps me with this treating.

Both Lees believe that God put something here to cure all illnesses:

> The Lord put these things here and that's what we use. Scripture says bitter herbs have more medicinal value. In the beginning that was all we had to use. We didn't have the pills and all the things we have now and even the people who used to sell patent medicines used to fix it in the bottles and carry it around and sell it.

The Lees specialize in treating "natural" illnesses. They do not treat patients who come to them with ailments complicated by "rooting." Rooting is considered to be "unnatural" and not suitable as medical treatment. The Lees are also quick to acknowledge pathological conditions that require modern medical assessment. For example, when one of their daughters was bitten by a poisonous spider, they took her to a physician in Pittsboro for treatment. As another example, one of their sons was treated for a serious heart disease at Johns Hopkins Hospital.

In summary, the Lees employ many remedies that appear to be empirically effective by objective standards. Some if used improperly are quite dangerous, while others may be placebos. The Lees' initial clients were primarily family members and neighbors, who then extended the referral networks so that the couple now serves a broad community in both Chatham and Lee counties. They now have clients as far away as Texas, California, and New York. When unable to go to

North Carolina, the distant patients write to Mr. Lee or consult him by telephone.


## DIAGNOSTIC SYSTEM

Mr. Lee's account of developing his diagnostic system describes a blend of old healing traditions with a tenacious commitment and arduous schedule. As a result of intensive work with herbs over the years, he has become highly skilled in locating medicinal herbs, of which he now has over 100. Various parts of plants are used for different purposes. His diagnostic method is similar to that found in the general African-American folk medical system. For example, he considers the effects of blood, phlegm, and bile. He regards blood as the most important health regulator. In the African-American folk medical system, blood and the balance of binary qualities associated with blood generation, volume, location, circulation, viscosity, purity, and temperature are "primary" diagnostic indicators. Blood is either good or bad (blood purity), fast or slow (circulation), high or low (quantity and location), hot or cold (temperature), and thick or thin (viscosity). Illness signifies an imbalance in one or more of these factors.

People who have good blood are less susceptible to illnesses such as colds and do not get sick very often. People with bad blood may have sores that do not heal quickly, and then may pass blood. Diabetes, venereal disease, and food poisoning are all causes of bad blood. People with bad blood may "fall out" (faint), have dizzy spells or fits and spasms. Their skin may be "scaly," "dead," "fuzzy looking," or irritated.

People with high blood have blood that goes to their heads where it stagnates and does not work its way down again. A person with high blood pressure has too much blood. Low blood means insufficient volume and blood that is not circulating or going up in the body as it should.

Blurriness of the eyes, pain in the head and eyes, and "falling out" are signs of either high or low blood. Sluggishness or a lack of energy may indicate low blood. Mr. Lee looks at the veins in the crook of the arm and on the back of the hands to judge whether the blood is high, low, or in balance.

Changes in the season affect a person, particularly when winter turns to spring. Mr. Lee said that "a person is like a tree, the sap is in the roots and only starting to rise in the spring, so a person is weaker. By winter a person is built up." Cool temperature can slow the blood and cause susceptibility to arthritis or a cold. The blood becomes warmer and moves faster with activity.

Blood that is too warm can cause rashes; if it is cold for too long, it may bring on a cold or other respiratory problem or arthritis.

Thick blood does not flow fast and has a lot of pressure behind it. Mr. Lee says that "if it is not circulating right, it clogs up the veins and may cause a stroke or brain damage." Thin blood means an imbalance between red and white blood cells. Low, thin blood is "tired blood."

Age and sex affect the blood. Babies and old people have thin blood. With aging, the blood first thickens and then thins down again around 55 or 60 years of age. Mr. Lee explains that "the older a person becomes, the cooler he becomes, because he has less blood. Women have more and thicker blood than men, that is why they can withstand the cold better."

Mr. Lee describes how the brain affects the blood. "Half of the brain is for thinking and all the things that come in the mind, and the other half is for the nerves. Most people have a stroke on the left side which is the thinking part, the blood piles up and causes an imbalance."

Phlegm is the second most important factor in determining health. Phlegm is already in the body:

> When a person is exposed to damp cold air he inhales it and the temperature goes through the entire body, and the darkness goes on in a person until he becomes congested. The phlegm and cold air get into the intestines or around them or in the side or back. If the blood is not circulating right, because it has become cold and slowed down, then phlegm may start becoming congested and get into the lungs and cause wheezing.

Staying cold and wet too long brings on phlegm, causing a reaction in the system where phlegm keeps collecting until it produces a cold. Mr.

Lee listens to how a person coughs and spits to determine how congested and how deep in the lungs and chest the phlegm is. He explained that

> the gall, which is attached to the liver, produces bile which helps break down food and helps eliminate impurities. If a person complains of a "foul" or "sour" stomach, or their food tastes bitter, or their mouth is not clear in either talking, or breath, then something is wrong with the liver.

Numerous other factors are considered in judging the state of health. For example, Mr. Lee often has dreams about people that may give clues to what is wrong with them. Or something significant may happen; for example, a bird whistling may be a warning of death. He also experiences flashes of insight he finds extremely difficult to describe. He has not been able to teach anyone this skill and considers it a gift from God.

Symbolism as well as other aspects of the lives of people in the lowlands have great significance in diagnoses. While we derogate symbolism and magic in this context, we must admit a certain consistency in their observations of symptoms and their prognoses of disease, which are often empirically sound. Despite this commonsense approach, however, they try to harmonize the objective facts with the traditional symbolic frame of reference.

### HERBAL REPERTOIRE

For his therapeutic herbs, Mr. Lee has drawn almost exclusively on indigenous plants and also introduced naturalized vegetation on his farm. The appendix lists a selected sample. According to Mr. Lee, "a person becomes ill when impurities or germs enter the blood system by eating, drinking, using or touching unclean things, or by being unclean oneself." A blood purifier such as goldenseal (*Hydrastis canadensis* L. Ranunculaceae) or sarsaparilla (*Menispermum canadense*) may be taken to eliminate these impurities, which are carried out of the system through perspiration, urine, and other body wastes. Pine top (*Pinus strobus* L. Pinaceae) tea should be taken for colds. "It causes a certain amount of water to come out of the blood, because the blood becomes hot, resulting in perspiration which eliminates the impurities from the blood."

Mr. Lee has developed a working frame of reference for classifying his plants based on four main features: (1) strength of taste, (2) degree of efficacy, (3) rate of reaction, and (4) toxicity.

The relative strength of taste is best exemplified by contrasting two extremes, poke root (root of the pokeweed *Phytolacca americana*), which has a very strong taste, and mint (*Mentha arvensis*), which has a mild taste. Overall quantity of course also affects taste.

The degree of efficacy is based on: (1) the age of the herb, (2) the amount used, and (3) system response. A young root may not be as efficacious as an old root; for example, a one-year-old root of pokeweed will not be as potent as a five-year-old root. Furthermore, the more roots or leaves one uses in preparing a remedy the stronger it will be. Finally, a strong herb will cause an immediate systemic reaction; a person "can feel it working on the problem." For example, grip grass (*Sisyrinchium*) is classified as strongly reactive; in contrast, catnip has a medium reaction.

Rate of reaction may be defined by comparison with a very active herb such as rabbit tobacco (*Gnaphalium obtusioflium*), which "stimulates a person right away," while a mildly active herb such as plantain (*Plantago major*) has a slow rate of response.

A "powerful" herb may be either poisonous, for example, nightshade (*Solanum nigrum*), or have harmful side effects only if used improperly, for example, poke root. Mr. Lee gives specific possible side effects associated with "powerful" herbs if not taken properly.

He describes how he takes various factors into account in the selection and preparation of herbs, for example, the season of the year, the appearance of the bark, and the smell and freshness of the plant. The season of the year is one circumstance that determines which part of a plant is used:

> In the winter, when the sap is settled, I use the root of a plant or the lower bark on a tree, while in the spring, the bark higher up on a

tree is better because the sap has risen and, therefore, the upper parts are stronger. The same is true of the leaves of some plants.

The moon also plays an important role in the planting, selection, and preparation of herbs for medicine. The best medicine is prepared when the moon is full because it "tastes better" and "holds its strength better."

He gets the bark from the north side of the tree in the spring "when the sap is rising and the sun does not take out the strength." In the winter he gets the bark from the bottom of the tree because the sap has settled. Most leaves and roots are usually dried in the shade to preserve their strength.

Smell is also important. "If it does not smell as I think it should then I don't use it." Roots that have sharp, pungent, or bitter smells are generally to be avoided. However, odor and taste are different; "most herbs have a bitter taste but they smell all right."

The freshness of the plant, as with pine top and red oak bark (*Quercus falcata* Fagaceae), is potentially significant for its effectiveness in treatment. Further analysis is needed to determine the actual role, if any, that the active principles of many of these herbs have in effecting the cures for which they are used.

Smell and taste are fairly classifiable sensory perceptions. Empirical efficacy is not easily reduced to a scientific scale. How "old" is a plant? What virtues are affected by height of growth, depth and size of root, and the extent of shade and sunlight? "High technological" measurements have as yet to be applied to the analysis of such factors. Mr. Lee has many ways of judging, using such criteria as color, texture, and form. He also classifies functional characteristics of taste and odor, which are given in the appendix together with treatments and nomenclature.

Most of Mr. Lee's materia medica is part of the general folklore (Porcher 1863; Krochmal et al. 1969; Morton 1974; Krochmal and Krochmal 1975; Hamel and Chiltoskey 1975), and the origins of the herbs and their applications are often traceable to American-Indian, African, and European traditions. He has, however, some personal favorite practices in the selection, combination, preparation, and administration of specific cures. For example, one remedy he has found effective for varicose veins is burdock (*Arctium minus*), dandelion (*Taraxacum officinale*), and white oak bark (*Quercus alba*) combined together in equal portions and made into a tea. To treat seizures he makes a tea from equal portions of catnip and the roots of black cohosh (*Cimicifuga racemosa*) and comfrey (*Cyanoglossum virginianum*). The roots of sarsaparilla and black cohosh are combined and preserved in corn whiskey as a treatment for diabetes and arthritis. If a patient has an extremely bad case of either ailment, then bear's-foot (*Polymnia uvedalia*) may be added.

Mr. Lee's system for classifying the herbs enters into his selection and preparation of the remedies. This reflects a "folk wisdom" that is not precisely verbalized but, nonetheless, holds in its essence the "old wisdom" of the tradition passed down from generation to generation. Familial and other established social networks still operate within the African-American community to meet the health needs of the people. The extended family often continues to be the chief resource in case of illness. When more authoritative answers are needed, the families may turn to elders in the community or to recognized practitioners. This is more common among older working-class rural people than among young middle-class urban residents (cf. Watson 1984; Payne-Price, this volume).

The people who come to the Lees,[5] however, are from every economic, social, and age level and from a variety of ethnic groups. While the practice of folk medicine is thought or felt to be dying out, this research has indicated a resurgence of interest, not only among the lay community but also some scientists. Such research findings may point to neglected leads in pharmaceutical research, possibly stimulating the discovery of additional useful data about the toxicity and therapeutic value of the herbs. The findings may also enhance our understanding of the process by which old knowledge is integrated with developing science.

NOTES

1. This work was made possible in part by support from the faculty research program in the Social Sciences, Humanities, and Education at How-

ard University from the Office of the Vice President of Academic Affairs 1979–80. The initial research was undertaken by Dr. Jane Philips and Dr. Arvilla Payne-Price.

2. The collected samples are kept in the Anthropology Laboratory at Howard University.

3. Over fifty hours of interviews have been tape-recorded and are kept at the Anthropology Laboratory at Howard University.

4. These two skills, although denied by unbelievers, are the inexplicable easing of pain and reduction of blisters from burns, and the staunching of bleeding. These phenomena have baffled scientists and have been accepted by some religious observers as due to the power of faith.

5. The Lees keep meticulous records that confirm every visitor.

REFERENCES

Duke, James
    1985    C.R.C. Handbook of Medicinal Herbs. Boca Raton, Fla.: C.R.C. Press.

Hamel, P., and M. Chiltoskey
    1975    Cherokee Plants and Their Uses: A 400 Year History. Sylvia, N.C.: Herald Publishing Co.

Kloss, Jethro
    1972    Back to Eden. Santa Barbara, Calif.: Woodbridge Press.

Krochmal, Arnold, and Connie Krochmal
    1975    A Guide to Medicinal Plants of the United States. New York: Quadrangle/The New York Times Book Co.

Krochmal, Arnold, Russell Walters, and Richard Doughty
    1969    A Guide to Medicinal Plants of Appalachia. Forest Service, U.S. Department of Agriculture, Agriculture Handbook No. 400.

Lust, John
    1974    The Herb Book. New York: Benedict Lust.

Meyer, Joseph
    1987    The Herbalist. Glenwood, Ill.: Meyerbooks.

Morton, Julia
    1974    Folk Remedies of the Low Country. Miami, Fla.: E. A. Seeman.

Porcher, Francis
  1863    *Resources of the Southern Fields and Forests, Medical, Economical and Agricultural.* Charleston, S.C.: Steam-Pow Press of Evans and Cogswell.

Reader's Digest
  1986    *Magic and Medicine of Plants.* Pleasantville, N.Y.: Reader's Digest Association.

Watson, Wilbur
  1984    *Black Folk Medicine: Central Tendencies in the Practice of Folk Medicine.* New Brunswick, N.J.: Transaction Books.

Weiss, Gaea, and Shandar Weiss
  1985    *Growing and Using the Healing Herbs.* Emmaus, Pa.: Rodale Press.

A Portion of Mr. Lee's Herbal Repertoire with His Working Frame of Reference

| Scientific name | Vernacular name given by Mr. Lee | Working frame of reference[a] | Use | Method of use and plant part(s) |
|---|---|---|---|---|
| 1. *Acorus calamus* L. Araceae | flagroot | STR, SR, A | gas, indigestion, heart burn, colic, upset stomach, menstrual cramps, ulcers, worms | Cut a root into ⅛-inch pieces, dry in the sun, chew or make a tea. Take a piece of root and make a tea. |
| 2. *Allium sativum* L. Liliaceae | garlic | ST, VSR, A | high blood pressure, colds, sore throat, cough, consumption, liver ailment, emphysema | Boil some garlic in water and drink. High blood pressure—take 3 to 4 cloves and put in a quart of water and take one tbsp 3 times a day. |
| 3. *Arctium minus* Schk. Compositae | burdock | MT, MR, MA | sores, swelling, coughs, colds, canker sores, gout, rheumatism, varicose veins, stomach trouble | Put 2 tbsp of chopped root to 2 cups of water, boil down to 1 cup and take 1 tbsp 1 time a day. For sores, boil one or two cups of roots in one quart of water and bathe the sores. For sores and swellings, bruise the leaf and place on the area. |
| 4. *Asclepias* spp. L. Asclepiadaceae | milkweed | UC, SR, A | sores, insect bites, wasp stings, poison oak and ivy, stop bleeding | Take 2 or 3 stems and break them. Apply sap directly to the sore or sting. Apply every 15 to 20 minutes. |
| 5. *Baptisia tinctoria* (L.) R. Br. | wild indigo | MT, SR, A | swellings, bruises, spider bites, insect bites, diabetes | Boil the roots in water and take 1 tsp a day for diabetes. Boil leaves in water and bathe the area affected. |

| # | Species / Family | Common name | Codes | Uses | Preparation |
|---|---|---|---|---|---|
| 6. | *Cassia marilandica* L. spp. Caesalpiniaceae | senna | MT, MR, A | laxative | Take 1 tsp of leaves and boil in a cup of water and drink. |
| 7. | *Cimicifuga racemosa* (L.) Nutt. Ranunculaceae | black cohosh | ST, VSR, VA | bronchitis, arthritis, rheumatism, fever, diabetes, prostate gland, heart trouble, stomach trouble, blood purifier, diarrhea, swelling, aphrodisiac, menstrual cramps, loss of appetite | Take 2-inch piece of root and place in a jar of 100% white corn whiskey. Take 1 tbsp 2 to 3 times a day. |
| 8. | *Chimaphila maculata* Nutt. Pyrolaceae | rat's vein | MT, MR, A | heart trouble, appetite builder | Chew the roots or fill a jar with roots and 100% corn whiskey. Take 1 tsp 3 times a day. |
| 9. | *Sanicula marilandica* Apiaceae | black snakeroot | ST, VSR, A | stomach trouble, snake, insect, and spider bites, fevers, sores | Chew a piece of root 2 times a day. For sores, mash up root and place on sore. |
| 10. | *Cyanoglossum virginianum* L. Boraginaceae | wild comfrey | ST, MR, A | ulcers, menstrual cramps, colds, wounds, swelling, diarrhea, gout | Boil 1 tsp of leaves in a cup of water and drink. |
| 11. | *Eupatorium perfoliatum* L. Compositae | boneset | ST, SR, A | colds, flu, pneumonia, fluid, fevers, coughs | Boil leaves in water and take 1 cup 2 times a day. |
| 12. | *Gaylussacia* spp. L. Ericaceae | huckleberry | MT, MR, A | diabetes | Take ½ dozen roots 6 inches long, boil in ½ gallon of water. Take 1 cup 3 times a day. |
| 13. | *Hexastylis virginica* (L.) Small Aristolochiaceae | heart leaf | UC, MR, A | hair dressing, dandruff | Take 1 cup of roots and stem and boil, strain, and then mix with petroleum jelly. |
| 14. | *Hydrastis canadensis* L. Ranunculaceae | golden seal | MT, MR, A | blood purifier, arthritis, stomach trouble, constipation, allergies, gout, sinus problems, fluid | Boil a piece of root in water and drink 1 cup. |

| Scientific name | Vernacular name given by Mr. Lee | Working frame of reference[a] | Use | Method of use and plant part(s) |
|---|---|---|---|---|
| 15. *Marrubium vulgare* L. Labiatae | horehound (cultivated) | ST, SR, A | chest colds, asthma, chicken pox | Boil 1 to 2 tsp of roots and leaves, steep, add honey. Drink 1 cup once a day. Boil down and make a syrup for colds. |
| 16. *Melia azedarach* L. Meliaceae | chinaberry | ST, MR, A | worms | Boil 1 cup of berries, steep 10 minutes, take 1 tbsp 2 to 3 times a day for a week. |
| 17. *Menispermum canadense* L. Menispermaceae | sarsaparilla | VST, VSR, VA | diabetes, high and low blood pressure, gout, arthritis, ear-aches, prostate gland, kidney problems, bladder and urinary tract problems, styes, boils, diarrhea, swelling, dandruff, sore or weak eyes, heart murmur, loss of appetite | Use the root. Cut up into pieces 2 inches long and fill a quart jar. Add 100% white corn whiskey. Take 1 tbsp 2 to 3 times a day. If a severe case then put in a 2-inch piece of black cohosh and a piece of bear's-foot root. Take 1 tbsp 3 times a day. For eye sores, boil root in water and put drops in eye. |
| 18. *Monarda didyma* L. Labiatae | balm, (Oswego tea) | ST, MSR, MA | Menstrual cramps, stomach trouble, nervousness | Boil the leaves in water and take two cups per day or as needed. |
| 19. *Nepeta cataria* L. Labiatae | catnip | MT, MR, VA | colic, thrush, diaper rash, insomnia, colds, arthritis, chicken pox, hives, diarrhea, fever, menstrual cramps, gas | Boil leaves in water. Take 1 cup for adults, 12 drops for young babies. |
| 20. *Panax quinquefolium* L. Araliaceae | ginseng | MT, MR, A | stomach aches, kidney and liver problems, diabetes, blood purifier, prostate gland, back and chest pains, aphrodisiac, nerves, consumption, low appetite | Put 4 or 5 pieces of root about 3 inches long in a jar and add 100% corn whiskey. Take 1 or 2 tbsp 3 times a day. |

| # | Species | Common name | Codes | Uses | Preparation |
|---|---------|-------------|-------|------|-------------|
| 21. | *Phytolacca americana* L. Phytolaccaceae | pokeroot | VST, VSR, VA, powerful | thyroid trouble, chest pain, fungal skin infections, arthritis, ulcers, laxative, ulcerated stomach cancer, spring tonic, impetigo, cysts | Dry the root and cut into small pieces ¼ inch long. Boil the root for itching about 45 minutes in one gallon of water or cut the root into pieces 5 or 6 inches long and take a bath in it. For laxative, boil poke salad (leaves) and add spring onions and bacon drippings. For chest pain, thyroid, and ulcers, boil about 3 roots in a quart of water, refrigerate, take 1 tsp 2 or 3 times a day. For cysts, boil 2 tbsp of roots in one pint of water for ½ hr until water turns milky. Cool and add 1 tbsp of 100% white corn whiskey to preserve. Take 1 tsp to 1-1½ tbsp 2 times a day. |
| 22. | *Pinus strobus* L. Pinaceae | white pine top | MT, MR, A | fevers, pneumonia, flu, colds, measles, whooping cough, soreness in chest | Take needles or tip ends and boil in a quart of water. Drink 1 or 2 cups several times a day. |
| 23. | *Polymnia uvedalia* L. Compositae | bear's-foot | MT, MS, A | colds, fever, stomach and kidney problems, heart problems, diabetes, arthritis, prostate gland, swelling, dandruff, eyewash, loss of appetite | Cut off 1- or 2-inch pieces of root and put in a jar. Add sarsaparilla root, fill jar with 100% white corn whiskey. Take 1 tbsp 2 to 3 times a day. Or chew a piece of root. |
| 24. | *Prenanthes trifoliolata* (Lass.) Fern. Compositae | gall-of-the-earth | ST, SR, A | blood purifier, arthritis, sores | Take 3 to 4 plants and place into 1 pint of water. Take 1 tsp 1 or 2 times a day. For sores break off the stem and put sap on the sore. |

| Scientific name | Vernacular name given by Mr. Lee | Working frame of reference[a] | Use | Method of use and plant part(s) |
|---|---|---|---|---|
| 25. *Prunus serotina* Ehrh. Rosaceae | wild cherry | ST, SR, A | coughs, cold, hoarseness, indigestion | Boil the bark and oak bark and mullein (*Verbascum thapsus*) together, strain and add honey, lemon, and whiskey to taste. |
| 26. *Quercus alba* L. Fagaceae | white oak bark | ST, SR, A | kidney, liver, and stomach problems, hemorrhoids, varicose veins, worms, wounds | Boil 1 tsp of bark in 1 cup of water and make a tea. |
| 27. *Quercus falcata* L. Fagaceae | red oak bark | ST, SR, A | malaria, coughs, low thin blood, hemorrhoids, varicose veins | Take 1 tbsp of red oak bark and white cherry bark and mullein and boil together in 1 quart of water. Take 1 tbsp each morning. |
| 28. *Rhus glabra* L. Anacardiaceae | red sumac | ST, SR, A | mouth sores, sore throats, wounds | Boil the berries and make a tea or chew the berries. |
| 29. *Salvia officinalis* L. Labiatae | sage | ST, SR, A | colds, congestion, sore throats, chicken pox, menstrual cramps, headaches | Make a tea from the leaves and take 1 cup before going to bed. |
| 30. *Sassafras albidium* (Nutt.) Nees. Lauraceae | sassafras | MT, MR, A | blood purifier, sores on body, stomach and bowel problems, colds, kidney problems, spring tonic, swelling | Boil 3 or 4 pieces of root 2 to 3 inches long until water turns red. Drink 2 or 3 cups a day. |
| 31. *Sisyrinchium* spp. L. Iridaceae | grip grass | ST, SR, A | purging and laxative | Take one or two bunches and add to a quart of water, boil and let steep. Take 1 cup. |

172

| # | Species | Common name | | Uses | Preparation |
|---|---------|-------------|---|------|-------------|
| 32. | *Solanum nigrum* L. Solanaceae | nightshade | UC, SR, A, powerful | poison ivy, insect bites, bee or wasp stings | Use the leaves and berries, mash them up and add some sweet milk. Sponge the area. |
| 33. | *Taraxacum officinale* Weber Compositae | dandelion | ST, SR, A | blood purifier, laxative, diabetes, fevers, urinary tract problems, kidney and liver problems | Boil the whole plant and take 1 to 2 ounces 2 to 3 times a day. |
| 34. | *Trifolium pratense* L. Fabaceae | red clover | MT, MR, MA | arthritis, cancer, liver problems, constipation, laxative | Use the flowers or dried leaves. Put 1 tsp to a cup and take 1 time a day. |
| 35. | *Verbascum thapsus* L. Scrophulariaceae | mullein | ST, SR, A | coughs, asthma, congestion, sore throat, colds, stomach trouble, bed sores, hemorrhoids, swelling, wounds, warts | Use 4 or 5 leaves and boil in water and drink. Add wild cherry bark and honey for a cough syrup. For hemorrhoids, boil a handful of leaves and mix with hog lard or petroleum jelly to make a salve. For bed sores, soak the leaves in water and bathe the area. |
| 36. | *Zea mays* L. Gramineae | corn silk | MT, SR, A | bed-wetting, mumps | Boil corn silk in water, take ½ cup or less 2 or 3 times a day. |

aLegend for Mr. Lee's working frame of reference

T = taste

R = reaction

A = active

V = very

S = strong

M= medium/mild

Powerful = poisonous

UC = unclassified

# CHAPTER 8

# Sandinista Cultural Policy

## Notes toward an Analysis in Historical Context

*David E. Whisnant*

A mong the themes that regularly emerge when Sandinista leaders speak of the role of culture in the revolution, two are particularly salient: the revolution's deep cultural roots, and the crucial involvement of Nicaragua's creative artists at every stage of the revolutionary process. Nearly fifteen years after leaving his native León as a rather callow and swaggering high school graduate to join the FSLN in the mountains, Omar Cabezas recalled the transforming power of his first political work in the Indian barrio of Subtiava.

> The Subtiavans were there even before there was a León, even before the Spanish conquest. . . . I left for the mountains confident mainly because I felt that Subtiava was behind me. . . . *Subtiava, that was power. . . .*
>
> Before the Subtiavans started marching, they beat their *atabales.* . . . And you felt a unity in the beat of the drums. . . . For this was the Indian awakening. . . . I realized at that moment they were marching not only in Subtiava but over all of Latin America— over history, over the future.[1]

Speaking at the Casa de las Américas in Havana almost simultaneously with Cabezas's recollections, novelist Sergio Ramírez, member of the

Governing Junta of National Reconstruction, made a statement later
quoted many times by other Sandinista leaders:

> The revolution has been a most important cultural fact of our his-
> tory not only because the people wove its multiple warp with imagi-
> nation and creative capacity, invented new forms of war and meth-
> ods of fighting, [and] resorted to their best traditions . . . but also
> because their poets, their musicians, and their painters took their
> places in the trenches and assaulted the enemy's positions.[2]

Thus at every stage the Sandinistas have portrayed the origins, development, and aims of the revolution as complexly interwoven with the
dynamics of Nicaraguan cultural history. Commander Henry Ruíz has
told how in its early days the FSLN was able to build "chains" of
support by using the cherished family and godparent links within
Nicaraguan *campesino* culture. Culture later became a central concern
in the structuring of the new government and in initial policy formulation: The decree establishing the Ministry of Culture was one of the
first half-dozen issued by the ruling junta the day after they entered
Managua. Six months later, Minister of Culture Ernesto Cardenal
asserted that "The revolution is culture, and our culture now is revolution; there is no distinction between revolution and culture." Early
reports of the Sandinistas' apparent success with cultural programs,
especially the widely acclaimed literacy crusade and the poetry workshops, disposed many outside Nicaragua to make a similar equation.[3]

Within Nicaragua itself, a consensus account of the relationship
between the political, social, and cultural aspects of the revolution
took shape rather quickly after 1979, and has been repeated upon
many occasions by Sandinista leaders. It goes something like this:
Through the agony of conquest, the years of internal strife, and new
foreign domination following independence, and particularly the recent decades of U.S. cultural imperialism facilitated and encouraged
by the puppet Somoza dictatorship, the authentic culture of Nicaragua
survived. Though fragmented and suppressed, it maintained its integrity, its vigor, and its genius for resistance. At length it formed the
strongest and most durable substratum of the Sandinista movement—

an inexhaustible reservoir of will and strength, a referential reality against which the movement's directions could be checked. The victory of the Sandinistas in 1979 was thus among other things a warrant of the ancient legitimacy and resurgent vitality of that culture, whose honoring and nurturing therefore had to be provided for legally and institutionally within the new government. Responsive to their cultural mandate, the Sandinistas began immediately to build an entirely new cultural apparatus within the country: insistently independent of foreign domination, democratic, decentralized, and deeply respectful and supportive of national cultural traditions.[4]

Like many consensus versions of events, this one contains substantial elements of easily documentable truth. Of the history of cultural imperialism, for example, there can be no doubt. But like all national cultural histories, that of Nicaragua is also more complex than can be comprehended within such a paradigm. Local elites, for example, frequently not only proved brutally insensitive to the cultural identity and interests of the majority of ordinary people (as when vast numbers of campesinos were dispossessed of their land in the elite-controlled conversion from subsistence agriculture to the production of coffee and cotton for export), but also often welcomed and facilitated foreign economic and cultural intervention and domination (Booth 1985:11–26).

This essay therefore attempts to sketch an analytical framework within which the cultural dimensions of the Sandinista revolution can be more adequately comprehended in relation to the complex histories of both the revolution and Nicaragua itself: the cultural development of Nicaragua prior to the revolution; the sources of and influences upon the formation of the Sandinistas' cultural ideas and assumptions; the actual role of culture in the revolution, both as an enabling and empowering resource and as a confusing and frustrating impediment; and the Sandinistas' successes and failures in embodying their cultural ideas and policies in operating programs. That is to say, I attempt at the first level to sketch some of the more readily apparent cultural dimensions of the various stages of the Sandinista revolution.

Beyond that, however, I also try to comprehend the more fundamental relationship between culture and revolutionary ideology insofar as the perils peculiar to it emerge in particular forms in the Nicaraguan context: the intractabilities (social or intrapsychic) of historical cultural formation; the tension between the need for postrevolutionary stability and an ideological commitment to artistic freedom (which may lead in practice to destabilizing criticism of the emergent state); the seductive tendency—perhaps especially prominent among an internationally oriented (and thus to some degree culturally *disoriented*) intellectual elite in a state undergoing decolonization—to romanticize and sanitize the national cultural past; and the perennially problematic linking of state-sponsored cultural programming (informed by whatever ideology) with national power and prestige. Hence, central to my analysis is the contention that conceptions of culture are inseparable from both power and ideology, and therefore inevitably interactive with each. I attempt here, that is to say, an essay on some aspects of the politics of culture as they may be seen in the recent history of Nicaragua.[5]

CULTURE AS PREAMBLE

When the Sandinistas finally entered triumphantly into Managua in 1979, they faced a task of cultural reconstruction burdened by a tragic national cultural history four and a half centuries long and many layers deep.

Indeed, as the Sandinistas began to reach backward toward their remotest cultural origins, even the precolonial experience of Nicaragua presented to them not a tranquil and reassuring panorama of cultural unity to be recovered and celebrated, but a rather turbulent and disquieting diversity, disunity, and conflict reinforced by geography and other factors. As both Helms and Radell have outlined, eastern Nicaragua, on the one hand, was peopled prior to the Conquest by hunting and gathering Indian groups culturally related to South America. On the other hand, the salubrious climate and rich volcanic soils of the Pacific coast supported more sedentary agricultural Indians, culturally related to Mesoamerica. Moreover, a generally low and uneven population density created sectors of relatively autonomous cultural development even within the eastern and western regions, as well as differences in political power and cultural influence (Radell 1969:32–38; Helms 1975).

The Conquest further complicated the situation, in some respects extending prior cleavages and disparities, and in others clearing the slate and starting over with new ones. Radell pointed out that "the Indian culture regions of pre-Columbian Nicaragua coincide closely to the later colonial administrative areas." Granada was founded at the center of a large existing Indian population, for example, and most upper-class Spaniards settled there; the earliest nonindigenous residents of León, in contrast, were mostly low-ranking Spanish foot soldiers stationed to forestall Cortez's threatened moves southward from Mexico.

Even more important culturally than any of these factors, however, was the genocidal destruction of the native population and the consequently irremediable reorganization of the cultural map of the country. As the sixteenth century opened, Nicaragua had approximately one million native inhabitants. Nearly half were sold into slavery in the single decade between 1527 and 1536. Tens of thousands more died of epidemic diseases or were exterminated by the Spanish. By the 1570s, a mere remnant of about 8,000 remained.[6]

The impact of the culturally genocidal Conquest did not fall uniformly upon the country, however; it was less severe as one moved eastward from the Pacific coast through the central highlands and toward the Atlantic coast. Indeed, in the period between the Conquest and Independence, western Nicaragua culturally was progressively Hispanicized and homogenized, while the Atlantic coast, increasingly isolated from that dynamic, maintained more racial, cultural, and linguistic diversity and autonomy, which in turn led much later (along with other factors) to an enduring Atlantic coast hostility to the "Spanish" Nicaraguans of the Pacific coast.

The arrival of political independence in 1838 had considerably less meaning within the cultural sector than one might at first assume. Most of the indigenous population was gone, their communities, languages, lifeways, and expressive practices forever erased. The majority of the population (centered on the west coast) had long since become *mestizo,* Catholic, and Spanish-speaking. The separation of the

Atlantic coast had been exacerbated by English buccaneers, who for a century and a half manipulated the remnants of the local indigenous population as pawns in their struggle against the Spanish for military and commercial control of the area. Hence the dominant language of the Atlantic coast was English, and the dominant religious orientation was Protestant, especially after Moravian missionaries arrived in 1849.[7] Thus what is now known as Nicaragua was—as it began its "independence"—in fact two countries, as it would remain for another century and a half.

On the west coast, the focus of national identity where the major urban centers, most of the population, and virtually all national institutions were concentrated, two dynamics with profound cultural implications operated from the earliest days of independence: the rise of Positivism and Liberalism, and persistent U.S. intervention in Nicaragua's internal affairs.[8]

Throughout Latin America, positivistic thought gained its strongest adherents among the agricultural, commercial, and professional elites. Woodward has distilled the essence of positivistic values and assumptions as they manifested themselves in liberal regimes throughout Central America: obsession with material development, anticlericalism, faith in scientific and technical education, willingness to subordinate political democracy to economic growth and prosperity, emulation of European and North American values, capital, and leadership, and insensitivity to the desires and needs of the working classes (Woodward 1985:156).

Culturally speaking, the implications of such a perspective were disastrous for the few scattered surviving remnants of indigenous cultural forms and practices, and even for the widespread mestizo, Hispanicized, Catholic working-class culture that had developed following the Conquest. The vernacular cultures of the urban working class and the subsistence-agriculture-based campesinos alike were arrogantly depreciated by the modernizing, Europeanizing elites of León, Granada, and Managua. Virtually no aspect of those cultural systems—land-tenure patterns, family and community structure, diet, customs and ceremonies, economic relationships—escaped radical transformation under the Liberal agenda.[9]

Such patterns of transformation were furthered by the growing intervention of the United States after the promulgation of the Monroe Doctrine in 1823 and the ensuing struggles for control of the Nicaraguan canal route. The episode with the most cultural implications was of course the William Walker intervention of the late 1850s. According to *Frank Leslie's Illustrated Newspaper,* Walker and his troops were "shedding their blood and sacrificing their lives" in Nicaragua not only to establish progressive government, but also to bring cultural enlightenment. One article, accompanied by an elegant engraving, envisioned "A Future Venice in Nicaragua." As for the natives, the journal harbored no "mawkish sympathy" for "the miserable, hybrid, wretched creatures that form the mass of the population of the Central American states." "The only way to purify and enlighten such people," it judged, was "with powder and ball."[10]

Practically speaking, what Walker did as soon as he managed to have himself elected president of the country was to declare English the official language, legalize slavery, and institute vagrancy laws to force peasants to work for large landowners. For its part, the United States immediately recognized Walker's as the legitimate government of Nicaragua, inaugurating an era of direct intervention in the country's cultural (and other) affairs that was to last more than a hundred years.

Though the Walker episode itself was short-lived, the broader and more durable patterns of Liberal subservience to North American and European culture can be glimpsed in, for example, the musical culture of Nicaragua's urban centers in the late nineteenth century. In a series of biographical sketches of about forty prominent Nicaraguan musicians and composers born in the century between 1811 and 1911, Gilberto Vega Miranda telegraphed the essential details: Trained for the most part by European-educated teachers (or their Nicaraguan students), most composed within the dominant European forms (symphonies, operas, concertos, oratorios) and performed on European instruments (strings, winds, piano) within the bounds of established European performance practices. Miranda's lone reference to the popular song "Zopilote" by Luís Felipe Urroz (1857–1915)—"who knew how to extract the general sentiment from a folkloric melody"—

evokes the cultural conflict and loss: In the song an Indian, baptized against his will, is converted into a predatory bird (*zopilote*), which sings and dances at night on the outskirts of the "*colonía indígena*."[11]

Thus, as the nineteenth century closed, the outlines of two and a half centuries of cultural loss and tragedy were clear. Any culture that could reasonably have been called indigenously Nicaraguan was practically extinct; the replacement post-Conquest, pre-Independence, subsistence-agriculture-based, Hispanicized vernacular culture itself had been decimated and dispersed by the Liberal-Positivist drive toward agroexport-based "modernization"; urban Liberal elites were in full control of cultural norms and institutions, in which European and North American forms were dominant; culture itself (of whatever complexion) was a concern subordinate to the perennial factional political struggles over the direction of economic development and the division of spoils; a major east-west cleavage divided the country culturally as well as in many other respects; and the relatively sparse population (barely half a million at the turn of the century, or an average of fewer than ten per square mile) was concentrated principally in the three urban areas of León, Managua, and Granada on the Pacific coast.

However, such a cultural tragedy had not developed with the wholly supine acquiescence of the entire populace. As Jaime Wheelock Román has demonstrated, instances of resistance can be documented all the way back to the Conquest. A major episode of what may in some respects be understood as cultural resistance emerged, for example, at the turn of the century during the Zelaya presidency (1894–1909). Although Zelaya was a classical Liberal whose major policies (infrastructure development, stimulation of agricultural export commodities, expropriation of communal lands, forced labor drafts, increased foreign investment) were beneficial to the elite and disastrous for campesinos, his nationalism and expansionism led him to oppose U.S. intervention and to end once and for all British control of the Atlantic coast.[12]

Zelaya's opposition to Yankee imperialism led to his own forcible replacement (with the help of U.S. marines) by the successive, short-lived, U.S.-approved regimes of José Madriz, Juan Estrada, and Adolfo Díaz. Rebel general Benjamin Zeledón (*"el indio"*), killed leading an armed insurrection of peasants and poor artisans against Díaz, became—paradoxically, since he was backed by Liberal coffee growers—a minor cultural martyr. And when his body was paraded before the public, it was viewed by the 17-year-old Augusto Sandino.[13]

A full analysis of the cultural significance of Sandino in the Sandinista revolution lies far beyond the scope of this paper, but several points are essential. Sandino was first of all the illegitimate son of a coffee grower and a peasant woman, and was very conscious of carrying within himself both Indian blood and some of the fundamental cultural conflicts of Nicaragua's national history.[14] He insisted that

> I am Nicaraguan and I am proud that in my veins flows, more than any other, the blood of the American Indian, whose regeneration contains the secret of being a loyal and sincere patriot. (Marcus 1985:396)

Hence Sandino's anti-imperialist challenge had a strong racial and cultural—as well as political and economic—basis. "The Yankees *say* according to the Monroe Doctrine," he observed, " 'America for the Americans' " but

> They *interpret* the Doctrine as "America for the Yankees." But so that the blond beasts will not continue in their deception, I recast the phrase as follows: the United States of North America for the Yankees. Latin America for the indolatinos. (Ramírez Mercado 1984: I, 259 and I, 270)

Thus Sandino's fundamental importance as the focal cultural hero and the center of the emergent legitimizing cultural myth of the Sandinista revolution is beyond question. More than any other single figure in Nicaraguan history except the nationally venerated poet Rubén Darío (to whom I will return presently), Sandino collected and focused the national cultural history for *los muchachos* of the 1960s and 1970s. The seeds he planted had to lie mostly dormant, however, during the long

Somoza night to come. Like the children of Israel, Sandino's children faced forty years in the wilderness before their deliverance.

The cultural landscape of Nicaragua during the Somoza dynasty has yet to be mapped in detail, but the image projected by both the Sandinistas themselves and many independent observers is not attractive: the accelerated decimation of vernacular culture (especially in rural areas) as a result of the regime's economic policies; the emergence of Managua as the center of "national" culture; the manipulative exacerbation of tensions between the east and west coast areas; the increasing hegemony of U.S. culture; the starvation of national cultural institutions; and the repression of free cultural expression.

From 1934 through 1979 public policy in Nicaragua was shaped principally by the Somoza dynasty's brutal drive for personal wealth.[15] In that process, the lives and culture of the majority of Nicaragua's ordinary people were both neglected and ground up by the regime as the increasingly concentrated ownership of agricultural lands drove hundreds of thousands of campesinos into poverty-ridden urban barrios, and the few public services and institutions that had ever been available deteriorated. Such a pattern of national "development" made of the entire country one vastly underdeveloped periphery feeding the insatiable maw of the Managua metropole.

Viewed from a cultural perspective, both the metropole-periphery polarization and the particular character of metropole cultural development were disastrous. Compounding the losses attendant upon cultural neglect and destruction evident elsewhere in the country, Managua itself was a veritable wonderland of cultural skewings, ironies, and contradictions. As Nicaraguan intellectual Mariano Fiallos Gil lamented in the 1960s, a respectable system of national cultural institutions had for the most part never been built. During the early years of the Somoza regime, Christiana Chaves described in a personal letter how she was continuing without pay the work of her father, who for a salary of 16 *córdobas* a month had labored for years to nurture the tiny National Museum, which lacked even a building of its own. Chaves noted that such institutional starvation had been compounded by earthquake, fire, and systematic private and commercial looting of archeological sites.[16]

Thus the domination of the cultural metropole by the United States occurred at once actively (both prior to the Somoza regime and later in collaboration with it) and by default. The U.S. hold on the country began in earnest with the toppling of Zelaya. By the late 1920s the intrusion of North American commercial culture was already evident in a proliferation of advertisements in Nicaraguan newspapers for Yankee automobiles, toothpaste, cigarettes, patent medicines (including Adalina sleeping pills for children), foods, appliances, tools, and office machines.

In subsequent decades the avalanche continued, until by the 1950s a large majority of products advertised were of U.S. origin. The media were also saturated with the creations of North American mass culture. The issue of *La Prensa* that published lavish reports of the funeral of Anastasio Somoza García in 1956 offered Nicaraguan readers "Mutt and Jeff" and "Buck Rogers" comics, reports on U.S. major league athletics, and their choice of a half-dozen Hollywood movies at Managua theaters.[17] During the early days of July 1979, just before the Sandinistas entered Managua, seventeen of the city's thirty-one movie theaters were showing U.S. films, seven out of eight of *La Prensa*'s comics were from the United States, and the Somoza-owned television system (linked to the Chase Manhattan Bank through the Banco Nicaragüense) was feeding viewers a steady diet of U.S. big league baseball, Hollywood films, Disney cartoons, and the fundamentalist Christian PTL Club.[18]

The few leftover scraps of support the Somozas threw to national cultural development were aimed very selectively, and frequently combined with rigorous cultural repression. Sandinista leaders (a number of them intellectuals, novelists, and poets) have recalled repeatedly, for example, the Somoza regime's attempts to censor books they wanted to read, or wrote and tried to publish.[19]

One of the most dramatic and widely known events of cultural repression was the destruction by Somoza's National Guard troops of Ernesto Cardenal's peasant community at Solentiname in 1977. Cardenal's imaginative attempts to encourage local people to examine their lives, express themselves, and develop a heightened political consciousness through poetry, graphic art, Bible study, economic cooperation, and intense political reading (of Marx, Mao, Castro, and others) began in 1966 and attracted worldwide attention. As Cardenal himself indicated when he later referred to Solentiname as "a little pilot plan for certain things that the revolution is now doing on a larger scale," the experiment was both complexly cultural and intensely political. "The most important thing we learned in our dialogues with Ernesto," said one member of the community, "was that the system had to be changed. The only way forward was to take up arms." Thus some members went to Costa Rica to receive military training. Somoza of course found such developments intolerable, and National Guard troops therefore laid waste to the whole enterprise: buildings, library and archeological collections, studios, workshops, and exhibits.[20]

Thus, in the same sense that the destruction of Solentiname was an apt metaphor for much of the tragic pre-1979 cultural experience of Nicaragua, so was the task of national cultural reconstruction prefigured in many aspects of the Solentiname experiment itself: its relationship to the complexly layered national cultural history; its stock of cultural ideas and assumptions (especially its perhaps somewhat romantic conception of and preference for working-class culture); its choice of culturally reconstructive approaches; and its conception of the role of culture in the larger revolutionary process.

## THE REVOLUTION AND IDEAS OF CULTURE

Comprehending fully the Sandinistas' cultural ideas and assumptions—and the process through which they were formed—would require far more complete biographical information and analysis than is thus far available for any of the participants, with the possible exception of Ernesto Cardenal.[21] Yet a few tentative inferences may be drawn.

It is clear, for example, that the radical student movement in Nicaragua had an important formative influence upon many Sandinistas, and that certain cultural assumptions, ideas, and activities figured importantly in that movement. The interests of students and indigenous people came together as early as 1822 when a group of students joined some artisans of León's Indian barrio of Subtiava to attack a militia headquarters. But such organized student activity was infrequent until the present century. In the early 1930s students tried to establish a student federation, and in the 1940s they mounted their first tentative moves against the Somoza regime. In the early 1950s they agitated in favor of university autonomy, and at the end of that decade several were killed and over eighty wounded when the National Guard fired on a demonstration (Wheelock Román 1975; Cabezas 1985).

A pivotal figure in infusing the student movement with a sense of Nicaraguan culture as a source of strength and direction was Mariano Fiallos Gil, who became rector of the National University at León in 1957. Having been neglected, starved, manipulated, and repressed for years by the government, the university was a pathetic shell when Fiallos took over. But he envisioned a major role for the institution in a national "resurrection," and turned it into a forum for the open discussion of national issues and experimentation with new educational and social programs. He created an experimental theater group, instituted a series of courses and conferences on the arts, started a museum of popular art, and attached the long dormant national schools of music and art to the university. Sergio Ramírez Mercado later called Fiallos's work "a vital experiment with Nicaraguan culture" (Ramírez Mercado 1971:15, 94–109, 186).

Much of the cultural activity at the university was organized by a group of radical students (including Sergio Ramírez) who were publishing a new literary journal called *Ventana,* which directly addressed social, political, and cultural issues. The journal drew political energy from a series of radical student activities of the late 1950s and literary models from various writers and literary movements linked to progressive social change, including North American writers such as Langston Hughes, Thomas Merton, the Beats, and Faulkner; Chinese poetry; Quechua poetry; Nicaraguan poets Rubén Darío, Ernesto Cardenal, Salomón de la Selva, and others. An "anti-editorial" in the October 1960 issue of *Ventana* declared that literature "is no pastime or diversion; it is a vehicle of culture, a way to life and truth." A year later, the group—which Sergio Ramírez Mercado later described as "the cultural counterpart to the Frente Sandinista"—organized a "culture week" at the university, featuring musical and theatrical presentations and discus-

sions of the relationship between the poet and society, between indigenous culture and Nicaraguan poetry, and related topics.[22]

The student movement of the 1960s—at least the *Ventana* wing of
it—aroused and focused several of what were to become central cultural elements of the Sandinista movement: the preeminence of poet
Rubén Darío (1867–1916) as the intellectual fountainhead for a resurgent cultural nationalism, and of Sandino as its charismatic hero and
an emphasis upon the creative revolutionary potential of what was
regarded as Nicaraguan national culture.

Despite the fact that Darío was most famous for his role in the
birth of the Modernist movement in Spanish poetry, which emphasized form over content, and despite his having spent most of his life
outside Nicaragua and having produced a corpus of work much of
which had little to do with Nicaragua, he came to be regarded—as he
was called when the Sandinistas established the Order of Rubén Darío
prize in poetry—"the highest exponent of Nicaraguan culture." As a
champion of indigenism, Darío had proclaimed in his *Prosas profanas*
(1896) that "if there is poetry in our [Latin] America, it is to be found
in the old things: in Palenké and Utatlán, in the legendary Indian and
the refined Inca," and he understood resistance to cultural conquest as
a permanent feature of that culture. That perspective naturally made
him especially wary of *los norteamericanos*—indeed somewhat preco-
ciously so, since he died before the period of the most pervasive and
brutal North American intervention.

Sandinista Minister of Culture Ernesto Cardenal characterized all
later Nicaraguan poetry as proceeding from Darío, and Darío himself
as the "precursor of the Revolution." Cardenal traced a direct line
from Darío through Sandino to FSLN founder Carlos Fonseca Amadór. The revolution, Cardenal said, "was a dream of Darío. And a
decision of Sandino. And a strategy of Carlos Fonseca."[23] My point
here is not that the complex cultural history matches such an elegant
paradigm, but that the paradigm itself arose and functioned as part of
the conceptual ground on which the Sandinistas launched and guided
the revolution.

With the advent of the FSLN, Darío's emphasis on the creatively
resistant strains within indigenous culture flourished as never before,

but it had never been entirely absent since the poet's death almost a half century earlier. It persisted as a major concern of the Vanguardia poets in the late 1920s and 1930s, and Mariano Fiallos Gil picked up the theme in the late 1950s and urged a whole generation of young radical students to explore it.[24]

The nature and importance of specifically Marxist ideas about culture in the Sandinistas' analysis of Nicaraguan cultural history and in their formulation of cultural history are difficult to assess, both because detailed analysis of the political development of individual Sandinista leaders for the most part remains to be done, and because the little that has been done already makes it clear that their commitment to Marxist ideology varies both in intensity and in emphasis, and derives from widely differing cultural as well as political experiences.

Both Tomás Borge and Carlos Fonseca Amadór joined Nicaragua's own Communist movement as early as the mid-1950s, but that particular involvement was unlikely to have supplied any of the cultural ideas later characteristic of the FSLN, since at the time the Communist PSN (Partido Socialista Nicaragüense) was so Stalinist in orientation that it viewed even Sandino himself contemptuously. As a very young man Fonseca himself traveled and studied in Russia. But Ernesto Cardenal first became enamored of Marxist thought fairly late in life, through a process he insists had more to do with the time he spent with Thomas Merton living "*la vida comunista*" at the Gethsemani monastery and studying scripture than it did with studying the usual sources. "I came to the revolution through the Gospel," he has said. "It was not by reading Marx, but through Christ. It can be said that the Gospel made me a Marxist." The younger Sandinista theorist Ricardo Morales Avilés (b. 1939) takes a relatively hard Marxist view of cultural matters—so much so that he is strongly critical of Cardenal and of what he sees as the well-intentioned but misguided romanticism of his Solentiname experiment.[25]

An analytical tack potentially more useful than simply trying to measure Sandinista cultural ideas and practice against some established version or other of Marxist cultural theory is suggested in Harry Vanden's assessment of the broader ideology of the Sandinista insurrection. Sandinista ideology, Vanden observes, is "a very flexible and non-sectarian Third World Marxism . . . carefully applied to the specific conditions of Nicaragua." More specifically, it is the Marxism of Ché, Fidel, and Ho Chi Minh—the Marxism of the postcolonial Third World, one persistent element of which has been a resurgence of cultural nationalism and independence.[26]

Certainly one aspect of older Marxist formulations that the Sandinistas substantially modified was its characteristic depreciation (indeed intolerance) of indigenous culture and cultural differences within the body politic. In this respect they were in agreement with some other Latin-American Marxists (especially in Peru, Bolivia, and Mexico) who at least since the 1920s had been arguing that progressive social change had to be linked to (perhaps even based primarily upon) the cultural heritage, thought systems, and practices of indigenous peoples (Vanden 1982: 35, 129–140, 177–181, 207, 219–223, 274, 288).

Both their emerging understanding of the prerevolutionary cultural experience of the nation and the more urgent postrevolutionary necessity to formulate policy and programs demanded that from such a many-stranded complex of sources, influences, and ideas the Sandinistas construct a coherent analytical perspective, select some guiding principles, and mark out directions for cultural development in the new Nicaragua.

Nicaragua's prerevolutionary history impelled the Sandinistas to emphasize first of all that, from the earliest days of Spanish colonialism to the most recent PTL Club television broadcast, their cultural past was marked by cultural imperialism and what they came to call ethnocide. "The most important characteristic of the Nicaraguan bourgeoisie's cultural attitude," Sergio Ramírez Mercado had said, "has been its desire to import a model." Linked fatally to that desire has been the United States' insistence upon "denationalizing" Nicaragua, turning its citizens into cultural copies of Díaz and Somoza, and sending them Air Force Band concerts and crates of *Reader's Digest*.[27]

The Sandinistas emphasize, however, that the colonial-imperial history has been paralleled by a countervailing dynamic of cultural resistance, coeval with the Conquest itself and reaching unbroken through Zeledón and Sandino to the spontaneous uprising in the Indian barrio of Monimbó in February 1978.[28] Hence for the Sandinistas the inescapable logic of the cultural past demanded that a central aim of cultural policy and programming be anti-imperialist cultural liberation (Cardenal 1980:163–167).

Fortunately, the colonially and imperialistically enforced syncretism of Nicaraguan culture has proved in some instances to be a strength rather than an impediment to that liberation. A dramatic example of the utility of cultural syncretism in resisting domination appears in the fiesta of *el torovenado*. Blending the most salient attributes of the (Spanish) bull—strength, haughtiness, brutishness—with those of the (Indian) stag—alertness, sagacity, agility—el torovenado is an emblem of cultural syncretism. The fiesta shows, according to Carlos Alemán Ocampo, how in acts of agile cultural resistance indigenous people are perennially able to incorporate repeated efforts at cultural domination as new sources of strength. The fiesta is intended, Ocampo suggests, "to protest, to denounce, and to explain to people how things are." It limns "the cultural stance against conquest, cultural penetration and political opportunism" (Ocampo 1981:2).

The particular character of the postrevolutionary challenge— flowing substantially, but not completely, out of national cultural history—evokes certain additional emphases. Perhaps the most important are cultural revitalization and democratization. Sandinista Minister of Culture Ernesto Cardenal commented repeatedly upon the former. "[Our] revolutionary culture has been a re-encounter with origins. And this re-encounter, the re-creation of a new life. . . . Our patrimony, which before was unseen, has been made present." Likewise, democratization has been conceptually central, perhaps sharing with anti-imperialism the honor of strongest emphasis. "If before [the revolution] culture was the closed preserve of a minority," Cardenal has declared, "now it will be . . . the right of the masses."[29]

Finally, Nicaragua's principal theoreticians of culture view cultural change and development as both conceptually inseparable from and practically essential to development in other sectors. "To political development and the immense effort to move beyond economic underdevelopment," Cardenal has observed, "we have joined cultural transformation," so that the restructuring of a new society is a "political duty" of the new culture.[30]

## THE POLICY CHALLENGE

Within the cultural arena, therefore, the Sandinistas have met many aspects of the analytical and conceptual challenge in an impressive fashion. Among the Sandinista leadership the level of conceptualization of the whole issue of culture is very high in comparison with many wealthier, larger, and supposedly more "advanced" nations. Only during the brief New Deal years, for example, did the United States approach with anything like comparable vision, imagination, and enthusiasm the task of conceiving and implementing a democratic cultural policy, and its successes were modest and in most cases of rather limited duration. The more recent flourish of cultural programming at the federal level has on the whole been conceptually timid, elitist, and funded at barely a pilot level.[31]

By contrast the Sandinistas have articulated (as I sketched briefly above) a highly conscious set of analytical and programmatic concepts, directed toward correcting the cultural distortions of the past, building upon the cultural givens of the present, and looking toward a vital and democratic cultural future. Nor is an awareness of and commitment to those concepts by any means limited to Ernesto Cardenal and other Ministry of Culture officials; they are quite generally evident in the thought of most members of the junta. Virtually every member of the FSLN National Directorate has spoken and written of the role of culture in social reconstruction with a sensitivity and sophistication rarely encountered among political leaders in the United States.[32]

As a consequence of the high general level of awareness of the importance of culture as a base and guide for change in all areas of public policy, cultural concepts, policies, institutions, and programs have been projected as playing an important role in social, economic, and political reconstruction. More specifically, the Sandinistas made extensive and fundamental changes in cultural policy itself, and consequently in cultural institutions and programs. For certain institutions and programs, the initial results have been very substantial, and have consequently already been written about rather extensively: the literacy campaign, the poetry workshops, the Centers for Popular Culture, and (to a lesser extent) graphic arts and experimental theater.[33]

These better-known efforts constitute only a small sector, however, of the much more extensive developments projected in the cultural arena. In view of the fact that the country was so bereft of public cultural institutions of any consequence prior to 1979, the task facing the new Ministry of Culture was formidable. Though hampered by the war's drain on the economy, and consequently reduced in most cases to relying on volunteers rather than paid professional staff, the Ministry initiated an impressive array of efforts to construct an infrastructure of cultural institutions and to inaugurate cultural programs throughout the country. At their best they have not only used well the limited available resources but even managed to turn calamity to advantage. In response to the Reagan administration's grain embargo, for example, the Ministry of Culture staged a corn festival (*Feria del Maíz*), in May 1981, celebrating the historical and mythical importance of corn in the culture in order to raise people's spirits, direct their energies, and rally their support for the national effort of survival and reconstruction.[34]

However energizing at a moment of crisis, such events still are of limited use in the broader restructuring of cultural institutions, which requires longer-term strategy and may not produce as dramatic results, from a public relations standpoint. Prior to 1979, for example, almost no books or journals were being published in the country except on a relatively small scale by universities and large private banks, which during the Somoza period had to some degree filled the void created by the regime's default in the area of cultural institutions and programming.[35] After the revolution, both the Ministry of Culture itself and Editorial Nueva Nicaragua established publications programs, oriented rather directly, as one would expect, toward encouraging and supporting the revolution. Thus some of the earliest books to appear under the new regime's imprimatur were those by Sergio Ramírez Mercado and Carlos Fonseca on Sandino, Jorge Eduardo Arellano's on Darío, Cardenal's on Solentiname, several collections of eulogies of the heroes and martyrs of the popular uprisings in Monimbó and Subtiava, volumes of poetry by Daisy Zamora and Rosario Murillo (both respected poets prior to the revolution), and speeches and policy statements on culture by Sandinista leaders.

Archives, libraries, and museums also received substantially increased attention and a level of public support that, though limited by required expenditures for arms, they had never before enjoyed. The overall aim was to establish them securely, to disperse them widely throughout the country in order to make their collections and services easily available, and to make them useful instruments of renewed national pride, identity, and social-political reconstruction. Corollary efforts were directed toward the conservation and restoration of historical buildings (such as Sandino's birthplace and Darío's home) and the collection of folk and popular culture—ranging from foodways and herbal remedies to slogans painted on walls during the revolution.[36]

Prior to 1979, music and film were virtually virgin territory with respect to policy (hence funding), but the Sandinistas nevertheless addressed them with vigor and imagination. As already indicated above, musical production within Nicaragua before 1979 had been dominated (at least so far as official legitimation was concerned) by western European and North American popular and art music forms; formal presentation occurred primarily in the principal west-coast cities. But from the 1960s onward, new politically progressive currents such as *nueva canción* appeared in Latin American music, and were eventually felt in Nicaragua. Two years before the Sandinistas entered Managua, a crowd of more than 3,000 at a human rights festival in Managua responded enthusiastically to themes rarely heard before in Nicaraguan music. A few months after the triumph, Tomás Borge observed that "with such songs as these [it is] impossible not to have a revolution, and . . . with a revolution such as ours, it would be impossible not to have songs such as those we have." Music flourished with encouraging new developments: The National School of Music was reopened, the Nicaraguan Symphony Orchestra was reorganized, a National Chorus and a musical journal were started, and phonograph record production was inaugurated with compositions such as Carlos Mejía Godoy's *Misa campesina nicaragüense*. Such performers as Salvador Bustos and Salvador and Katia Cardenal later helped to energize the new *volcanto* (from *volcán* = volcano and *canto* = song) musical movement.[37]

A parallel development occurred in film. The task was no less than to create a national film industry from the ground up, initially using the meager production facilities of PRODUCINE—which had made public relations films for various Somoza enterprises, training films for the National Guard, and the like—and the skills gained by the small War Correspondents Corps in the FSLN. The new Nicaraguan Institute of Cinema (INCINE) was structured into the Ministry of Culture from the beginning. Assisted by politically oriented filmmakers from other countries, INCINE began to produce historically based fictional films (such as *Alsino y el cóndor*), news programs, and documentaries.[38]

Thus by any reasonable measure—especially if one defines that measure to be the sophistication of current cultural programming in most countries, which after all is not very high—the Sandinistas made remarkable strides both conceptually and programmatically. But the endemic hazards of making cultural policy in a revolutionary context are both numerous and well known, and signs indicate that the Sandinistas have not escaped them entirely.

## THE HAZARDS OF CULTURAL POLICY MAKING IN A REVOLUTIONARY CONTEXT

Recent history provides numerous examples of the ways nation-states undergoing revolution or convulsive social-political change (as well as, of course, those that are not) manipulate culture in terms of their ideologies, their unique histories, and the pressures they encounter in various international arenas. The examples that come most easily to mind are the American and French revolutions of the late eighteenth century, the Russian and Mexican ones of the early twentieth, Fascist Italy and Nazi Germany of a quarter-century later, the United States during the Great Depression, a long list of former imperial colonies that have emerged as new nations since World War II, Cuba and China in the 1960s, and Nicaragua itself.

Since substantial comparative analysis is not possible here, these other cases must serve in a merely suggestive way to contextualize more broadly one's sense of the inescapable complexity of cultural policy within a revolutionary context—and perhaps therefore to soften any impulse to blame the Sandinistas for not "solving" problems that have so consistently proved fiendishly resistant to solution.[39] Nevertheless, the Sandinistas did encounter substantial difficulties in forming cultural policy and constructing cultural institutions and programs in the midst of their own particular historical circumstances, difficulties that must be taken into account in the present analysis. Doing so reminds us once again of the complex linkages between ideology, the realities of power, and conceptions of culture.

In 1972 Ernesto Cardenal visited Cuba's new national school of art, housed in the facilities of a former Havana country club. The artists he met seemed refreshingly modest and dedicated to integrating their work into the larger effort of national reconstruction. "Their preoccupation," Cardenal observed, "is that poets and artists should be one with the people." And yet the students told him that the director of the school was more interested in the country's new sports program than in the arts, because sports stars won medals for Cuba in international competition, while artists did not (Cardenal 1972:73–75).

Several of the inherent pitfalls of forming cultural policy in a revolutionary context are implicit in the incident: the inescapable tension between official ideology and aesthetic values on the one hand, and day-to-day bureaucratic practice on the other; the conflict between the needs of individual artists for creative freedom and support, and the drive of the state for stability and legitimacy vis-à-vis both its own people and the international community; and (by no means least) the perdurable limits of frail human beings engaged in ideologically guided enterprises situated in fragile socially constructed realities.

Among the Sandinista leadership, both Bayardo Arce Castaño and Sergio Ramírez Mercado have spoken of some of the potential risks of post-1979 cultural development in Nicaragua: ideological dogmatism (and therefore creative narrowness) in the arts, and the temptation to reflect only a narrowly conceived "revolutionary reality" in artistic production. Rosario Murillo has also noted the temptation to institutionalize certain modes of creation (such as Cardenal's *exte-*

*riorismo* in the poetry workshops) and the corollary tendency to engage in self-censorship in the face of the dominance of such modes.[40]

But the first seven years of the Sandinista government suggest that the risks are even broader than these cautions imply, even if one avoids invoking the usual simple-minded and self-congratulatory cant about cultural freedom and vitality in capitalistic democracies.

In the first place, revolutionary ardor tempts one to project cultural changes on a scale not likely to be realized in the short or medium term with available resources. Before the revolution, Cardenal has said, the green uniforms and helmets of the police were "symbols of terror and death," but now the police are writing poetry. The difference, he says, is "between the horror and a smile, between those who tortured and assassinated, and those who now love and write poetry" (Cardenal 1972:73–75).

And yet in many areas of cultural activity the changes have in fact been hesitant and slow. In sports, for example, the Ministry of Culture projected a decisive turn away from the urban-based, elitist, professionalized North American–derived sports of the Somoza era (baseball and boxing in particular) toward a dispersed, egalitarian system geared to mass voluntary participation. Yet two years after the Sandinistas took over, the Sandinista newspaper *Barricada* still regularly carried major articles on big-league sports in the United States and virtually none on local sports events of the kind originally envisioned.[41]

More serious, however, than the logistical difficulty of effecting rapid change where such change is relatively easily conceivable are the deeper structural intractabilities of historical cultural formation. It is one thing to speak of forming a culture that is "democratic, anti-imperialist, popular, and national," as Cardenal consistently has, but the cultural system of ideas, practices, values, predispositions, assumptions, and institutions that was in place when the Sandinistas entered Managua was split east-to-west, class-stratified, urban-dominated, complexly amalgamated and factionalized racially, mestizo, macho, and in many respects (e.g., technologically) irreversibly global-villaged.

This psychic and historical residue emerged in perplexing and painful ways, especially with respect to the Miskito problem and the role of women in the new society. The psychic and institutional strength of the macho ideal in Latin American society makes the problem of women's role formidable indeed. Nevertheless, both the prominent and undeniably crucial role of women in the FSLN and the new government, and the egalitarian thrust of Sandinista ideology, made avoiding the issue virtually unthinkable. Moreover, Nicaraguan women are mobilized, determined to play a central role in shaping the new social order, and linked to the supporting network of the international women's movement. A solution would also appear to be possible—however long and arduous the process may prove to be—largely without external interference or manipulation.[42]

The staggering historical complexity of the Miskito problem, by contrast, makes it difficult even to conceive of a workable approach.[43] The poignancy of the Sandinistas' initial naive hopes for national cultural unity has been noted as repeatedly as the tortuous problem itself has been outlined: the ancient geophysical and cultural division of the country; the manipulation and exacerbation of that division by successive external and internal groups (the British, North American corporations, Moravian missionaries, the Somozas, the U.S. government acting in concert with Contra mercenaries); factionalisms and conflicts among racially and culturally distinct Atlantic coast groups themselves; and the Sandinistas' own bumbling efforts to deal with the problem under the dual pressures of a broad need for national reconstruction and U.S. efforts at destabilization. Bourgeois crystallized the problem as of 1984 as follows:

> By the end of the fifth year, tensions with ethnic minorities had become an Achilles heel of the Nicaraguan Revolution: militarily, the Atlantic Coast region where the minorities lived had exploded into an arena of bitter fighting; politically, accusations of human rights violations against the indigenous population had damaged the Revolution's international image; and morally, the inability to incorporate minorities . . . into a full participation in the revolutionary process had contradicted Sandinista political principles (Bourgeois 1985:201)

Thus, the Atlantic coast dilemma perhaps put Sandinista cultural theory and practice to a more severe test than any other single problem and has revealed that the road to national cultural unity, independence, and vitality will be long and arduous.

Suggestions here and there also indicate that the Sandinistas—like the leaders of every revisionist enterprise (those who have led the black power, native American, and feminist movements in the United States, for example)—have sometimes been rather romantically selective in their characterization of Nicaraguan cultural history. For a revolution that so strongly emphasizes the culture of common (and especially rural) people, it is important to bear in mind that the Sandinista leadership is drawn heavily from the urban bourgeoisie. Perhaps deriving partially from needs induced by their own inevitable cultural dislocation and alienation, the tendency to idealize lower-class culture is ever present and tempting. To distinguish finely between the relative importance of objective reality and inner need as sources of Omar Cabezas's excitement upon hearing the drums of Subtiava would be a daunting endeavor.

Equally troublesome is the corollary danger of sanitizing national cultural history in order to make "national" culture more serviceable as an energizing and legitimizing resource. Thus patterns of internal factional strife and collaboration (León liberals with William Walker, Miskitos with Somoza), no less present in Nicaraguan than in any other national history, are rarely mentioned.

Similarly, it is one thing for Cardenal to assert, as he has frequently, that Rubén Darío is the father of all Nicaraguan poetry—which consequently is characteristically proud, nationalistic, and resistant to external domination from whatever quarter—and another to deal with the actual literary record, which is quite mixed. It is true, on the one hand, that Salomón de la Selva (1893–1958) was implacably opposed to Somoza, and that his spirit and that of Darío flourished later in the Grupo Gradas poets of the 1960s, the Ventana group that proclaimed itself the generation that would not betray Nicaragua, and the still younger soldier and brigadista poets of the poetry workshops. But it is also true that the Ventana group's "we will not betray" declaration had such force partly because it was a response to the whining plaint of the "Betrayed Generation" of Nicaraguan poets who found their heroes among the Beat poets of the United States and proclaimed that "We don't belong to any country."

Thus Nicaraguan poets have in fact been strongly divided in their political ideas and alignments. Within the Vanguardia movement, Pablo Antonio Cuadra wrote poems against the U.S. Marine occupation and was twice imprisoned for anti-Somoza activity, but the movement on the whole was elitist, pro-Somoza, and enamored of European-style fascism. Within the younger Generation of 1940, Ernesto Mejía Sánchez was forced into exile for ten years over his opposition to Somoza, and Ernesto Cardenal participated in the April Rebellion (1954) against him. But another of the generation, the romantic dandy Carlos Martínez Rivas, tried to help shore up Somoza's image at the very time of the April Rebellion by organizing a celebratory cultural event for the Somocista newspaper *Novedades* and thirty years later insisted to interviewer Steven White that "I have no ideas, no ideals, and no ideology."[44]

Moreover, the very notion of "revolutionary culture" is inescapably problematic. Among the Sandinistas, characterizations of the relationship between culture and the revolution range from Bayardo Arce Castaño's rather commonsensical assertion that "cultural activity is an inherent part of the revolution itself," to Cardenal's categorical but nonetheless romantic equation of revolution and culture, to Ricardo Avilés's more instrumental statement that "cultural struggle is . . . one front of the revolutionary struggle." In a more nuanced way, Sergio Ramírez Mercado, while admitting that revolution is in some practical ways costly to a person who wants to be "just" a writer, maintains that it is more importantly an event of enormous creative potential. It is, he says, "first and foremost a great human event that completely transforms lives, creates multiple new histories, events, heroisms, villainies, happiness and sorrow," all of which become the stuff of new literature.[45]

Even if some or all of that is true, however, the notion of revolutionary culture—like all such global notions, of whatever theoretical construction or ideological stripe—in its insistence upon total congruence between theory and reality carries a potential both for misapprehension of cultural complexity and contradiction and for preferential skewing of institutions and programs. Poet and newspaper editor Pablo Antonio Cuadra—first a supporter and then an opponent of the Sandinistas—has spoken darkly of the dangers of "cultural *dirigismo*" and of throwing off one cultural imperialism only to fall prey to another emanating from what he calls the "culturally gray" countries of the Communist bloc.[46]

Although Cuadra's view begs the whole question of whether culture in contemporary socialist or Communist countries can legitimately be characterized by such a sweepingly pejorative term as "gray," and whether state-derived dirigismo is either essentially different from or worse than the usual modes of cultural legitimation and control under advanced corporate capitalism, the danger he fears cannot lightly be dismissed: that as culture is wedded to (and conceived specifically in terms of) nationalism, a new national cultural myth— partly clarifying and energizing, partly obfuscating and stultifying— will be created and placed in the service of both abstract political ideology and all too concrete political power. Eric Hobsbawm and Terence Ranger's collection of essays on the British penchant for inventing cultural "traditions" and using them in the service of British imperialism—in highland Scotland and Wales, in Victorian India and colonial Africa, and indeed on the Miskito coast of Nicaragua, though Hobsbawm and Ranger do not treat this case—shows the usefulness of cultural manipulation in establishing political hegemony.[47]

Thus the cultural agenda that faced the Sandinistas was awesomely daunting: to throw off historical cultural imperialisms without encouraging new ones as they engaged in the essential tasks of forming supportive political relationships, establishing their own legitimacy on the international scene, and seeking economic and military aid; to maximize the positive aspects of their authentic cultural past without blinking its contradictions; to forge a functional national culture that bridged historical hostilities and distrust without riding roughshod over legitimate and durable differences; to create a sensitive and stable array of national cultural institutions and programs that would be serviceable in all of these ways at the same time that the country was burdened by the necessity to defend itself against a sworn enemy with a hundred times its population and thousands of times its economic and military power; and, not least, to tolerate, amidst its drive for order and stability, the irreducibly messy and potentially disloyal and destabilizing unpredictability of the individual and collective creative process.

To guard against impatience as well as critical arrogance and intolerance, it is well to remind oneself—as Daisy Zamora did in an interview three years after the Sandinistas entered Managua—not only of the perplexity, fear, vacillation, nostalgia, and suffering that are inescapable amidst such circumstances, but also that if the Sandinistas accomplished even a modest portion of such an agenda, they would not only have worked a near miracle in terms of analytical sophistication, institutional structure, and actual programs, but would also have done what no nation in the world, "advanced" or otherwise, has yet demonstrated a reliable ability to do. As Zamora reflected, discussing what the Ministry of Culture was to be and do in the revolution "was like talking about the creation of a world" (White 1986:96).

## NOTES

The following abbreviations are used:

BCV:    *Barricada Cultural: Ventana*
CPN:    Steven White, ed., *Culture and Politics in Nicaragua: Testimonies of Poets and Writers* (New York: Lumen Books, 1986)
HPC:    *Hacia una política cultural de la revolución popular Sandinista* (Managua: Ministry of Culture, 1982)
NIR:    Thomas W. Walker, ed., *Nicaragua in Revolution* (New York: Praeger, 1982)
NFFY:   Thomas W. Walker, ed., *Nicaragua: The First Five Years* (New York: Praeger, 1985)

1. Omar Cabezas, *La montaña es algo más que una inmensa estepa verde.* Quotation from translation by Kathleen Weaver (1985:40). An excellent collection of statements by Sandinista leaders Bayardo Arce, Tomás Borge, Carlos Núñez, Luis Carrión, Daisy Zamora, and Daniel Ortega on cultural aspects of the revolution may be found in *HPC.*

Readers will note that I have employed several terms to refer to various elements and manifestations of Nicaraguan culture: *traditional, national, indige-*

*nous,* and *vernacular.* In view of the enormously complicated cultural history of the country, each of these terms (as well as, I believe, any other conceivable term) is problematic in some respect(s). Acutely aware of the inadequacy of all such terms, I have alternated among them as one or the other seemed less inadequate or misleading in a particular context.

The initial research for this article was conducted during a National Endowment for the Humanities Faculty Summer Seminar at Tulane University led by R. Lee Woodward, Jr. I am grateful to the staff of Tulane's Latin American Library (and especially to Cecilia Montenegro Teague) for their splendid cooperation and assistance. For useful comments and suggestions on earlier drafts of this article I am indebted to Julie Franks, Archie Green, John Heyl, John Sinnegen, and Lee Woodward.

2. Sergio Ramírez Mercado (1982a:15, 16). The wording used by Ramírez in the text of his speech was "La revolución ha sido *un* hecho más importante de nuestra historia," but the speech was headlined in *BCV* as "La Revolución: *El* hecho cultural más grande de nuestra historia." The latter form prevails in all subsequent quotations I have seen, and appears in at least one translation of the speech.

3. Ruíz quoted in John A. Booth (1985:141). Ernesto Cardenal (1982g:175). The earliest brief monograph on the Sandinista cultural programs was Charles Stansifer (1981). It was followed by David Craven and John Ryder (n.p., 1983?) and Elizabeth Dore (1985:413–22). A good selection of pre-1979 poetry appeared in Steven F. White (1982). The literacy crusade was the subject of Sheryl Hirshon (1983). Interviews with some of the best known Nicaraguan writers are collected in Margaret Randall (1984) and in *CPN.*

4. For statements in which some of these elements figure prominently, see Ernesto Cardenal (1980), Julio Cortázar (1983), and Eduardo Galeano (1981).

5. I am grateful to Julie Franks for helping me to sharpen my sense of this connection. The approach I apply here has emerged neither in the broader scholarly analyses of the revolution nor in the few existing detailed analyses of specific cultural programs. Stansifer (1981) begins with Rubén Darío; *NIR* and *NFFY* contain four brief essays on selected cultural programs; Booth (1985) devotes fewer than three pages to cultural policy; Carlos M. Vilas (1986) does not mention culture at all. Craven and Ryder (1983) is prefaced by a précis of Nicaraguan social and political history from the midnineteenth century forward, but the cultural strand of that history is curiously absent.

6. Radell (1969:66–80). Radell's figures are based on a meticulous and rigorous analysis of the best available contemporary records; there seems little reason to doubt their accuracy.

7. For a brief survey of the Atlantic coast in relation to the revolution, see Philip A. Dennis (1981).

8. On Liberalism and Positivism's impact throughout Latin America in the nineteenth century, see E. Bradford Burns (1980), especially pp. 5–17, and R. Lee Woodward, Jr. (1971), especially pp. *ix–xiii* and 12–14; on agroexport monoculture see Jaime Wheelock Román (1975).

9. For illustrative details on, for example, the privatization of Indian communal lands and prohibitions against growing traditional subsistence crops, see Booth (1985:11–14, 20–21).

10. *Frank Leslie's Illustrated Newspaper,* February 7, 1856 and June 6, 1857, as reproduced in *The War in Nicaragua as Reported in Frank Leslie's Illustrated Newspaper* (1976), pp. 146–147, 158, 182–184. An excellent discussion of the Monroe doctrine in relation to Nicaragua may be found in Karl Bermann (1986:19 ff). The most important of the many treatments of the William Walker episode are listed in Woodward (1985:334–335).

11. Gilberto Vega Miranda (1982). The original date of publication is not given but appears to be about 1945. Gilberto Vega Miranda was apparently a co-conductor of the orchestra of the National Guard, which he described as "la única banda que tenemos en Nicaragua."

12. Booth (1985:22). For a more extensive discussion of the Zelaya regime, see Benjamin Teplitz (1973). For a comprehensive history of U.S. imperialism in Nicaragua, see Karl Bermann (1986). The long history of Nicaraguan resistance to foreign intervention is chronicled in Jaime Wheelock Román (1974).

13. George Black (1981:9). On September 27, 1981, the official Sandinista newspaper, *Barricada,* carried a full page of articles (p. 3) on Zeledón, under the headline "Nuestro pueblo, dueño de su historia."

14. The literature on Sandino is of course vast. My few remarks here are based upon Bermann (1986:192–194); Booth (1985:41–50); and Sergio Ramírez Mercado (1984).

15. The literature on the Somoza dynasty is both large and constantly growing. See, for example, Richard Millett (1977) and Bernard Diederich (1981). Briefer discussions are available in Walter LaFeber (1983) and Booth (1985:51–95).

16. Undated (probably early 1960s) article by Fiallos Gil (1965); Christiana Chaves (1939).

17. *El Diario Nicaragüense* (Granada), July 1929 and January 10, 20, and 27, February 11, and March 19, 1931; *La Noticia* (Managua), September 22, 1934 and November 8, 1940; *El Centroamericano* (León), July and August 1937; *La Prensa,* October 2, 1956. For a broader analysis of the importance of comic strips and other forms of popular culture within larger patterns of economic imperialism in Latin America, see two books by Ariel Dorfman (1972), which by 1983 had gone through 24 printings, and (1983). Still broader in its treatment of the problem is Thomas L. McPhail (1981), especially pp. 189–197 on Latin America.

18. Black (1981:38); *La Prensa,* July 1, 1979, p. 21. In my necessarily very brief sketch here I have chosen not to include contemporaneous cultural developments in León and Granada, some of which became quite important in the Sandinista period. I have also excluded the cultural activities of the Banco Central and private banks. These receive brief discussion in Stansifer (1981) passim, which takes a somewhat more sanguine view than mine of cultural developments during the Somoza period.

19. See, for example, Luis Carrión (1982:54) and the Ernesto Cardenal interview in Philip Zwerling and Connie Martin (1985:45).

20. Cardenal quotation from Ernesto Cardenal (1981a:3). Subsequent quotation from Margaret Randall (1983a:85). On Solentiname, see Ernesto Cardenal (n.d., 1982b,d) and several articles by Cardenal in *HPC,* pp. 169–175, 217–244, and 216–273.

21. Most of the available biographical information on Sandinista political and cultural leaders is scattered through a host of their speeches, interviews, and articles on a variety of subjects and has yet to be collected or analyzed. See, for example, Margaret Randall (1983b:7–12; 1984); the documents and interviews in *CPN;* and Bruce Marcus (1982). For Cardenal, Jorge Eduardo Arellano (1979) is a good place to begin.

22. *Ventana* 5 (October 1960):1–2; 9 (n.d.; before June 12, 1961):8–11; 10 (n.d.; before October 1961):1, 6; 11 (n.d.; early 1962?):4. On the founding and purposes of the journal, see Sergio Ramírez Mercado's comments in *BCV* (January 30, 1982):3; *CPN,* pp. 75, 78–81; and Ramírez Mercado (1982b).

23. Decree No. 927 published in *Nicaráuac* 2 (7):99. Darío quotations from Harry E. Vanden (1982:42). Cardenal quotations from Ernesto Cardenal, "Rubén Darío revolucionario," in *HPC,* pp. 235–238.

24. A few of Pablo Antonio Cuadra's remarks on the Vanguardistas' interest in indigenous culture may be found in *CPN,* pp. 20, 23. See Fiallos Gil's

discussion in Mariano Fiallos Gil (1964). Evidence of sustained interest can be seen in Jorge Eduardo Arellano (1977a).

25. On the PSN, see Vanden (1982:48), Booth (1985:138), and Diederich (1981:68). In an interview in *CPN*, p. 20, Pablo Antonio Cuadra commented on the PSN's hostility to Nicaraguan nationalism (cultural or otherwise). Cardenal quoted by Paul W. Borgeson, Jr., "The Poetry of Ernesto Cardenal" (Ph.D. dissertation, Vanderbilt University, 1977), p. 63. On the differences between Avilés and Cardenal, see "Ernesto Cardenal: la misión liberadora de la poesía," in Ricardo Morales Avilés (1981:114–120).

26. Vanden (1982), passim. The emerging cultural politics of the Third World in the period immediately before the Sandinista triumph were adumbrated in a series of conferences on cultural policy organized by UNESCO in the 1970s. See David E. Whisnant (1983a:21–27). The area conference for Latin America and the Caribbean took place in Bogotá in January 1978. A summary of its proceedings was published in *Intergovernmental Conference on Cultural Policies in Latin America and the Caribbean* (Paris: UNESCO, 1978).

27. See, for example, Ernesto Cardenal (1981b, 1982d:5). Ramírez Mercado's remarks are in *CPN*, p. 83.

28. Wheelock Román (1974) covers the period to 1881. References to the Monimbó episode abound in Sandinista commentary on the revolution. See, for example, Instituto de Estudio del Sandinismo (1982).

29. Cardenal (1982a:10–12, 17). Cf. Cardenal interview in Zwerling and Martin (1985:44). Cardenal (1982c:272).

30. Cardenal (1982a:12, 26). See also Tomás Borge (1982:25–33).

31. The literature on New Deal cultural programs is vast. On the centrally important issue of their egalitarian character, see Jane DeHart Mathews (1975:316–339). For a survey of the pre–New Deal period see Grace Overmyer (1939). A useful though conceptually limited overview of issues in more recent U.S. cultural policy formulation and administration is available in Kevin V. Mulcahy and C. Richard Swaim (1982). Useful comparisons are available in Augustin Girard (1970), Nils G. Nilsson (1980), and Eric W. White (1975).

32. A representative sample of their statements on culture may be found in *HPC*.

33. See, for example, Hirshon (1983). Marya Jiménez has spoken of her role in the workshops in Jiménez (1983) and in an interview in *CPN*, pp. 106–113. Very useful statements are Ernesto Cardenal (1982f:225–32) on poetry work-

shops; Ross Kidd (1983:190–201); Alejandro Bravo (1983); and David Kunzle (1983:141–157) on graphic art. Additional details on the CPCs are available in the first three numbers of *La Chacalaca* (Apr.–Dec. 1982). For the poetry itself see Kent Johnson (1985).

34. *Nicaráuac* 2 (Dec. 1981): 55, 61–75.

35. See Stansifer's (1981:6–8) brief discussion.

36. On museums see Cardenal (1982a:19–20; 1982e). On libraries see Cardenal (1982g). On cultural conservation, see Emilia Torres (1982) and Cardenal (1982c:271; 1982g). In 1985 the Ministry of Culture published *Cocina Nica,* brief selections from Angélica Vivas's earlier treatment of Nicaraguan foodways, *50 años de cocina.*

37. *Gaceta Sandinista,* 2 (May 1977): 9, Ernesto Cardenal (1982g:172), and Tomás Borge (1982:27). On *nueva canción* see Nancy Morris (1986). Albums released by Luís Enrique and/or Carlos Mejía Godoy include *La nueva milpa* and *El son nuestro de cada día* (both Madrid: CBS Records, 1978), *Amando en tiempo de guerra* (San José, 1979), *Convertiendo la oscuridad en claridad* (Managua: Ministry of Culture, 1980), *La misa campesina nicaragüense* (Managua: Ministry of Culture, 1981), *Un son para mi pueblo* (San Francisco: Paredon, 1983), *La tapisca* (Enigrac, 1985), and *Canto épico del FSLN* (México, D.F.: Enigrac/Discos Pantagrama, 1985). Performed in a less traditional style but thematically related are Guardabarranco (Salvador and Katia Cardenal), *Si buscabas,* and Salvador Bustos, *Tragaluz,* (both Oakland, Calif.: Redwood Records, 1985).

38. John Ramírez (1984); Jorge Abelleira (1981); Alfonso Gumucio Dagrón (1982). Pertinent interviews with foreign filmmakers involved in the Nicaraguan film industry are available in *Nicaráuac* 2 (Jan. 1981):165–68 and *BCV* (June 4, 1983):2–3.

39. See Philip V. Cannistrano (1971); Sheila Fitzpatrick (1970); Lewis D. Wurgraft (1971); Mark N. Hagopian (1974:240–42) (China); Frederick C. Turner (1968:254–306). Alan Wald (1981) has commented perceptively on the American left's "perennial difficulty in explaining the connections between politics and culture."

40. Bayardo Arce Castaño (1982, 1983); Sergio Ramírez Mercado (1982b). Murillo quoted in "Entre la libertad y el miedo," *BCV* (Mar. 7, 1981), included in *CPN,* pp. 100–05.

41. See Eric A. Wagner (1985) and *BCV* (Sept.–Oct. 1981) passim.

42. Pre-1979 FSLN statements on women's needs and rights may be found in "The Historic Program of the FSLN" (1969), reprinted in Marcus (1982:13–

22), and *Gaceta Sandinista* (Oct. 1976):3, 10. Brief overview analyses are available in Elizabeth Maier (1980); Susan E. Ramírez-Horton (1982); and Maxine Molyneux (1985:145–62). Testimonies of Nicaraguan women are collected in Margaret Randall (1981), and of several women writers in Randall (1984).

43. The mass of available literature on the Miskitos makes it unnecessary to discuss the problem extensively here. It began to be treated seriously in the literature as early as 1943; see Emilio Alvarez Lejarza's (1943) pamphlet, reprinted in *Nicaragua Indígena* (Managua: Organo del Instituto Indigenista Nacional, 1969), pp. 35–49. An early book-length scholarly treatment was Mary Helms (1971). Since 1979 there has been a flood of scholarly and journalistic analyses of the problem. See, for example, Manuel Ortega Hegg (1982) and several discussions by Philippe Bourgeois (1981; 1982:303–18; 1985). Another full-length analysis is Craig Dozier (1985). The Ministry of Culture devoted the entire October 1982 issue of *Nicaráuac* to the Atlantic coast problem. Titles 89 and 90 of Article IV of the new Nicaraguan constitution, adopted in November 1986, grant broad cultural recognition and rights, as well as considerable social and political autonomy, to Atlantic coast groups. On the new constitution, see *Envio* 6 (January 1987):14–31.

44. This brief discussion is based almost exclusively upon *CPN*, passim. On the political conservatism of the *vanguardistas* see Jorge Eduardo Arellano (1977b).

45. Arce Castaño (1983); Cardenal (1982g:175); Ramírez Mercado interview with Steven White in *CPN*, p. 77.

46. Cuadra interview with Steven White in ibid., pp. 29–36.

47. Eric Hobsbawm and Terence Ranger (1983). The dynamic is not limited to conservative political perspectives; my own (1983b) study of systematic cultural intervention in the southern mountains of the United States examines the well-meaning cultural manipulations indulged in by liberal cultural missionaries as the region opened to capitalist economic "development" (and, concurrently, to an intense popular interest in its purportedly unsullied "native" culture). See David E. Whisnant (1983b). Thirty years ago, Frantz Fanon (1961) warned of similar dangers.

REFERENCES

Abelleira, Jorge
    1981    Entrevista paralela con el Cine y la TV Nicaragüense. *Barricada Cultural: Ventana* (December 12): 2–4.

Alvarez Lejarza, Emilio
1943    *El problema del indio en Nicaragua.* Managua: Editorial Nuevos Horizontes. Reprinted in *Nicaragua Indígena*, pp. 35–49. Managua: Organo del Instituto Indígenista Nacional, 1969.

Arellano, Jorge Eduardo
1977a   Ed., *25 poemas indígenas.* Managua: Universidad Centroamericana.
1977b   *Panorama de la literatura nicaragüense*, pp. 57 ff. Managua: Editorial Nueva Nicaragua.
1979    Ernesto Cardenal: de Granada a Gethsemany (1925–1957). *Boletín Nicaragüense de Bibliografía y Documentación* 31 (September): 25–43.

Avilés, Ricardo Morales
1981    *Obras: no parearemos de andar jamás*, pp. 114–20. Managua: Editorial Nueva Nicaragua.

*Barricada Cultural: Ventana*

Bermann, Karl
1986    *Under the Big Stick: Nicaragua and the United States since 1848.* Boston: South End Press.

Black, George
1981    *Triumph of the People: The Sandinista Revolution in Nicaragua.* London: Zed Press.

Booth, John A.
1985    *The End and the Beginning: The Nicaraguan Revolution*, 2d ed. Boulder, Col.: Westview Press.

Borge, Tomás
1982    La cultura es el pueblo. *Hacia una política cultural de la revolución popular Sandinista.* Managua: Ministerio de Cultura.

Bourgeois, Philippe
1981    Class, Ethnicity, and State among the Miskitu Amerindians of Northeastern Nicaragua. *Latin American Perspectives* 8 (Spring): 22–39.
1982    The Problematic of Nicaragua's Indigenous Minorities. In *Nicaragua in Revolution*, ed. Thomas W. Walker. New York: Praeger.
1985    Ethnic Minorities. In *Nicaragua: The First Five Years*, ed. Thomas W. Walker, pp. 201–16. New York: Praeger.

Bravo, Alejandro
    1983    Cultura popular en León: CPC Antenor Sandino. *Barricada Cultural: Ventana* (July 19).

Burns, E. Bradford
    1980    *The Poverty of Progress: Latin America in the Nineteenth Century.* Berkeley: University of California Press.

Cabezas, Omar
    1985    *La montaña es algo más que una inmensa estepa verde.* Translated by Kathleen Weaver as *Fire from the Mountain: The Making of a Sandinista.* New York: New American Library.

Cannistrano, Philip V.
    1971    The Organization of Totalitarian Culture: Cultural Policy and the Mass Media in Fascist Italy, 1922–1945. Ph.D. dissertation, New York University.

Cardenal, Ernesto
    1972    *En Cuba,* pp. 73–75. Buenos Aires: Ediciones Carlos Lohlé.
    1980    Cultura revolucionaria, popular, nacional, antiimperialista. *Nicaráuac* 1 (May–June): 163–68.
    1981a   Revolution and Peace: The Nicaraguan Road. *Journal of Peace Research* 18(2): 3.
    1981b   La unidad contra el imperialismo. *Nicaráuac* 2 (December): 103–07.
    1982a   La democratización de la cultura. In *Colección popular de literatura nicaragüense.* Managua: Ministerio de Cultura.
    1982b   Aprender la revolución. *Barricada Cultural: Ventana* 42 (October 10): 3–5.
    1982c   La cultura de la nueva Nicaragua: un cambio de todo. *Hacia una política cultural de la revolución popular Sandinista.* Managua: Ministerio de Cultura.
    1982d   La democratización de la cultura, No. 2. In *Colección popular de literatura nicaragüense.* Managua: Ministerio de Cultura.
    1982e   Defendiendo la cultura, el hombre, y el planeta. *Nicaráuac* 3 (January): 149–152, and *La Chacalaca* 1 (April): 6, and 2 (July): 71.
    1982f   Talleres de poesía: socialización de los medios de producción poéticos. In *Hacia una política cultural de la revolución popular Sandinista,* pp. 225–32. Managua: Ministerio de Cultura.
    1982g   La cultura: primeros seis meses de revolución. *Hacia una política*

cultural de la revolución popular Sandinista, pp. 173–75. Managua: Ministerio de Cultura, and *Barricada Cultural: Ventana* (October 4): 4.

n.d. *El evangelio en Solentiname. Volumen primero.* Managua: Ministerio de Cultura.

Carrión, Luis

1982 El arte en las fuerzas armadas. *Hacia una política cultural de la revolución popular Sandinista.* Managua: Ministerio de Cultura.

Castaño, Bayardo Arce

1982 El difícil terreno de la lucha: el ideológico. In *Hacia una política cultural de la revolución popular Sandinista,* pp. 17–24. Managua: Ministerio de Cultura.

1983 Tanto arte . . . tanta actividad cultural. *Barricada Cultural: Ventana* (July 19): 2–4.

*Chacalaca, La*
1982

Chaves, Christiana

1939 Letters to Erwin P. Dieseldorff, July 18 and September 19. Dieseldorff Collection, Box 152, Folders 3 and 4, Tulane University Library.

Cortázar, Julio

1983 Discurson en la recepción de la Orden Rubén Darío. *Casa de las Américas* 23 (May–June): 130–34.

Craven, David, and John Ryder

1983? *Art of the New Nicaragua.* N.p.

Dagrón, Alfonso Gumucio

1982 Cine obrero sandinista. *Plural* 11 (2a época) (July): 35–40.

Dennis, Philip A.

1981 The Costeños and the Revolution in Nicaragua. *Journal of Interamerican Studies and World Affairs* 23 (August): 271–96.

Diederich, Bernard

1981 *Somoza and the Legacy of U.S. Involvement in Central America.* New York: E. P. Dutton.

Dore, Elizabeth

1985 Culture. In *Nicaragua: The First Five Years,* ed. Thomas W. Walker. New York: Praeger.

Dorfman, Ariel
>   1972    *Para leer el pato Donald: comunicación de masa y colonialismo.* Mexico, D.F.: Siglo Veintiuno Editores.
>   1983    *The Empire's Old Clothes: What the Lone Ranger, Babar and Other Innocent Heroes Do to Our Minds.* New York: Pantheon Books.

Dozier, Craig
>   1985    *Nicaragua's Mosquito Shore: The Years of British and American Presence.* University: University of Alabama Press.

Fanon, Frantz
>   1961    On National Culture. In *The Wretched of the Earth,* pp. 206–48. New York: Grove Press (1968).

Fitzpatrick, Sheila
>   1970    *The Commissariat of Enlightenment: Soviet Organization of Education and the Arts under Lunacharsky, October 1917–1921.* Cambridge: Harvard University Press.

*Gaceta Sandinista*
>   1976    2 (October): 3, 10.
>   1977    2 (May): 9.

Galeano, Eduardo
>   1981    La revolución como revelación. *Nicaráuac* 2 (December): 109–14.

Gil, Fiallos
>   1965    Los primeros pasos de la Reforma Universitaria en Nicaragua. *Ventana* 2 (July): 59.

Gil, Mariano Fiallos
>   1964    Introducción al estudio del proceso cultural centroamericano. *Ventana* 1: 3–63.

Girard, Augustin
>   1970    *Cultural Development: Experience and Politics.* Paris: UNESCO.

Hagopian, Mark N.
>   1974    *The Phenomenon of Revolution.* New York: Harper & Row.

Helms, Mary
>   1971    *Asang: Adaptations to Culture Contact in the Miskito Community.* Gainesville: University of Florida Press.

1975    *Middle America: A Culture History of Heartlands and Frontiers.* Englewood Cliffs, N.J.: Prentice-Hall.

Hirshon, Sheryl
    1983    *And Also Teach Them to Read.* Westport, Conn.: Lawrence Hill.

Hobsbawm, Eric, and Terence Ranger (eds.)
    1983    *The Invention of Tradition.* London and New York: Cambridge University Press.

Instituto de Estudio del Sandinismo
    1982    *Porque viven siempre entre nosotros: héroes y mártires de la insurrección popular sandinista en Masaya.* Managua: Editorial Nueva Nicaragua.

Jiménez, Marya
    1983    *Poesía de la nueva Nicaragua: talleres populares de poesía.* Mexico, D.F.: Siglo Veintiuno Editores.

Johnson, Kent (ed.)
    1985    *Poems from the Sandinista Workshops in Nicaragua.* San Rafael, Calif.: West End Press.

Kidd, Ross
    1983    A Testimony from Nicaragua: An Interview with Nidia Bustos, the Coordinator of MECATE, the Nicaraguan Farm Workers' Theatre Movement. *Studies in Latin American Popular Culture* 2: 190–201.

Kunzle, David
    1983    Nationalist, Internationalist, and Anti-Imperialist Themes in the Public Revolutionary Art of Cuba, Chile, and Nicaragua. *Studies in Latin American Popular Culture* 2: 141–57.

LaFeber, Walter
    1983    *Inevitable Revolutions: The United States in Central America.* New York: W. W. Norton.

Leslie, Frank
    1976    *The War in Nicaragua as Reported in Frank Leslie's Illustrated Newspaper, 1857–1860.* Managua: Fondo de Promoción.

Liss, Sheldon B.
    1984    *Marxist Thought in Latin America.* Berkeley: University of California Press.

McPhail, Thomas L.
    1981    *Electronic Colonialism: The Future of International Broadcasting and Communications.* Beverly Hills, Calif.: Sage Publications.

Maier, Elizabeth
    1980    Mujeres, contradicciones y revolución. *Estudios sociales centroamericanos* 27 (Sept.–Dec.): 129–39.

Marcus, Bruce (ed.)
    1982    *Sandinistas Speak: Speeches, Writings, and Interviews with Leaders of Nicaragua's Revolution* New York: Pathfinder Press.
    1985    *Nicaragua: The Sandinista People's Revolution.* New York: Pathfinder Press.

Mathews, Jane DeHart
    1975    Arts and the People: The New Deal Quest for a Cultural Democracy. *Journal of American History* 62 (September): 316–39.

Millett, Richard
    1977    *Guardians of the Dynasty.* Maryknoll, N.Y.: Orbis Books.

Ministry of Culture
    1982    *Hacia una política cultural de la revolución popular Sandinista.* Managua: Ministerio de Cultura.

Molyneux, Maxine
    1985    Women. In *Nicaragua: The First Five Years,* ed. Thomas W. Walker. New York: Praeger.

Morris, Nancy
    1986    Canto porque es necesario cantar: The New Song Movement in Chile 1973–1983. *Latin American Research Review* XXI: 117–36.

Mulcahy, Kevin, and C. Richard Swaim (eds.)
    1982    *Public Policy and the Arts.* Boulder, Colo.: Westview Press.

*Nicaráuac*
    1981

Nilsson, Nils G.
    1980    *Swedish Cultural Policy in the 20th Century.* Copenhagen: Swedish Institute.

Ocampo, Carlos Alemán
    1981    El torovenado y la resistencia cultural. *Barricada Cultural: Ventana* (October 31): 2

Ortega Hegg, Manuel
  1982    El conflicto etnia-nación en Nicaragua: un acercamiento teórico
          a la problemática de las minorias étnicas de la Costa Atlántica.
          *Estudios sociales centroamericanos* 11 (January): 125–38.

Ortega Saavedra, Humberto
  1979    *50 años de lucha sandinista,* pp. 75, 93, 115. Managua: Ministerio
          del Interior.

Overmyer, Grace
  1939    *Government and the Arts.* New York: W. W. Norton.

Radell, David R.
  1969    An Historical Geography of Western Nicaragua: The Spheres of
          Influence of Leon, Granada, and Managua, 1519–1965. Ph.D.
          dissertation, University of California, Berkeley.

Ramírez, John
  1984    Introduction to the Sandinista Documentary Cinema. *Areito* 10
          (37): 18–21.

Ramírez-Horton, Susan E.
  1982    The Role of Women in the Nicaraguan Revolution. In *Nicaragua
          in Revolution,* ed. Thomas W. Walker, pp. 147–60. New York:
          Praeger.

Ramírez Mercado, Sergio
  1971    *Mariano Fiallos: biografía.* León, Nicaragua: Editorial Universi-
          taria de la U.N.A.N.
  1982a   La Revolución: el hecho cultural más grande de neustra historia.
          *Barricada Cultural: Ventana* 56: 15–16.
  1982b   Cultura de masas y creación individual. In *Hacia una política
          cultural de la revolución popular Sandinista,* pp. 157–66. Managua:
          Ministerio de Cultura.
  1984    *Augusto C. Sandino: el pensamiento vivo,* 2d ed., 2 vols. Managua:
          Editorial Nueva Nicaragua.

Randall, Margaret
  1981    *Sandino's Daughters.* Vancouver: New Star Books.
  1983a   *Christians in the Nicaraguan Revolution.* Vancouver: New Star
          Books.
  1983b   Conversando con Sergio Ramírez: 'Hay aquí una fuerza centri-
          fuga. *Barricada Cultural: Ventana* (July 19): 7–12.
  1984    *Risking a Somersault in the Air: Conversations with Nicaraguan Writ-
          ers.* San Francisco: Solidarity Publications.

Stansifer, Charles
   1981    *Cultural Policy in the Old and the New Nicaragua.* Hanover, N.H.:
           American Universities Field Staff.

Teplitz, Benjamin
   1973    The Political and Economic Foundations of Modernization in
           Nicaragua: The Administration of José Santos Zelaya 1893–
           1909. Ph.D. dissertation, Howard University, Washington,
           D.C.

Torres, Emilia
   1982    Lineas de trabajo para los CPC—1983. *La Chacalaca* 3 (Decem-
           ber): 5–8.

Turner, Frederick C.
   1968    *The Dynamics of Mexican Nationalism.* Chapel Hill: University of
           North Carolina Press.

United Nations Educational, Scientific and Cultural Organization
   1978    *Intergovernmental Conference on Cultural Policies in Latin America
           and the Caribbean.* Paris: UNESCO.

Vanden, Harry E.
   1982    The Ideology of Insurrection. In *Nicaragua in Revolution,* ed.
           Thomas W. Walker. New York: Praeger.

Vega Miranda, Gilberto
   1982    Músicos nicaragüenses de ayer. *Boletín nicaragüense de bibliografía
           y documentación* 48 (July–August): 51–72.

Vilas, Carlos M.
   1986    *The Sandinista Revolution: National Liberation and Social Transfor-
           mation in Central America.* New York: Monthly Review Press.

Wagner, Eric A.
   1985    Sport after Revolution: A Comparative Study of Cuba and Nica-
           ragua. In *Nicaragua in Revolution,* ed. Thomas W. Walker, pp.
           291–302. New York: Praeger.

Wald, Alan
   1981    Remembering the Answers. *The Nation* (December 26): 708–
           10.

Walker, Thomas W. (ed.)
   1982    *Nicaragua in Revolution.* New York: Praeger.
   1985    *Nicaragua: The First Five Years.* New York: Praeger.

Weaver, Kathleen (transl.)

  1985   *Fire from the Mountain: The Making of a Sandinista.* New York: New American Library.

Wheelock Román, Jaime

  1974   *Raíces indígenas de la lucha anticolonialista en Nicaragua.* Managua: Editorial Nueva Nicaragua.

  1975   *Imperialismo y dictadura: crisis de una formación social.* México: Siglo Veintiuno Editores.

Whisnant, David E.

  1983a   International Perspectives on Cultural Policy Formulation: The UNESCO Conferences. *New Jersey Folklore* 8 (Spring): 21–27.

  1983b   *All That Is Native and Fine: The Politics of Culture in an American Region.* Chapel Hill: University of North Carolina Press.

White, Eric W.

  1975   *The Arts Council of Great Britain.* London: Davis Poynter.

White, Steven (ed.)

  1982   *Poets of Nicaragua.* Greensboro, N.C.: Unicorn Press.

  1986   *Culture and Politics in Nicaragua: Testimonies of Poets and Writers.* New York: Lumen Books.

Woodward, R. Lee, Jr. (ed.)

  1971   *Positivism in Latin America, 1850–1900: Are Order and Progress Reconcilable?* Lexington, Mass.: Heath.

  1985   *Central America: A Nation Divided.* New York: Oxford University Press.

Wurgraft, Lewis D.

  1971   The Activist Movement: Cultural Politics on the German Left, 1914–1933. Ph.D. dissertation, Harvard University.

Zwerling, Philip, and Connie Martin (eds.)

  1985   *Nicaragua: A New Kind of Revolution.* Westport, Conn.: Lawrence Hill.

CHAPTER 9

# Women's Culture and
# Its Discontents

*Micaela di Leonardo*

A nthropologists are familiar with the experience of being raided for useful concepts by scholars from other disciplines and, indeed, by purveyors of popular culture. The anthropological terms ethnocentrism, culture shock, and assimilation, for example, have all passed into common parlance in postwar America. This conceptual pillage is not always unsolicited: Since the 1920s, many anthropologists—Margaret Mead being the most obvious example— have made concerted efforts to popularize anthropological concepts and findings.

This paper is concerned with a widespread current instance of self-conscious borrowing from anthropology by feminist scholars from other disciplines. The term borrowed is "culture," the neologism "women's culture." The route of transmission, or at least one road in use, runs through the burgeoning field of cultural history, whose practitioners have been engaged in a growing love affair with some kinds of anthropological discourse for the past two decades. In considering the meanings and implications of women's culture, though, I shall sketch out my own path of intellectual discovery, from fieldwork to feminist theory to the women's culture issue and, finally, to the problematic nature of the inscriptions of gender in anthropological theories of culture.

In keeping with the theme of this volume, this paper is concerned with the politics of culture, and in a very basic way: how social power (and perceptions of power) enter into constructions of the culture concept itself. Specifically, I address the questions of the linked constructions of power, morality, and culture; of the political uses of constructions of our own histories and of the lives of "exotic" others; and of the politics of conceiving cultural difference.

My own fieldwork experience involved cultural difference in an ironic way. As I wrote in *The Varieties of Ethnic Experience,* "the usual ethnographic encounter was in a sense reversed: instead of learning to understand members of a different culture, I learned that I had not understood members of my own."[1] As a third-generation Californian Italian-American, I studied a cross-class population of Italian-Americans in California. My research involved both participant-observation and historical analysis, and I was concerned with the past and present intersections of kinship, class, ethnicity, and gender in my informants' lives.

Over the course of the fieldwork, as I read more literature in the area and as my acquaintance with my informants deepened, I began to realize that both scholarly and popular discourse (including my own) on American white ethnicity tends to identify folk models with analysis. That is, rather than considering the relations between received notions and observable realities, we all tend a priori to accept the notions themselves. Thus the literature is filled with descriptions of warm, nurturant ethnic families and various white ethnic types: repressed, fatalistic Irish; emotionally excitable but intellectually stolid Italians; shrewd, entrepreneurial Jews. What was even more interesting was my informants' use of the same ethnic symbolism to label very different social realities. Thus individuals with very large or very small kin groups, with relatives who saw one another every day or once a month, or with stay-at-home or career women mothers would all label themselves as having grown up in "typical, close Italian families," which they assumed had survived unchanged since emigration. Whether at the grass roots or in scholarly literature, Americans tend to conceive ethnicity as a reality to be asserted rather than to be assessed empirically, as an unvarying entity rather than as a historical process.[2]

When I considered the lives of my women informants, I found

parallel patterns. Ethnic scholarship stereotypes Italian-American women as traditional working-class wives and mothers. It neglects their historical labor force participation and emphasizes their power in the home through the use of moral influence—a constellation of cultural constructions that students of nineteenth-century American and European prescriptive literature (not to mention late twentieth-century antifeminist literature) will find familiar.

My own women informants broke this stereotype from the outset.[3] Their life histories revealed extraordinarily varying household worlds and patterns of labor force participation, and their political perspectives ranged from left to right, from feminist to antifeminist. There were, however, gender commonalities for the population as a whole. I discovered a fundamental pattern of gender differentiation in the ways informants perceived themselves as ethnic actors. Men, across class and age ranges, tended to claim their ethnic identity through their kinswomen's activities, their "ethnic" labor. Men would refer, for example, to their grandmothers' Sunday dinners, their aunts' Christmas cookies, their mothers' Easter feasts. Such a male definition of ethnic identity clearly poses a problem for the female members of the group: Under this rubric they can claim ethnic identity only if they provide the nurturing, symbolically laden environment for which men can take credit.

How did these Italian-American women identify themselves? They took varying stances, but all my informants negotiated their ethnic identities with clear knowledge of the dominant male ideology (which incidentally is also reflected in mass media images of "traditional" nurturing Italian-American women). Some women accepted the male model and gloried in their competent execution of housework and mothering tasks, their spiritual guidance of their families. This stance was often associated with deprecation of "modern" American women. Other women disputed the male model by splitting ethnic identity by gender and denigrating Italian-American men while lauding Italian-American women. One woman professional provided herself with a gendered ethnic pedigree: "My grandmother was the first women's libber."[4]

I discovered, in other words, one example of women's expression of agency within the constraints of male domination—a process that is now well-trodden ground in feminist scholarship. But what sorts of agents were these women? I had to consider not only how they negotiated their ethnic identities vis-a-vis Italian-American men, but also vis-a-vis all other perceived social actors. And while some women's declared superiority to "Americani" was amusing, it was no longer so humorous when others defined themselves in terms of their control over dependent and adult children. The process ceased to be amusing altogether when women's self-definitions included expressions of racism, classism, homophobia, and xenophobic nationalism. This fieldwork experience forced me to learn an important feminist lesson: Attending to women's agency does not necessarily entail entire approbation of women's morality.

I wish to broaden the canvas in discussing a second segment of my field research. In the process of mapping individuals' kin and friend networks, I discovered an unlabeled category of labor. My women informants were clearly involved not only with housework, childcare, and market labor, but also with the work of kinship. I define kin work as the conception, maintenance, and ritual celebration of cross-household kin ties, including visits, letters, telephone calls, presents, and cards to kin; the organization of holiday gatherings; the creation and maintenance of quasi-kin ties; decisions to neglect or to intensify particular kin relations; the mental labor of reflecting about all these activities; and the creation and communication of altering images of family and kinship vis-a-vis the images of others, both folk and mass media. All these activities require time, intention, and skill beyond the execution of housework, childcare, and market labor. They were nearly always accomplished only by my women informants, and I believe that in fact kin work is an unlabeled category of women's work in American society in general. We can easily point to indirect evidence for this contention: the fact that kin-work tasks can be seen as extensions of women's household responsibilities for childcare and cooking; the existence of a vast body of prescriptive literature—women's popular magazines—that enjoins the correct execution of kin-work tasks; and the vehement responses of audiences over the past few years to my talks on kin work.[5]

As I revised an article on kin work and its implications for feminist theory, I began to have a visceral understanding of the literary critics' term *intertextuality* (which refers, in part, to writers' lack of control over readers' perceptions of their work). My article originally focused on what I conceived as a problematic trend toward materialist reductionism in feminist theory. That is, feminist scholars were tending to concentrate on economic determinants of women's lives and implicitly denying the equal force of culture and consciousness. In a changed intellectual climate, though, my article began to "read" as supportive of "women's culture" voices in feminist discourse. I was forced to make further revisions in the text to prevent a reading in of such presumptions.

What do I mean by this? In order to gain a sense of the common thread in, and variations of, the women's culture concept in recent feminist writing from a number of disciplines, consider the following set of descriptive quotations:

> *literary criticism:* "Women's culture forms a collective experience within the cultural whole, an experience that binds women writers to each other over time and space."[6]
> *political theory:* "There is always a women's culture within every culture."[7]
> *social theory:* "The bedrock of women's consciousness is the obligation to preserve life. Now as in the past, women judge themselves and one another on how well they do work associated with being female."[8]
> *political history:* "Women's culture is the ground upon which women stand in their resistance to patriarchal domination and their assertion of their own creativity in shaping society."[9]
> *psychology:* "Women not only define themselves in a context of human relationship but also judge themselves in terms of their ability to care."[10]

Let me describe some of these interpretations of women's culture across a range of disciplines. In literary criticism, Elaine Showalter has used the term to indicate transhistorical and cross-cultural connections and commonalities among women writers. Most recently, she has pluralized the term to indicate the existence of varying traditions among women writers. In philosophy, Sarah Ruddick has constructed the notion of maternal thinking, which is cognate to women's culture; political theorist Jean Elshtain has used this concept to buttress her notion that women are innately pacifist, although she has since moved from this position. In psychology, Carol Gilligan has posited a women's mode of ethical thinking based on the achievement of cooperative social relations rather than the application of abstract moral laws. In linguistics and folklore an emphasis has been placed on women's speech, folk traditions, and popular performance. In American and European women's history, many scholars have delineated the self-conscious nineteenth-century creation of "women's sphere" among bourgeois white women, and have noted its emphasis on nurturant loving relations among kinswomen and female friends. In labor history, a number of scholars have focused on women workers' creation of shopfloor work cultures. In sociology, Jessie Bernard has claimed a transhistorical and cross-cultural separate women's world. And finally, feminist anthropologists have offered numerous ethnographically specific descriptions of separate women's domains within particular societies, from Yolanda and Robert Murphy's delineation of Mundurucu women's separate houses and working groups to Rayna Rapp's narrative of the sex-segregated domains of a French peasant village.[11]

There is also the simultaneous American feminist popular cultural phenomenon of "women's culture," which refers both to notions of women's a priori sisterhood and to institutions of alternative feminist cultural production—bookstores, bars, music festivals, journals, and newspapers. Some participants in grass-roots women's culture invoke the invented tradition (in the Hobsbawm and Ranger sense) of primeval matriarchy.[12] These claims for the existence of prior social worlds in which women ruled are most often buttressed by reference to genuine goddess worship in a variety of ancient societies. For example, Patricia Roth, in reviewing a new book on women workers in the sex industry, asserts:

> I think of the difference between modern-day pornographic images
> and ancient matriarchal archetypes, typified in goddess replicas that

have come down to us, as well as in belly-dancing and other woman-identified forms of erotica. These archetypes expressed the primal life-force which was woman, woman as mother, as life-giver, and as the earth herself.[13]

Such claims confuse the structures of supernatural worlds with those of the social worlds that give rise to them and are, as I have written in another context, the despair of feminist anthropologists.

Clearly, the discourse on women's culture is a realm of multiple meanings. Can we disentangle the referents? Of what use is the concept? Of what harm? Is it (in one or more interpretations) accurate? And finally: What relation does it bear to anthropological cultural theories? In what follows, I shall attempt to address these questions and to link a consideration of women's culture and gender and cultural theory back to the kin-work concept. Finally, I shall return to the issue of the politics of culture through the multiple issues thrown into relief by the problematics of the women's culture phenomenon.

First, it seems to me that feminist historians' excavations of genuine white middle-class women's spheres in nineteenth-century United States and Europe and the contemporary popular cultural phenomenon are the principal ethnographic touchstones to which feminist theorists refer in their discussions of women's culture. These two sets of phenomena serve as resource wells for the creation and elaboration of notions of feminine nature.

To take the most extreme, least nuanced American interpretation as an ideal type: There is an idea abroad in the land that there is an entity, women's culture, that represents an *Ur*-form of women's nature and has the same characteristics across time and space. These characteristics include moral superiority to men; cooperative rather than competitive social relations; selfless maternality, and benevolent sexuality. Thus women's culture embodies the notion of an authentic feminine selfhood that has been distorted, accreted over by male domination. Political scientist Joan Cocks labels this set of claims concerning women's nature a counterhegemonic effort to conceive the female self as "the [patriarchal] order's perfect opposite."[14] Obviously, such a notion entails the muting or outright denial of women's less pleasant characteristics. It bears false witness to a variety of forms of female action, including lying, theft, competition, the abandonment of children, torture, and murder. All of these activities are part of some historical and cross-cultural female realities not necessarily explained by male domination.

This vision of women's culture also entails, in its celebration of women's nurturant bonds with one another, the denial of divisions among women—on the basis of race, class, region, generation, nationality, and sexual preference. Such divisions may often separate individual women more than a putative bond of common womanhood joins them. The recent heightening of the "debate on difference" in feminist theory, though, has had some effect on the women's culture discourse. Recent work in American women's history, for example, focuses on specific instances of women's cultural worlds that are framed by extragender differences. Kathy Peiss and Christine Stansell, for example, explore the worlds of nineteenth-century working-class women in New York City in two overlapping periods, and Nancy Hewitt considers the ways in which the white middle-class model of nineteenth-century woman's sphere does not apply to black American women.[15]

It is important, though, not only to criticize an ideal-typical version of women's culture, but also to consider the range of interpretations given to it. At one end is a simple biological reductionism that would claim that women are literally hormonally superior to men. Such a stance neatly inverses male-superior biological arguments, and is often associated with varieties of feminism labeled radical or cultural.[16]

Far more common is a reliance on the presumption that childcare is a universal female responsibility, and that this state of affairs has global psychological entailments in terms of gendered personalities: women's weak vs. men's strong ego boundaries, the cultural devaluation of the female, etc. This argument was first articulated by psychoanalytic sociologist Nancy Chodorow and has been widely influential not only among feminist social scientists but in the humanities, particularly in literary criticism, where feminists have used it as a frame for the investigation of relations among female characters and writers.[17]

Finally, some theorists, such as literary critic Elaine Showalter, rely on a notion of women's universal "colonization" to assert cultural commonalities for women across time and space. Such a perspective bears some relation both to the assertion that women are universally perceived as "natural" in relation to men's "cultural" status and to Lacanian feminist literary criticism, which proceeds from an assumption that the Freudian "possession of the phallus" should be construed metaphorically on the level of language, and thus that language itself is a male realm from which women are excluded.[18]

Many texts from which I have drawn in order to lay out the range of interpretations of the women's culture concept cite feminist social theory and, in most cases, feminist anthropologists to ground their arguments. What do these anthropologists actually say about the cultural implications of gender divisions in society? Specifically: Whose culture theories are being used or abused here? What do they have to say about the moral evaluation of (gendered or nongendered) cultural worlds? And finally, how do they frame intra- and intercultural variation: How do they attempt to encompass vast variations in human perceptions of social reality, variations linked to but not determined by differences in material circumstances?

Feminist anthropologists, like adherents of the women's culture concept, range widely over a continuum in their interpretations of the relations between gender and culture. The continuum itself, however, bears a very different structure. While women's culture writers commonly assume gendered cultural homogeneity and differ on explanations for it, feminist anthropologists differ in terms of both explanatory level and claims of universal gendered cultural difference.

At one pole are two groups of universalists: British anthropologists Edwin and Shirley Ardener and Americans Sherry Ortner and Michelle Rosaldo. The Ardeners are Elaine Showalter's source for the notion of women as universally muted or colonized. Edwin Ardener's influential early paper draws on French structuralism and medium-range theory in British social anthropology to propose a model of the relation between male and female symbolic worlds when men dominate society and symbolic discourse.[19] Sherry Ortner also makes use of structuralism to posit the universal symbolic association—male:culture, female:nature—as a means of explaining women's universal subordination.[20] Michelle Rosaldo makes a structurally similar argument, but her dichotomy is lodged in the sphere of social organization: Women are universally relegated to the lower-status domestic domain while men inhabit the public world.[21] Rosaldo also integrates Chodorow's psychoanalytic model into her argument, claiming that women's responsibilities for childcare articulate with their confinement in the domestic world, and that girls' and boys' differential senses of self derive from this unified psychological/social organizational reality.

Ortner's work sparked much debate and a significant collection of articles, edited by Marilyn Strathern and Carol MacCormack.[22] This volume of theoretical and ethnographic essays investigates cultural constructions of gender and of the natural and human worlds in a wide variety of ethnographic contexts. Its contributors demonstrate that not only are women not universally associated with nature (vs. male culture) but that many societies do not even dichotomize the human and natural worlds as we do in the West. Ortner has since written, with Harriet Whitehead, more abstractly about gendered universals. She now argues that "gender" and "prestige" are universally and simultaneously culturally constructed.[23]

Contributors to the Strathern and MacCormack book, and others who consider regional cultural constructions of gender and their associations with other cultural constructions—such as scholars who have written about honor, shame, and sexuality in the Mediterranean—lie between the universalizing and anti-universalizing extremes of the continuum.[24] At the anti-universalizing end are scholars, such as Nicole-Claude Mathieu and Penelope Brown, who are skeptical about the possibility of cross-cultural comparison of gendered social realities.[25] These anthropologists join with nonfeminist predecessors in a concern with two problems: the difficulty of attaining knowledge of other minds, and the associated tendency to attribute to others one's own cognitive templates.

But this radical anti-essentialist end of the spectrum is not the one most attractive to Western feminist scholars outside anthropology. Perhaps because of the historical realities of the nineteenth-century cultural constructs of Moral Mother/True Woman, and the institution of separate spheres for white bourgeois women, these scholars have found extraordinary salience in the anthropological vision of women as everywhere dominated by men, everywhere inhabiting a separate social domain, and perhaps everywhere of higher moral character as well.

This vision and its embodiment in the notion of women's culture is not merely academic, in either sense of the word. In a recent Equal Employment Opportunity Commission affirmative action suit against Sears Roebuck, feminist historian Rosalind Rosenberg testified that nineteenth-century American women created a women's culture that stressed nurturance, home, and children, and that this unselfish, non-competitive *geist* discouraged them from seeking difficult, well-paying jobs in the labor market.[26] These theoretical constructs and their sources, then, have contemporary political implications.

Thus far I have identified an issue, women's culture, in feminist theory; constructed a taxonomy of its appearance in a variety of texts; and considered a range of feminist anthropological approaches to gender and culture upon which nonanthropological feminist scholars have (and have not) relied in their constructs of women's culture. I would like now to return to two classic texts (now nearly fifteen years old) in feminist anthropology to suggest a different pattern of borrowing and influence.

Women's culture writers heavily cite the Chodorow and Ortner (and sometimes Rosaldo) articles in the collection *Woman, Culture, and Society* (Rosaldo and Lamphere 1974). I have noted that they use these texts to emphasize notions of universal psychological and symbolic entailments of women's childcare responsibilities. I would like to suggest two neglected essays in the collection as equally fruitful candidates for borrowing. Louise Lamphere, in "Strategies, Cooperation, and Conflict among Women in Domestic Groups," considers differing types of kinship and social organization structures and the patterns of alliance and fissure that they encourage between women.[27] Jane Collier, in "Women in Politics," attempts to redraw the map of "the political" as defined in anthropology.[28] She considers women a priori as political actors, and in so doing looks at patterns of women's struggles with one another for individual gain in households. These two articles stress precisely the themes that the women's culture concept tends to elide: the material variations in women's lives that give rise to differing female perspectives on social reality, and the cross-cultural ubiquity of women's (often quite ruthless) struggles against, as well as cooperation with, one another.

I would also like to recommend the much less cited of the two bibles of feminist anthropology, *Toward an Anthropology of Women*, edited by Rayna Rapp. The contributors to this volume tend far more than those in *Woman, Culture, and Society* to stress the varying historical and political-economic contexts in which women experience their lives, and from which they make decisions concerning appropriate actions and negotiate senses of themselves and others. In the Rapp book Anna Rubbo, for example, writes about the historical process of proletarianization in rural Colombia and its effects on both women still living in the countryside and those who have migrated to the city.[29] She considers not only changing sexual divisions of labor and women's shifting resources for survival, but also the ways in which they conceive these shifts, their associations with men and children, and even changing conceptions of the supernatural related to shifting political-economic realities.

Taking into account material differences in women's lives and the realities of conflict between women leads us to four contentions that have been implicit in my argument thus far. First, women's agency may have varying moral contents. We cannot automatically evaluate women's actions as morally superior to men's. (And in so doing we leave unexamined our criteria for moral judgment.) This is the lesson I learned in the field, and not heeding it often entails a neglect of the related second point: Women, like men, are social actors who employ strategies to achieve desired ends. Their strategies may appear on the surface as nurturant or selfish actions, as cooperative or competitive behavior, and most often take place within the material and ideological constraints of some form of male domination. Of course the strategies of one group of women may function as constraints on another group, as the historically uneasy relations between domestic servants and their mistresses attest.

The third point is that sentimentalizing women's common primary responsibility for children obscures the fact that the cultural construction of mothering (and fathering) has varied enormously across time and space; and that, most importantly, we can observe women's use of the maternal role as a symbolically charged stratagem to gain power under extremely constraining circumstances. Some of my women informants' efforts to control their adult children through kin work provided poignant illustration of this point: Their strategies largely failed in the face of overwhelming economic and cultural forces encouraging the social autonomy of adult American children.

Finally, "women's cultures" have been historically, economically, geographically, and culturally contingent phenomena. They do not necessarily include all women in particular populations and may be characterized as much by conflict as cooperation. To cite several contemporary American ethnographic examples: While we may learn something by looking at the commonalities among Chicana cannery workers in California, white middle-class lesbians in a Midwest college town, and Caribbean domestic workers in New York City, we will learn as much or more by taking the differences in these women's lives seriously.[30]

Thus, to return to kin work, I have now revised my article to make clear my women informants' consciousness of the power in domestic domains to be gained through kin work; the ubiquity of conflict as well as cooperation over kin-work activities; and the historicity of these activities as gendered labor. That is, kin work is part of "women's culture" in the sense I am criticizing, in that it involves obligations women heed to nurture kin and foster relations among kin and friends, and in that it involves cooperating networks of women. But it is also part of women's culture in three neglected senses. First, we must pluralize "culture" because the differences in kin work perceived and performed by women in different situations are as important as the commonalities. Second, it is an area in which women act strategically to influence others and gain desired ends. And third, women may and do perceive their interests as conflicting with those of other women, and may act accordingly.

This formulation of the problem, however, assumes that feminist scholarship, in whatever discipline, exists in an intellectual vacuum. Actually, the feminist anthropologists whose work supplied theoreti-

cal ballast for women's culture writers had themselves relied on pre-
and nonfeminist theories of cultural process. How *has* anthropological
cultural theory dealt with gender? What models has it provided for
borrowing or revision by feminists?

I am now beginning to consider prominent anthropological theories of cultural process in terms of their treatments of gender divisions,
and am looking in particular at issues of agency, sharedness, stratification, and moral evaluation. That is, do theories of culture allow for
women's as well as men's sentience and effective action? How do they
deal with differences, particularly intracultural differences, in perception? How do they treat hierarchical social difference? And finally, do
they implicitly or explicitly provide frameworks for judging the different moral worth of different groups of humans? In this last section, I
shall offer some very preliminary and sketchy answers to these questions through a consideration of two traditions in anthropological
cultural theory.

The Marxist tradition envisions the human creation of culture as
the process of separation from nature through self-conscious operations upon it—the activities (productive labor) that reproduce human
life. While the writings of Marx and Engels are somewhat ambiguous
about the productive status of the biological reproduction of humans
and the provisioning of households, in general women are not considered to be part of this definitionally human labor process. (Victorians
that they were, Marx and Engels did not conceive of women as un-
marked workers outside households.) Women, in this scheme, thus
emerge as occupants of an unchanging domestic sphere just in time for
Engels to assert their loss of equality, the "world-historic defeat of the
female sex," through the rise of private property.[31]

Nevertheless, twentieth-century Marxist writing on ideology and
consciousness has built on Marx's understanding of the linkages between differing material situations and differing perceptions of social
reality. This writing has in turn inspired feminist work on women's
distinct visions—and actions in relation to—social processes in different historical and cultural contexts.[32]

The Marxist heritage with regard to issues of moral evaluation is
equally ambiguous. On the one hand, Marx's apocalyptic vision of the

historic role of European proletariats in bringing about socialist revolution has given rise to a tradition of ennobling portrayals of oppressed
groups—a tradition, of course, by no means originating with Marx.
Marxist methodology, though, prescribes the attempt to analyze
groups' and individuals' perceptions and actions in terms of their objective places in social and economic structures.[33] We might then trace both
feminist essentialist portrayals of women's moral superiority and feminist materialist, morally neutral analyses of women's linked political-
economic situations and perceptions back to Marxist traditions.

Despite the existence of considerable work in twentieth-century
Marxism on cultural process, feminist anthropologists directly influenced by Marxist research have tended to focus on issues of labor,
economy, and politics rather than on culture and consciousness.[34] Structuralism, in contrast, has had a major shaping effect on feminist anthropological models of culture through Sherry Ortner's early use of Lévi-
Straussian analysis. Women lack agency in the Lévi-Strauss vision:
They are the objects of primary human (male) exchange that literally
creates culture. Lévi-Strauss acknowledges the counterfactual, contradictory character of this model in a well-known passage in *The Elementary Structures of Kinship* (1969): "woman could never become just a sign
and nothing more, since even in a man's world she is still a person, and
since insofar as she is defined as a sign she must be recognized as a
generator of signs."[35] But there is no allowance in Lévi-Strauss's model
for women's generation of signs, and Ortner's feminist account inherits
this legacy. Similarly, Ortner (1974) carries forward the structuralist
tendency to elide intracultural difference and, under this heading, to
ignore extragender stratification. Finally, Ortner adds to Lévi-Strauss's
insistence on the primacy of binary categories in human thought, and
on universal human (male) self-definition in opposition to nature, the
assertion of a universal identification of female with (degraded) nature.
She thus implicitly evaluates male thought as unfairly denigrating to
women. Women appear in her model only as objects of this categoriza-
tion; a further logical operation is necessary to define women's moral
superiority through this process of cognitive victimization.

Cultural theory in anthropology has been fed by many streams.
Marxism and structuralism must be joined, at a minimum, by evolu-

tionism, structural-functionalism, various schools of symbolic analysis, ethnoscience, poststructuralism, and interpretation to begin to form an adequate account of anthropological conceptions of cultural process, and thus to investigate the place of gender in those conceptions. But my work to date indicates that feminist scholars have inherited from most cultural theory traditions difficulties in attributing agency to female actors, in allowing for intracultural differences in perceptions—particularly those based on social stratification—and in attributing different moral worth to subsets of human populations.

Let us look, for example, more closely at Sherry Ortner's recent formulation in this light. In their introduction to the edited collection, *Sexual Meanings,* Ortner and Whitehead (1980) make the claim that "the cultural construction of gender tends everywhere to be stamped by the prestige considerations of socially dominant male actors."[36] My concern is to look behind the hidden metaphor here: What is under the stamp? I believe that we need to problematize, to investigate explictly the issues of cultural sharedness and difference before we generalize about universals in the cultural construction of gender. To reverse the trend in interdisciplinary borrowing upon which I commented at the opening of this piece: I am inspired by some recent trends in Marxist social, labor, and cultural history. Many scholars in these fields are concerned with the forms of consent and resistance created by dominated groups, whether feudal peasantry, proletarianized artisans, or modern industrial workers. Other scholars concern themselves with total cultural landscapes and the ways in which different groups make use of them. How is the same language used to different ends? How can we document the use of different cultural constructs?[37]

If we consider kin work within this frame, it emerges as a phenomenon through which women both resist and consent to male dominance, and in which different actors use the same language to very different ends. Resistance can operate in at least two ways. Women may use the female assignment of kin work tasks to claim for themselves decision-making power over social events and relations with kin, and, as I have mentioned, they may attempt to use kin work to maintain control over relatives, particularly adult children.

The fact that the potential for such control has been undermined by economic and social shifts in this century may be related to the second form of women's resistance: simply refusing to do kin-work tasks. Many of my women informants reported cutting back on kin-work activities as their labor force participation increased. A letter to Ann Landers expresses the perspective of the fed-up kinworker who sees no compensation accruing:

> Why is it that all the married women of America are supposed to write all the letters and send all the cards to their husbands' families? My old man is a much better writer than I am, yet he expects me to correspond with his whole family. If I asked him to correspond with mine, he would blow a gasket.[38]

Some feminists, however, laud women's kin-work activities in a celebration of women's morality, as does Carol Gilligan: "Women's place in man's life cycle has been that of nurturer, caretaker and helpmate, the weaver of those networks of relationships on which she in turn relies."[39]

There is, then, a great deal to be investigated under the stamp of the prestige considerations of socially dominant males. The agentless frameworks of some schools of culture prevent us from seeing that cultural constructions are, after all, human creations, subject to struggles over interpretation by groups as parts of larger struggles over social power.

In this piece, I have picked up a knotty problem by two separate threads: the use and abuse of anthropological cultural theory by feminist theorists, and the problematic inscription of gender in cultural theories. I have only a provisional story to tell, but clearly, although the women's culture concept carries its discontents within itself, they are not discontents of its own making.

NOTES

1. Micaela di Leonardo (1984).

2. See di Leonardo (1984), particularly pp. 22–25 and 96–157.

3. The following analysis draws from di Leonardo (1984), pp. 191–229.

4. See di Leonardo (1984), p. 223.

5. See di Leonardo (1984), pp. 194–205, and (1987), pp. 440–53.

6. Elaine Showalter (1982).

7. Judit Moschkovich (1981).

8. Temma Kaplan (1982).

9. Gerda Lerner (1980).

10. Carol Gilligan (1982).

11. See Showalter (1982, 1985); Sarah Ruddick (1980); Jean Bethke Elshtain (1983, 1987); Gilligan (1982); Sally McConnell-Ginet, Ruth Borker, and Nelly Furman (1980); Rosan A. Jordan and Susan J. Kalcik (1987); Carroll Smith-Rosenberg (1975); Nancy Cott (1979); Susan Porter Benson (1987); Barbara Melosh (1982); Jessie Bernard (1987); Yolanda and Robert Murphy (1985); Rayna Rapp (1975).

12. Eric Hobsbawm and Terence Ranger (1983).

13. Patricia Roth (1987).

14. Joan Cocks (1984).

15. Kathy Peiss (1985); Christine Stansell (1986); Nancy A. Hewitt (1985).

16. See the discussion of radical and cultural feminism in Janet Sayers (1982), pp. 187–92.

17. Nancy Chodorow (1978).

18. See Showalter (1982) for a summary of these positions.

19. Edwin Ardener (1975).

20. Sherry Ortner (1974).

21. Michelle Zimbalist Rosaldo (1974), pp. 67–88.

22. Marilyn Strathern and Carol MacCormack (1980).

23. Sherry Ortner and Harriet Whitehead (1980).

24. See, for example, Jane and Peter Schneider (1976).

25. Nicole-Claude Mathieu (1978); Penelope Brown (1981).

26. On this issue, see Jon Weiner (1985); Karen J. Winkler (1986); Rosalind Rosenberg (1986); Alice Kessler-Harris (1986).

27. Louise Lamphere (1974).

28. Jane Fishburne Collier (1974), pp. 89–96.

29. Anna Rubbo (1975).

30. Patricia Zavella (1987); Susan Krieger (1983); Shellee Colen (1985).

31. See, for example, Marx's contradictory treatment of the "animal" functions of eating, drinking, and procreating in the "Economic and Philosophic Manuscripts," in Karl Marx (1975), pp. 279–400, esp. pp. 326–29, and Frederick Engels (1940), esp. p. 50.

32. I refer here to a very large and internally contentious field of writing labeled "Western Marxism." See New Left Review (1977) and Perry Anderson (1976). A relatively recent exemplary feminist text is Nancy Cott (1987).

33. See Steven Lukes (1985).

34. For example, see the work of Kathleen Gough, Eleanor Leacock, Helen Safa, Karen Sacks, and María Patricia Fernandez-Kelly.

35. Claude Lévi-Strauss (1969).

36. Ortner and Whitehead (1980), p. 12.

37. Here, again, I can only refer to exemplary texts such as E. P. Thompson (1963); George Rulé (1979); David Montgomery (1979); Jean-Christophe Agnew (1986).

38. Letter to Ann Landers printed in *Washington Post* (April 15, 1983).

39. Gilligan (1982).

REFERENCES

Agnew, Jean-Christophe
    1986    *Worlds Apart: The Market and the Theater in Anglo-American Thought, 1550–1750.* Cambridge: Cambridge University Press.

Anderson, Perry
    1976    *Considerations on Western Marxism.* London: New Left Books.

Ardener, Edwin
    1975    Belief and the Problem of Women. In *Perceiving Women,* ed. Shirley Ardener, pp. 1–28. London: Dent.

Benson, Susan Porter
    1987    *Counter Cultures: Saleswomen, Managers and Customers in American Department Stores, 1910–1919.* Champaign-Urbana: University of Illinois Press.

Bernard, Jessie
    1987    *The Female World from a Global Perspective.* Bloomington: Indiana University Press.

Brown, Penelope
    1981    Universals and Particulars in the Position of Women. In *Women in Society,* ed. The Cambridge Women's Studies Group, pp. 242–54. London: Virago Press.

Chodorow, Nancy
    1978    *The Reproduction of Mothering.* Berkeley: University of California Press.

Cocks, Joan
    1984    Wordless Emotions: Some Critical Reflections on Radical Feminism. *Politics and Society* 13(1): 27–58.

Colen, Shellee
    1985    "Doing Domestic" for the Green Card: West Indian Women's Experiences. Paper presented in the American Ethnological Society "domestic workers" symposium at the Meetings of the American Anthropological Society, December, Washington, D.C.

Collier, Jane Fishburne
    1974    Women in Politics. In *Woman, Culture, and Society,* ed. Michelle Z. Rosaldo and Louise Lamphere, pp. 89–96. Stanford, Calif.: Stanford University Press.

Cott, Nancy
    1979    *The Bonds of Womanhood: Woman's Sphere in New England, 1780–1835.* New Haven, Conn.: Yale University Press.
    1987    *The Grounding of Modern Feminism.* New Haven, Conn.: Yale University Press.

di Leonardo, Micaela
    1984    *The Varieties of Ethnic Experience: Kinship, Class and Gender among Italian-Americans in Northern California.* Ithaca, N.Y.: Cornell University Press.
    1987    The Female World of Cards and Holidays: Women, Families and the Work of Kinship. *Signs: Journal of Women in Culture and Society* 12(3): 440–53.

Elshtain, Jean Bethke
    1983    On Beautiful Souls, Just Warriors and Feminist Consciousness. In *Women and Men's Wars,* ed. Judith Stiehm. Oxford: Pergamon Press.
    1987    *Women and War.* New York: Basic Books.

Engels, Frederick
    1940    *The Origins of the Family, Private Property and the State.* New York: International Publishers.

Gilligan, Carol
    1982    *In a Different Voice: Psychological Theory and Women's Development.* Cambridge, Mass.: Harvard University Press.

Hewitt, Nancy A.
    1985    Beyond the Search for Sisterhood: American Women's History in the 1980s. *Social History* 10(3): 299–321.

Hobsbawm, Eric, and Terence Ranger (eds.)
    1983    *The Invention of Tradition.* Cambridge: Cambridge University Press.

Jordan, Rosan A., and Susan J. Kalcik (eds.)
    1987    *Women's Folklore, Women's Culture.* Philadelphia: University of Pennsylvania Press.

Kaplan, Temma
    1982    Female Consciousness and Collective Action: The Case of Barcelona, 1910–1918. *Signs: Journal of Women in Culture and Society* 7(3): 545–66, esp. p. 546.

Kessler-Harris, Alice
    1986    Equal Employment Opportunity Commission vs. Sears Roebuck and Company: A Personal Account. *Radical History Review* 35 (April): 57–79.

Krieger, Susan
    1983    *The Mirror Dance: Identity in a Woman's Community.* Philadelphia: Temple University Press.

Lamphere, Louise
    1974    Strategies, Cooperation, and Conflict among Women in Domestic Groups. In *Woman, Culture, and Society,* ed. Michelle Z. Rosaldo and Louise Lamphere, pp. 97–112. Stanford, Calif.: Stanford University Press.

Lerner, Gerda

    1980    Politics and Culture in Women's History: A Symposium. *Feminist Studies* 6(1): 26–64, esp. p. 53.

Lévi-Strauss, Claude

    1969    *The Elementary Structures of Kinship*, p. 496. Boston: Beacon Press.

Lukes, Steven

    1985    *Marxism and Morality.* Oxford: Oxford University Press.

McConnell-Ginet, Sally, Ruth Borker, and Nelly Furman (eds.)

    1980    *Women and Language in Literature and Society.* New York: Praeger.

Marx, Karl

    1975    Economic and Philosophic Manuscripts. In *Karl Marx: Early Writings,* ed. Quentin Hoare. New York: Vintage.

Mathieu, Nicole-Claude

    1978    Man-Culture and Woman-Nature? *Women's Studies International Quarterly* 1: 55–65.

Melosh, Barbara

    1982    *The Physician's Hand: Work Culture and Conflict in American Nursing.* Philadelphia: Temple University Press.

Montgomery, David

    1979    *Workers' Control in America: Studies in the History of Work, Technology, and Labor Struggles.* Cambridge: Cambridge University Press.

Moschkovich, Judit

    1981    —But I Know You, American Woman. In *This Bridge Called My Back: Writings by Radical Women of Color,* ed. Cherríe Moraga and Gloria Anzaldúa, pp. 79–84, esp. p. 82. Watertown, Mass.: Persephone Press.

Murphy, Yolanda and Robert

    1985    *Women of the Forest,* 2d ed. New York: Columbia University Press.

New Left Review (ed.)

    1977    *Western Marxism: A Critical Reader.* London: New Left Books.

Ortner, Sherry

    1974    Is Female to Male as Nature Is to Culture? In *Woman, Culture, and Society,* ed. Michelle Z. Rosaldo and Louise Lamphere, pp. 67–88. Stanford, Calif.: Stanford University Press.

Ortner, Sherry, and Harriet Whitehead (eds.)
    1980    *Sexual Meanings: The Cultural Construction of Gender and Sexuality.* Cambridge: Cambridge University Press.

Peiss, Kathy
    1985    *Cheap Amusements: Working Women and Leisure in Turn-of-the-Century New York.* Philadelphia: Temple University Press.

Rapp, Rayna
    1975    Men and Women in the South of France: Public and Private Domains. In *Toward an Anthropology of Women,* ed. Rayna (Rapp) Reiter, pp. 252–82. New York: Monthly Review Press.

Rosaldo, Michelle Zimbalist
    1974    Woman, Culture, and Society: A Theoretical Overview. In *Woman, Culture, and Society,* ed. Michelle Z. Rosaldo and Louise Lamphere, pp. 17–42. Stanford, Calif.: Stanford University Press.

Rosaldo, Michelle Z., and Louise Lamphere (eds.)
    1974    *Woman, Culture, and Society.* Stanford, Calif.: Stanford University Press.

Rosenberg, Rosalind
    1986    What Harms Women in the Workplace. *New York Times* (February 27).

Roth, Patricia
    1987    Women Who Sell Sex: Can Workers' Control Bring Power into Whores' Hands? *Gay Community News* 14 (July 5–11): 8–9.

Rubbo, Anna
    1975    The Spread of Capitalism in Rural Colombia: Effects on Poor Women. In *Toward an Anthropology of Women,* ed. Rayna (Rapp) Reiter, pp. 333–57. New York: Monthly Review Press.

Ruddick, Sarah
    1980    Maternal Thinking. *Feminist Studies* 6(2): 342–67.

Rulé, George
    1979    *Ideology and Popular Protest.* New York: Pantheon.

Sayers, Janet
    1982    *Biological Politics: Feminist and Anti-Feminist Perspectives.* New York: Tavistock.

Schneider, Jane and Peter
  1976    *Culture and Political Economy in Western Sicily.* New York: Academic Press.

Showalter, Elaine
  1982    Feminist Criticism in the Wilderness. In *Writing and Sexual Difference,* ed. Elizabeth Abel, pp. 9–36, esp. p. 27. Chicago: University of Chicago Press.

Showalter, Elaine (ed.)
  1985    *Feminist Criticism: Essays on Women, Literature and Theory.* New York: Pantheon.

Smith-Rosenberg, Carroll
  1975    The Female World of Love and Ritual: Relations between Women in Nineteenth Century America. *Signs: Journal of Women in Culture and Society* 1(1): 1–29.

Stansell, Christine
  1986    *City of Women: Sex and Class in New York, 1789–1860.* New York: Knopf.

Strathern, Marilyn, and Carol MacCormack (eds.)
  1980    *Nature, Culture and Gender.* Cambridge: Cambridge University Press.

Thompson, E. P.
  1963    *The Making of the English Working Class.* New York: Random House.

Weiner, Jon
  1985    Women's History on Trial. *Nation* 241 (September 7): 161, 176, 178–80.

Winkler, Karen J.
  1986    Two Scholars' Conflict in Sears Sex-Bias Case Sets Off War in Women's History. *Chronicle of Higher Education* (February 5): 1, 8.

Zavella, Patricia
  1987    *Women's Work and Chicano Families: Cannery Workers of the Santa Clara Valley.* Ithaca, N.Y.: Cornell University Press.

# CHAPTER 10

# Christian Missionaries, Western Feminists, and the Kikuyu Clitoridectomy Controversy

*Dallas L. Browne*

The recent settlement of African and Middle Eastern populations in Europe has focused public attention on the issue of female circumcision. Swedish women's groups oppose the practice of this custom in Sweden (Levin 1980). In Britain, the Women's Action Group on Female Excision and Infibulation seeks the international abolition of this practice (Hayter 1984). In their article "The International Crime of Genital Mutilation," Robin Morgan and Gloria Steinem (1980:100) expressed their indignation at sluggish efforts by African governments to change this custom. Fran Hosken, the most widely read American authority on this subject, has repeatedly lamented the lack of international support for the abolition of clitoridectomy (Hosken 1981). Yet, despite government support Lord Kennet, Baroness Gaitskell, and other British parliamentarians failed to secure the passage in 1983 of a bill titled "The Prohibition of Female Circumcision" (Hayter 1984:323). Many African and Middle Eastern women support the continuation of this custom, although they are the alleged "victims" whose bodies are being mutilated and violated.

Do African and Arab women suffer from a form of false consciousness that encourages blind allegiance to tradition even when it harms them, or are some Westerners being culturally biased and narrow-minded?

Efforts to change such traditions raise many questions. Why and how do issues related to female sexuality become political boundary markers? Who has the right to decide what customs are sexually oppressive or offensive? How do Western observers know when and if Third World women are in a position to assert what they want for themselves when discussions of sexuality arise in other cultures? Should minority groups living in Europe and America be legally forced to discontinue practices fundamental to their culture? Will legal pressure eradicate such private behavior or merely drive it underground?

This paper argues that individuals in Africa, the Middle East, Europe, and elsewhere have the right to decide what is to be done with their bodies, as long as this does not harm others. If clitoridectomy is abolished, this decision must be made by the women practicing this custom. To deny them the choice over what is to be done with their own bodies diminishes their liberty and may suggest that they are not intelligent enough to know what is good for them or how to get what they need.

## VITAL DATA

An estimated 70,000,000 women in Africa and the Middle East have had clitoridectomies (Hosken 1981). Most reports suggest that girls voluntarily underwent such surgical operations at the urging of their parents, although forced submission has also been reported (Kenyatta 1938, Hosken 1981, Murray 1976, Sindzingre 1977, El Dareer 1983). When the Sudan recently proposed abolishing clitoridectomy, Asma El Dareer's survey of 3,210 females and 1,545 males indicated that nearly five times as many women and seven times as many men favored continuation over abolition (El Dareer 1983:138).

## FIELDWORK

From 1972 to 1978 I lived, worked, and conducted fieldwork in Nairobi, Kenya. Most of my work was among members of an ethnic group known as the Kikuyu. The Kikuyu are an agricultural people, whose traditional land has been partially absorbed by Nairobi as it expanded. The land is owned by patrilineages, and before the British entered Kenya women were not allowed to own or inherit land. Women acquired the right to use land from their husbands. They grew maize and beans and later added coffee and tea. Women traded food items, and men controlled cash crops. Although men held formal power, women had access to power through institutions such as the women's council and woman-to-woman marriage. Kikuyu culture has been compelled to adapt to two sets of external forces: first British colonial rule, from 1896 to 1963, and later rapid urbanization, from 1963 to the present, especially in Nairobi. A remarkable blend of traditional and modern culture is crystallizing in communities such as the one I studied, known as Kawangware.

The primary focus of my research in Nairobi was the control of urban communities exercised by elders' councils. I learned of female circumcision ceremonies quite by accident. I lived with a branch of former paramount chief Kinyanjui's family in Kawangware. One of the sons was scheduled for circumcision. Returning late from errands in town I missed the van that took the men and boys to the ceremony. Our neighbor was a woman named Mama wa Njoki, from whom we often bought beer that she brewed. She felt sorry for me and asked me to ride to the ceremonies with her, her daughter, and the women from our compound who were going to the ritual. Once there, I got swept up in the flow of events and incidentally became privy to information about clitoridectomy. When we arrived at the farm I was pushed along by a crowd of women rushing the girls off to the area where the clitoridectomies were taking place. Although some Kikuyu men teased me later, I felt privileged that the women trusted me enough to allow me to witness the proceedings. As a stranger, my sex was almost neuter, and this along with the excitement of the moment helped me witness the ceremony. From that night on I took great interest in clitoridectomy and the role of women in Kawangware.

I began to ask many Kikuyu women about clitoridectomy. Some Nairobi women with whom I spoke viewed efforts to abolish the custom as evidence of neocolonial racial supremist attitudes among some European women. They claimed that European women subjected them to many indignities during the colonial era, made them care for European children, wash the dirty dishes and clothes of Europeans, and do any work considered too dirty or demeaning for European women. The Europeans discouraged marriage between European men and African women and degraded African women by insulting them and calling them bad names. These Kikuyu women thus felt that European women had oppressed them throughout the colonial era, and colonial episodes have left a legacy of mistrust. They questioned the depth of European humanitarian concern and suspected ethnocide or an attempt to destroy their indigenous culture as the real but hidden driving force behind reformers' zeal. This opinion was common among Kikuyu women with scant Western education, who spoke little or no English and who compared current attempts to abolish this custom with earlier missionary efforts.[1] This view sharply contrasts with that of Kikuyu women who have earned Western college degrees. Educated women overwhelmingly oppose clitoridectomy, regardless of tribal traditions, but also share the opinion that foreigners should not dictate how their culture should change.[2] African women from tribes that never circumcised their women are also outspoken opponents of clitoridectomy.[3]

Western-educated Kikuyu are generally unwilling to admit that the custom of clitoridectomy persists. Many educated women who, before I got to know them well, had denied that the custom still existed later showed signs of being embarrassed by revelation of its continuation. They had been taught by missionaries that such traditional customs were uncivilized and barbaric. Consequently they now treat them as if they were closely guarded national secrets. Before beginning fieldwork I was told repeatedly by several Western-educated Kikuyu that the custom had died in the early 1930s. Apparently, missionary campaigns against clitoridectomy merely drove it underground, where it secretly thrived.

Families practicing clitoridectomy live in encapsulated social networks and seldom discuss it with families that disapprove of it. Kikuyu lineages, or *mbaris,* such as mbari wa Njora, that have publicly denounced the custom, are not asked to participate. In fact, they are shunned. Most Kikuyu women who are not circumcised come from devout Presbyterian families, and their social networks consist of like-minded Kikuyu. Many families who practice clitoridectomy belong to the Roman Catholic or Orthodox churches, whose reputation for tolerating local customs has won them many converts. Presbyterian families on the one hand and Catholic and Orthodox families on the other represent two variants of modern Kikuyu culture. Politically and economically they were integrated by common membership in local branches of KANU and GEMA.[4] I estimate that over 40 percent of the Kikuyu women in Kawangware have been circumcised. Al-Saadawy and Smith confirm that at least 75 percent of the women in industrializing Egypt have undergone circumcision (Al-Saadawy 1977, Smith n.d.).

To understand why both historic and modern abolition campaigns have met with so little success, let us briefly define clitoridectomy, review the evolution of the clitoridectomy controversy in Kenya, and then draw conclusions about the issues of law, morality, and cultural self-determination. Throughout this account we will try to understand why millions of African and Third World women defend this custom while many Western women consider it humiliating, oppressive, brutal, mutilating, and savage. How do we account for this discrepancy?

TYPES OF CLITORIDECTOMY

Clitoridectomy is the partial or complete excision (removal) of the external female genitalia, ranging from removal of only the prepuce (outer fold, or foreskin) of the clitoris to excision of the entire clitoris together with the labia minora and/or majora. Four general types are distinguished by the extent of the surgery. The first type involves removal of the foreskin and occasionally the labia minora as well; the second, the labia minora and part of the clitoris; the third, the labia minora and the entire clitoris; and the fourth, the entire clitoris, the labia minora, and the labia majora. The fourth type is also called Sudanese or pharaonic circumcision and is common in the Sudan, Somalia, and Egypt. It may be accompanied by infibulation (sewing the vagina closed) to protect the virginity of unmarried girls. The

severity of the last two types of operations can cause lifelong complications if performed improperly. Tobe Levin and others have labeled
these two "unspeakable atrocities" (Levin 1980).

Cook (n.d.), Mustafa (1966), and Shandall (1967) claimed that
most Muslim women follow the first two types of clitoridectomy and
regard them as *sunna* (traditional). They avoid calling it mutilation.
Girls generally undergo these rituals before puberty, usually between
the ages of 6 and 12. The Kikuyu girls whose clitoridectomies I witnessed in Kawangware, Kenya, in 1977 ranged in age from 7 to 11.
While the girls exhibited anxiety, I saw no evidence of hysteria, brutal-
ity, or deliberate disfiguring. In most cases only the foreskin surrounding the clitoris was removed. The operation was seen as the counterpart of male circumcision and a necessary rite of passage bestowing
honor and adult privilege on deserving girls.

## CLITORIDECTOMY AND CIRCUMCISION CEREMONIES
## AMONG THE KIKUYU

Throughout several circumcision seasons from 1973 to 1977 I observed
ceremonies involving the first two types of clitoridectomy among
modern urban Kikuyu women. Just prior to their operation girls are
asked to declare the type they wanted; most choose the first, or mildest, type. Type two, noted above, was the only other option offered in
the observed cases. Since the initiates are minors, their parents and
their advisor or guardian make the selection, in consultation with the
young girl. The girls I talked to assented to their parents' wishes.

In Kawangware these operations were performed by a trained
female medical technician who worked for the Catholic health clinic
during the day, along with her husband, also a medical technician.
Both husband and wife were trained nurses, with special training in
the art of traditional circumcision. People trusted them. Twice yearly,
at the beginning of school vacations, they organized large circumcision ceremonies on an isolated farm just beyond the city limits. Children came in groups at night, in vans, cars, and minibuses, accompanied by many relatives and well-wishers. Everyone was in a festive

mood and sang Christian hymns on the way to the ceremonies and traditional circumcision songs on the way home. Such songs are collectively known as *karunguru,* after the beer (sometimes called *njohi ya murungu* in Kawangware) traditionally consumed the night prior to the circumcision.

Drinking of the ceremonial beer (*njohi*) begins semitraditional ceremonies lasting seven days.[5] Formal instruction of initiates and all-night dancing and singing of traditional circumcision songs then commence. A goat is slaughtered at the home of the initiate to signify the importance of the occasion. The beer that is consumed is made locally, with great ceremony. Just prior to initiation, all the hair on the head of the initiates is shaved off and all personal ornaments taken from them to impress upon them the fact that they are leaving one life—carefree childhood—and entering another—responsible adulthood. If a girl wants her ears pierced, it is done now. Traditionally, boys also pierced their ears, but seldom do so now. Well-wishers drop by for the next few days and expect to be offered food and drinks.

From the third to the fifth day after circumcision, initiates rest and continue to receive instructions on civic duties, proper hospitality, ideal treatment of one's spouse, sexual conduct and courtship, marital duties, obligations toward kin, and other topics vital to Kikuyu culture. On the fifth day, the girl's circumcision advisor (*muriaria*) ritually washes her with a weed known as *muthunga,* scrubbing the milk of the plant into small cuts on the side of the girl's forehead to indicate that she has undergone a pure Kikuyu circumcision. Many girls now forego this, fearing that it will "ruin their face." On the sixth day after circumcision, the girl's advisor/guardian/teacher brings food to the girl and sleeps at her home. By the seventh day the girl is considered mature and sufficiently healed but, because the number seven is considered a bad omen for travelers, does not begin to visit relatives and friends in her new adult status until early on the morning of the eighth day.[6]

In Kawangware, modern antiseptics are used and Western health standards are observed in the clitoridectomy. Private parts are cleansed, antiseptics applied, and a painkiller given. (The painkiller is injected, if such is the request, but most initiates avoid this practice since it is frowned upon by the community.) The scalpel is sterilized before and after use, and clean sterile bandages are applied.[7] Although I saw electric lights used, they were deliberately kept dim to create an aura of secrecy, mystery, and awe.

The operation and following ritual and feasting represent a substantial outlay of money for poor households. Money is diverted from many other domestic expenditures until the ceremony is successfully completed and the girl's identity securely established. Circumcision remains a central feature of Kikuyu identity. Its abolition could lead to a total breakdown of Kikuyu culture.

The clitoridectomies I witnessed were in most respects the female counterparts of male circumcisions, involving removal only of the foreskin. Given the tenacity of this custom, we must ask if it is wiser to strive for further reforms, such as hospitalization of participants and exclusive use of the mildest type of clitoridectomy, or to seek total eradication of the practice. Historically, eradication efforts have met with stiff opposition. To understand why, let us briefly review the history of the Kikuyu clitoridectomy controversy.

## HISTORICAL ANTECEDENTS: SISTERS IN AFFLICTION?

European colonial administrators sought military, economic, political, and cultural domination of Africa between 1890 and 1960. Absolute domination is difficult to achieve, for even in the most coercive social systems, such as South Africa's apartheid, people will maintain a semiautonomous underlife, for example, the black subcultures that flourish in such townships as Soweto (Sally Falk-Moore 1978). Complete autonomy is equally difficult to achieve. People worldwide have been drawn into global commercial and political systems so vast that semiautonomy and self-regulation of local matters is now widely accepted (Immanuel Wallerstein 1979).

Britain established Kenya Colony in the late 1800s. Efforts to establish the hegemony of British culture created conflict. Although Africans were incorporated into colonial empires based upon racial inequalities and subjugation, the Africans' semiautonomy prevented their complete alienation from their indigenous culture. Continued ownership of land and other productive, wealth-creating assets provided the objective basis for urban and rural semiautonomy. Moreover, Britain is a tiny nation, and its attempts to dominate the globe spread its modest population so thin that the collaboration of local opinion leaders became an essential component of the British system of indirect rule. Pragmatically, the salary of one Englishman in Kenya would pay for four Africans. Training and hiring Kenyan men and a few women was more profitable than hiring Englishmen, so limited training of locals was encouraged. Government-sponsored schools would have drained state treasuries, so mission schools also were encouraged. Consequently, new generations of Africans had learned the English language and history and had basic skills needed by the colonial powers. These new Kenyans were nominal Christians who had never known a time when they were not colonized. Despite this, they maintained two separate social worlds. In one, their own language and cultural symbols such as circumcision and clitoridectomy nurtured the Kikuyu's distinct identity, pride, and sense of self-worth. In the other, they followed British customs and culture. However, the two worlds were unequal; when they came into conflict, British culture prevailed, by force if necessary.

British colonial administrators were quick to encourage Christian missionary activity in Kenya, for many of them felt that conversion would pacify indigenous Kenyans and make them easy to control. Indigenous religion and culture were viewed as obstacles that retarded Westernization and the creation of new values in Africans that would make them servile and submissive. As long as Africans could favorably compare their own culture with English culture, the contrast would foment rebellion and the desire to restore independence. To make way for the new social order the traditional order was ruthlessly attacked. Africans were told that their customs were backward and savage. They were taught that salvation could be attained only by abandoning their cultural heritage and by slavishly imitating European customs and values.

Bridewealth, polygyny, and clitoridectomy were especially repugnant to agents of British culture, for they clashed with values cherished in England, such as the monogamous family. Early advocates of Western culture did not fundamentally understand Kenyan cultures, nor did they respect them. They held such cultures in utter contempt. Their actions were thus guided by ignorance and prejudice that left a trail of unresolved injustices.

Originally, many missionaries thought that bridewealth was a form of slavery. To their minds the transfer of wealth from the groom's family to the bride's amounted to the purchase of the bride, as if she became the property of her husband who was thereafter free to use her as a beast of burden. Anthropologists such as Louis Leakey later demonstrated that, contrary to these mistaken notions, bride-wealth was more like the European dowry than human bondage. Earlier revelations of this nature led some missionaries to take a some-what more sophisticated approach to their war against Kikuyu cul-ture, and to try to absorb or co-opt local cultures. However, since most of the missionary activity referred to here took place between 1890 and 1940, and Leakey's books on Kikuyu culture were not pub-lished until after 1940, few missionaries benefited from such anthropo-logical insights.

Terence Ranger (1972) noted that Bishop Lucas of Tanganyika had tried to Christianize the boys' initiation ceremony known as *jando.* By 1900 this had met with success, but similar efforts in 1905 to transform *malango,* the female circumcision ceremony, failed. Un-daunted, Kenyan missionaries, from 1910 on, tried to Christianize both male and female circumcision ceremonies. The missionary Dr. Philip succeeded in performing male circumcisions in mission hospi-tals, but when Mrs. Stevenson, another British missionary, invited traditional doctors to perform clitoridectomies in the hospitals, the experiment failed. Stevenson wrote that the operation she witnessed was "so brutal" she would never sanction another (Murray 1976) and subsequently became the bitterest opponent of the custom. She con-vinced Dr. Philip and other missionaries that the practice was evil and should be abolished. When asked why, she answered that "one of the women cried bitterly during the operation."

To many Kikuyu, Stevenson's extreme, almost hysterical reaction was childish. Pain and adversity are normal features of adult life. One major lesson taught to girls undergoing this operation was that pain and hardship must be endured. Stevenson's desire to have Kikuyu girls avoid hardship and pain seemed irresponsible to the women's *kiama* (council). Nevertheless, by 1915 Stevenson had persuaded some women, such as Lizzie Mwarania, Ruth Wangui, and Julia Mukani, to avoid the *mambura,* ritual training associated with clitoridectomy. As a result, they were ostracized by the women's council, which argued that their loyalty to the Kikuyu community was questionable. The three women became the first public opponents of their traditional customs at Tumutumu, Nyeri, in Kenya (Waruiru 1971).

To understand the council's reaction, let us review the significance of circumcision for the Kikuyu. First and foremost, cutting a person's genital flesh symbolically marks the passage from childhood to adulthood. Regardless of chronological age, uncircumcised persons are considered irresponsible children and not allowed to vote on important matters. When speaking of its significance, people occasionally draw analogies between circumcision and cutting the umbilical cord at birth. Unlike infants, initiates are taught by older women how to please their husbands, the rules of etiquette and hospitality to guests, and other traditional subjects that prepare women for responsible roles in society. Women are vital to Kikuyu economies because they grow most of the food crops, sell most crops in markets, and support children. Second, women's councils stress that a woman must learn to take the initiative in all communal duties, such as helping other women during and for a month after childbirth, preparing proper foods for weddings, funerals, initiation ceremonies, etc. At initiation, a woman is taught the family lineage in depth and meets many of her relatives during the festivities. She is also advised during the rituals which families or clans are hostile to her *mbari* (extended family). Third, by tradition, only circumcised women can hold public office. Fourth, only circumcised women can marry, and own or manage property, such as land or a business, that produces wealth. Finally, uncircumcised women are believed to be unable to conceive or reproduce because they are not responsible and thus not ready for the lifelong obligations that accompany parenthood. Clitoridectomy and circumcision are essential prerequisites for full citizenship.

Unaware of its deeper cultural and symbolic importance, missionaries first attacked clitoridectomy on the grounds that it was immoral, decadent, and devilish. They later mounted what is now a standard attack against clitoridectomy on medical grounds, after the death of Elizabeth Ndobi in 1920 during childbirth. On the basis of his postmortem, Dr. Philip concluded that Ms. Ndobi's clitoridectomy had resulted in "serious complications in the birth canal . . . fatal to childbirth." The extent to which his opinion was influenced by reformers' zeal is impossible to determine. However, Christopher Waruiru noted that by 1930 a Dr. Thomson claimed that under the "normal traditional operation the formation of scar tissue is *not* possible" (Waruiru 1971). Jomo Kenyatta described a traditional Kikuyu clitoridectomy: "with a stroke she [the circumcisor] cuts off the tip of the clitoris. And no other part of the girl's sexual organ is interfered with" (Kenyatta 1938:146). From my own observations, Kenyatta's testimony, and Thomson's statement, it seems that Dr. Philip may have overstated his case and improperly diagnosed the cause of Ms. Ndobi's death to lend credence to the medical case against clitoridectomy. After all, he was seeking to prove that it was a form of genital mutilation and, as such, reprehensible. Mrs. Stevenson actually labeled clitoridectomies "genital mutilation," and Western reformers have since repeated the same argument. Jomo Kenyatta (1938:128) used similar words in describing clitoridectomy:

> Clitoridectomy, like Jewish circumcision, is a mere bodily mutilation which, however, is regarded as the *conditio sine qua non* of the whole teaching of tribal law, religion and morality [for Kikuyu].

However, note that Kenyatta, unlike Dr. Philip, assigned no negative connotations to "bodily mutilation." His phrase was matter-of-fact description.[8]

The female circumcision controversy divided whole Kikuyu communities during the 1920s. Those who agreed with the missionaries' call for abolition were called *kirore* (a corruption of the Swahili term, *kidole,* for the thumbprint used to sign documents), and the pure Kikuyu who adhered to tradition were known as *karinga.* The karinga insisted that it was possible to simultaneously revere and maintain tradition and be a Christian. Since missionaries like Reverend Barlow (who started the clitoridectomy controversy), Philip, and Stevenson ostracized Kikuyu who favored female circumcision, and refused to recommend them for government jobs or allow their children to attend Christian-sponsored schools, the issue became central to the struggle for political control. It symbolized the quintessential expression of Kikuyu identity. The freedom to continue circumcising females also became a gauge of self-determination. The Kikuyu felt that this custom must be preserved to maintain any semblance of semiautonomy. British administrators realized that it was extremely risky to attack the custom because of its ability to ignite bloody and costly rebellion after several groups of Kikuyu embraced it as their cause célèbre. African urban professionals, white-collar workers, and skilled laborers, who had organized themselves into a mass movement known as the Kikuyu Central Association (KCA), rapidly adopted this cause, as did the Kikuyu Independent School movement and other African nationalist groups (Rosberg and Nottingham 1966).

When it became clear to colonial administrators that they could not win the battle without alienating both Kikuyu collaborators and rebels, they took the official position that clitoridectomies could be performed as long as the patient "consented." For some the announcement came too late. Kikuyu extremists formed a group called Watu Wa Mungu (People of God), which some believe was the forerunner of Mau Mau. The leaders of this sect claimed to hate European missionaries for trying to destroy their beloved culture. They claimed that Europeans were quarreling not only with the Kikuyu but, according to the newspapers, among themselves. They concluded that war was inevitable and advised their followers to retreat to the forest and make weapons. Most made bows and arrows and traditional poisons. They prayed frequently on hilltops for God's help that they might emerge victorious, and called upon other Kikuyu to join them. They roared like lions to make themselves seem more ferocious and to inspire awe in others. They also trembled and worked themselves into fits of fanatic religious zeal. Airplanes, they believed, caused famine, drought, and plagues of locusts. All who embraced this sect believed that they were immune to bullets.

Theirs was the blood of God; if bullets touched their blood, they reasoned, the bullets would turn into harmless water (National Archives of Kenya DC/KBU/3/2/1927).

Although they claimed to be defenders of pure Kikuyu tradition, most People of God members were ex-mission boys. They refused to pay bridewealth for women and seldom paid taxes. They seemed to represent an extreme reaction to the rapid and forced destruction of Kikuyu culture. Because they claimed that God inspired them through dreams, they were also commonly referred to as *waroti* (dreamers). As ascetics, they preferred sleeping on the ground. Their motto was "Independence in every possible thing." They took oaths of unity, later adopted by Mau Mau or freedom fighters. When they began to use their weapons to attack police posts, many were killed, including Munguru wa Karaha, Joseph Nganga wa Kiara, and Samuel Muinami wa Njuguna (National Archives of Kenya DC/KBU/3/2/1927).

In this manner, the "female circumcision controversy" became indirectly linked to early nationalist struggles and the use of cultural symbols to arouse violent resistance to the imposition of colonial rule. The assertion of the right to continue practicing African culture became a symbol of patriotism and a warning that the Kikuyu had a rendezvous with self-government.

Jomo Kenyatta argued throughout the 1930s that the moral demands of most churches were inconsistent with traditional beliefs and practices, because the outcome was detribalization. Bearing this in mind, the missions put local customs into three categories:

   a. Beliefs and customs that they felt did not fit with Christian principles, but which did not actively oppose Christian values, were viewed as innocuous. Therefore, they were to be allowed to die of their own accord. Ancestor veneration and the practice of *ugo* (magic) fell into this category.
   b. Customs such as sexually provocative dances and polygyny, regarded as incompatible with Christian principles, were to be actively opposed. Dances like the *mugoiyo, urigu,* and *gicukia* were vigorously denounced, and African Christians were prohibited from participating in them on pain of banishment from the church.

c. Customs regarded as medically or hygienically undesirable were
to be abolished, for example, exposure of the dead (the Kikuyu
traditionally did not bury their dead but placed their bodies in
the bush away from the family homestead) and clitoridectomy.
(Macpherson 1970:105)

Christian missionaries in Kenya felt that the first two categories of
Kikuyu customs would die out in time, even if not actively opposed.
When Kikuyu culture proved more resilient than Europeans imagined, they zealously mounted an all-out attack on mambura, especially
clitoridectomy. They claimed that it was merely unnecessary mutilation of women.

Because the Kikuyu traditionally believed that uncircumcised
women could not bear children, Reverend Barlow, who began the
controversy over clitoridectomy in 1912, first tried to prove to Kikuyu
Christian women that a normal healthy uncircumcised woman could
bear a child. Kikuyu custom held that this was impossible. By disprov-
ing this the missionaries were satisfied that they had completely undermined this institution, and that its total demise was imminent. As we
have seen, this was only one of five reasons that the Kikuyu valued
clitoridectomy, so they continued the practice. They perceived the campaign against it as attempted ethnocide or cultural genocide, because
women who followed missionary advice in essence lost the privileges
that accompany full citizenship in Kikuyuland. British culture was very
male chauvinistic and held status and power to be the exclusive preserve
of men. This attitude all but destroyed the "dual sex" systems of
Kikuyu authority that were common before British intervention. The
power of Kikuyu women's councils drastically declined under British
rule (Mazrui 1986:136).

Women became marginalized, excluded from access to traditional
structures of power and mobility. Since the British did not want to hire
or advance the mass of Kikuyu society in the emerging colonial structure, they left few alternative opportunities for Kikuyu women who
might abandon the traditional system associated with clitoridectomy.
Blindly the missionaries had created a "Catch 22." If the Kikuyu
women followed missionary teaching, most would not be absorbed by

the male-dominated evolving European colonial society. Clitoridectomy assured a woman's success in the old system. Why surrender
assured honor and success for uncertainty? This was unacceptable to
most women, and widespread resistance to the changes proposed by the
missionaries followed. The missionaries saw this as confirmation of the
backwardness of the majority of Kikuyu. Most Kikuyu women felt
that, given the choices available, what the missions were demanding
was irrational and unrealistic, as well as destructive of their culture. For
the majority of women, clitoridectomy assured a good marriage, economic security, and social acceptance, traditional symbols of success for
women. Without a clitoridectomy, a woman risked being labeled bad, a
poor marriage partner, a betrayer of custom, and a person who deserves
to fail by being reduced to poverty. Some of Nairobi's first prostitutes
were uncircumcised Kikuyu women, and this stigma still clings to all
uncircumcised Kikuyu women in the minds of many Kikuyu men.

As the controversy heated up, accusations and counteraccusations
were hurled by both sides. The kidole (women who complied with
the missionaries' wishes) were in the minority, but the missionaries
had the power to recommend these women for secure government
jobs or to get their children into good schools. Kidole formed a privileged elite.

The accusations became wilder and harder to prove. Karinga
(women who adhered to traditional practice), for example, claimed
that the missionaries wanted to abolish female circumcision so they
could marry Kikuyu girls and thereby gain access to the land. To
corral public opinion and gain government support for circumcision,
karinga and the KCA composed songs known as *muthirigu* (*mserego* in
Swahili). These were verses extemporized in marketplaces, attacking
individuals who called for the abolition of clitoridectomy. In one case
they sang:

> *Baru* (Reverend Barlow) *ni mugaru*
> *Na muka ni muchiaru*
> *Na mwari ni muchiaru*
> *Nguria makuroruo nuu!!*

meaning:

> Barlow, his wife, and daughter
> have delivered
> I wonder who
> will nurse them!

The song went on to state:

> The District Commissioner
> Is bribed with uncircumcised girls
> So that our land will go.

The missionaries and their allies in government were not amused. Teachers and government employees who openly opposed abolition lost their jobs throughout the 1930s. To avoid such reprisals, some people, such as Chief Gatere, circumcised their daughters privately while publicly denouncing circumcision for women. Others defiantly forced their daughters to be circumcised. If caught, mothers such as M. Wairimu were sentenced to six months in jail, because by 1930 such operations could be performed by "consent only." Abolition advocates began to believe that they were the only enlightened Kikuyu and that they alone were therefore fit to lead or administer the country and to save other Kikuyu from descent into barbarism.

From 1930 to the present, cultural activities in Kenya have been closely connected with politics. Cultural conflicts have encouraged nationalism and revealed inequalities in the new society emerging in Kenya.

The stress of rapid urbanization and modernization in Kenya has inspired a revival of traditional culture, and clitoridectomies appeared to be on the rise while I was doing my field work there. The strong support given to traditional culture by Jomo Kenyatta, Kenya's first president, lent additional legitimacy to a host of African traditions. Traditional dancers, for example, were encouraged to perform for dignitaries to demonstrate that politicians were proud of their heritage.[9] Rumor in Nairobi alleges that Tom Mboya, a Luo, had himself circumcised to gain the respect of the Kikuyu so that he could become vice-president of Kenya.[10]

Since female nurses perform clitoridectomies for a fee they have an economic stake in the custom and are among its staunchest supporters. Moreover, women who have undergone the operation and Kikuyu women who encouraged their daughters to undergo it are loath to condemn it. To do so would be admission of personal guilt and wrongdoing as well as condemnation of one's parents and ancestors, tantamount to sacrilege.

Culture is the handmaiden of Kikuyu politics. Since 1976, events at the Kamiriitha Community Educational and Cultural Center have illustrated this point. Kamiriitha, a Kenyan town of some ten thousand people, built the center through local self-help (harambee) efforts. Villagers organized a literacy program that produced dramas portraying local people's lives and experiences. An internationally renowned author, Ngugi wa Thiong'o, was commissioned to write the first play, which reflected the lives and values of many Kikuyu and was critiqued by ordinary Kikuyu before it was produced in a theatre that they constructed. The play was very successful and attracted a full house at every performance. Kenyan officials banned the play, however, because they felt that it encouraged class conflict. The playwright was detained, the theatre destroyed, and the center closed down.

The Kenyan government, which is trying hard to unify Kenya and develop a national identity, feared that the play might heighten class consciousness and lead to violence. Any custom viewed as divisive is discouraged. In light of this, the open revival of female circumcision ceremonies is seen in some Kenyan circles as yet another challenge to authority and the existing order. As such, it is greeted with fear, abhorrence, and often intolerance. Some believe that it could open old wounds between kidole and karinga. Emotions are so strong on this issue that violent clashes are feared that could retard or completely undermine the new nationalism.

Western activists can become unwitting pawns in an ongoing power game between local and national Kenyan interest groups. Feminists opposing clitoridectomy may even find themselves aligned with educated male chauvinists in Kenya of views antithetical to feminism (Ngugi wa Thiong'o 1983) who seek to destroy all sources of traditional and modern power capable of creating and sustaining rival power blocks. The alliance of these men with Western feminists implies that Kikuyu and other indigenous feminists are weak and manipulable. Should local feminists emerge as a rival source of power, they too will very likely be suppressed. In the meantime, it is convenient to use them and their opposition to clitoridectomy to crush a new Kikuyu bid for power inspired by the revival of such cultural symbols.

The women who perform these operations, the mothers who encourage daughters to submit to them, and the fathers, uncles, and brothers who condone them find themselves labeled criminal for upholding their traditions. Older women, already circumcised, are being asked to state that they were wrong or unwise to submit, and many simply refuse to accept this judgment. This could provoke a cultural backlash that local feminists are ill prepared to combat because of their small numbers.

Witness how some modern Kikuyu writers, such as Ngugi wa Thiong'o, and historians, such as Godfrey Muriuki, feel that it was almost a patriotic duty for a Kikuyu woman to resist missionary teaching on this subject. In recent years, the women's liberation movement in America has wholeheartedly embraced the missionary position on this subject. Despite her knowledge of the controversy and the vital symbolic role played by clitoridectomy in Kikuyu custom, religion, politics, economics, and fertility control, Fran Hosken campaigns against it with all the zeal of the old missionaries. She states:

> Women thus are socialized and politicized to join in proudly pointing to the importance of their cultural tradition and heritage that disenfranchises them legally, regards them as chattels and castrates their sexuality, besides robbing them of their children. (Hosken 1981)

As Pat Caplan has pointed out, Hosken underestimates the power of African women within their cultures. Caplan believes that Hosken is insensitive to continuing change within most African cultures when she asserts pejoratively that "a custom is beyond question in most of Africa" (Caplan 1981a:878). This suggests that Africans are the victims of cultural tyranny. Charitably judged, Hosken's statement is misleading.

Clitoridectomy became a political issue between the Kikuyu and Kenya's white settlers and missionaries, as well as a symbol of the struggle between African nationalists and British colonial power. Hosken praises the missionaries who condemned this practice. She even ridicules the argument that criticism from international women's groups could fuel a violent backlash, just as it did during the "female circumcision controversy" of the 1930s and the "Mau Mau" of the 1950s. Evidence from Kenya suggests that women's customs are seen as fundamental cultural boundary markers and, consequently, that suggestions to change women's customs can ignite volatile emotions, as they did in Iran over the custom of unveiling modern Iranian women.

## CLITORIDECTOMY IN THE UNITED STATES

We have seen how the clitoridectomy controversy became a rallying point for nationalists in Kenya, how it became politicized and entangled in complex ways with the further disempowerment of women. We have seen how Western feminists with sympathy and zeal have called for the abolition of this custom that they feel oppresses women. I have argued that African women have the right to make their own decisions. I want to conclude by looking at the paradoxes that attend the practice in the United States. Ironically, what was a sacred custom tied to other rights and duties among the Kikuyu appeals to some American women for cosmetic purposes. Other women have requested the operation for hygienic reasons, for example, to "reduce chafing and irritation" (Hodgkinson and Hait 1984:414).

A follow-up study of Western women several years after they selected cosmetic clitoridectomy revealed that "reduction of the labia minora may improve the physical comfort and sexuality of some women" (Hodgkinson and Hait 1984:416). Although many authors have argued that clitoridectomies provide a one-way ticket to the loss of sexual pleasure, this report suggests that an improved self-image can increase sexual enjoyment. The issue seems not yet settled. Kikuyu and Third World women do not view clitoridectomy as cosmetic surgery and so do not consult obliging plastic surgeons to operate on their daughters. In a recent telephone survey of gynecologists in the New York City area, I asked if they had ever performed a female circumcision. One replied, "How barbaric! Of course I would never consider it." Another stated, "I would only perform such an operation if the clitoris were cancerous." Many others claimed never to have heard of the procedure. The New York medical establishment echoes the sentiments of Baroness Masham, who testified before the British Parliament:

> [F]emale circumcision is a totally heinous thing. It is impossible to find a single circumstance in which such a barbaric procedure could be justified in a civilized society such as ours. (Hayter 1984:324)

Hostility toward minorities' custom of clitoridectomy merely drives the practice underground and increases the medical risk. If prejudice against the custom were not so strong, more women might bring their daughters to hospitals for the operation, thereby reducing the potential for harm. Officials at the National Institutes of Health in Washington, D.C., admitted that the growing number of female immigrants from areas where clitoridectomy is common means it may now be a practice in the United States, but that it is almost impossible to assess its extent if it occurs outside of hospital settings. Like gynecologists, they too seemed unaware that plastic surgeons are performing the procedure on Western white women of means. They were eager, however, to learn as much as possible about it. Medical intolerance may pose major cultural problems for many new immigrants.

Rather than outlaw this procedure, shouldn't we enable women eager for clitoridectomy to have it done in the safety of a hospital? No doubt Western women desiring this operation will fight both men and women seeking to limit their freedom to do what they will with their bodies. Should Third World women be any less empowered?

If determined people seek these operations in back alleys from nonmedical technicians, aren't we increasing the risk of physical injury from incompetence and unhygienic conditions, just as criminalization of abortion exposed Western women to medical abuse from unqualified quacks? Criminalization of clitoridectomy may also increase the risk that AIDS will be transmitted nonsexually via uncleaned razors or knife blades exposed to contaminated blood. Thus, criminalization, like prohibition of liquor and abortions, may prove to be unenforceable and thus more dangerous than encouraging women to have the procedure performed in hospitals. Like other women, Kikuyu women in the West need political power to protect their customs and secure their rights, but their minute numbers may exclude them from power at present. Westerners sincerely eager to help these women achieve better lives might listen rather than preach to them.

Third World women living in Western nations currently treat clitoridectomy as an embarrassing cultural secret they must hide from a hostile or indifferent world, because we make them ashamed of it. They resort to unqualified practitioners who perform the operation after agreeing, above all, never to reveal its existence. Our blind prejudice against this custom is imperiling innocent lives. These women dread subjecting their daughters to ill-prepared and equipped people as much as Western women, yet Western attitudes leave them little choice. Criminalization may create a thriving black market for unqualified, greedy, but daring individuals willing to risk the health of millions of women worldwide for a quick profit. Is this really the legacy we want to leave the next generation of women?

To approach this problem intelligently we need to make a clear distinction between the types and associated medical risks of clitoridectomy, rather than treat all clitoridectomies the same. Lori Heise (1989:B4) committed this mistake by presenting the worst health risks associated with the most severe type of clitoridectomy (pharaonic), as if they were typical of all types. Indiscriminate lumping of clitoridectomy with infibulation only further obfuscated the issues. Infertility, chronic urinary tract infection, and loss of sexual feeling are reported among populations practicing pharaonic clitoridectomy. Reliable statistics are too meager to permit an assessment of the incidence of these problems, but such problems are rarely associated with the milder forms of the operation, and failure to mention this is misleading. Lack of careful detailed analysis polarizes and inflames public opinion when it should be informed. Heise's article highlights the need for a more enlightened discussion of this issue. Beyond this, the various cultural settings of different groups of women need more analysis before specific recommendations are made. The average Western woman is adapting to demands substantially different from those faced by the average Kikuyu woman in Kenya.

Bearing the above in mind, imposing our moral values on others is normally unjustifiable in a pluralistic, multicultural society, where tolerance and inclusion are required more than intolerance and exclusion. Fostering intolerance of cultural difference nourishes bigotry. Male circumcision is now viewed by some as medically unnecessary and painful, yet it is socially and legally tolerated in most Western societies because we have grown accustomed to it. Distinctions can be made between custom and religious dictate, but if the law is to grant maximum freedom to individuals to determine private morality, how can we tolerate one custom and not the other without discriminating? This is all the more true when we consider that until 1945 we prescribed clitoridectomies for girls to cure chronic masturbation and curb promiscuity in America and England. Neither male circumcision nor minor clitoridectomy, as was performed on Kikuyu women, causes long-term injury or impairment of function of a body organ. Thus, choosing to have such an operation seems best left in the realm of private decision.

While I do not favor the sexual suppression of women, or condone unnecessary suffering, if Western women and men have a right to purely elective cosmetic surgery, then denying Third World women access to elective surgery of their choice seems tantamount to legal paternalism and denial of their comparable right of self-determination. Legislation to do so seems to slight the intelligence of these women and to treat them as minors. With one stroke of the pen, the mothers, grandmothers, and great grandmothers of Third World women would be converted into criminals who wantonly subjected their daughters to harmful acts. In essence we would rewrite their history and control the way they view their past, as well as their present. People once thought heroes could instantly become villainous friends. Perhaps Ngugi wa Thiong'o (1983:48) said it best. "How do you kill the right and the determination of a people to have a cultural life?"

When grappling with Western gender issues, do we really have the right to limit the liberty of others or to reinterpret their history? For Ngugi and millions of others the answer is clearly no. Is a Kikuyu immigrant to the United States, who lives in a socially encapsulated world, entitled to nontherapeutic surgery any less than an American woman, if not undergoing the operation causes her distress? For low-income, uneducated Kikuyu women in Kawangware, failure to circumcise may stigmatize one as "immoral," "wanton," "promiscuous," or "wayward" and therefore excellent as a lover but unfit to be a wife and decent mother, that is, unmarriageable. Such stigmatization can condemn to destitution a poor woman who needs a husband for survival. Surely, this is not what Hosken and others had in mind for these women.

Wouldn't it make more sense to support women worldwide who seek better educational and economic opportunities rather than to criminalize clitoridectomy? Kikuyu women in the diaspora who are well educated and have real career options outside of marriage usually abandon this practice. Doesn't their behavior indicate the best approach to this issue?

NOTES

1. Very few well-educated Kikuyu women have either participated in or supported this custom. Most believe it dangerous and life threatening, and so oppose it. By contrast, uneducated Kikuyu women, who tend to live in a socially encapsulated world, are its strongest supporters, especially if they are older. Support for this custom could evolve into a class market in urban areas.

2. Since outright prohibition seldom succeeds, whether in temperance campaigns against alcohol or international campaigns against clitoridectomy, and since higher education strongly correlates with abandonment of tradition, perhaps women who are anxious to see this custom end should put more effort into the education of Third World women rather than into crusades for the abolition and criminalization of clitoridectomy.

3. The Kikuyu term for circumcision is *irua*. Some writers view all types of circumcision, male and female, as forms of deliberate body mutilation. Most writers take a more moderate position and do not classify many types of circumcision as mutilation.

4. KANU stands for the Kenyan National Union, which has dominated Kenyan politics since Kenya became independent. GEMA, the Gikuyu/Embu/Meru Association, along with the Luo Union, was one of the most powerful voluntary associations in Kenya. Both were mutual-aid tribal unions with multiple functions. President Daniel arap Moi banned these unions because he feared that they would become centers for what some considered subversive political activity. Although Kenya has 42 ethnic groups, the 5 largest tribes make up over 90 percent of the population. A coalition of any 3 of the big 5 can control Kenyan politics. The Luo and the Kikuyu together comprise almost 40 percent of the population, and, since Moi is not a member of either group, some analysts believe he feared the potential of these tribal unions.

5. Symbolically the number seven is very important to Kikuyu. Prior to circumcision, one traditionally underwent a ritual second birth. During this ceremony a goat was slaughtered, and the child was coiled with the goat's intestines, symbolizing the umbilical cord. A woman would stay in the birth position, and the child would come close and pretend to emerge from her female organs. This was the climax of the ritual. After this the child wore a charm made of goat's skin on its wrist for seven days, symbolizing a readiness to be circumcised. This custom is observed mainly by members of the Kikuyu Orthodox Church in Kawangware.

In general, the seventh day is considered not good, a day of bad omen. If a Kikuyu were traveling, he would refuse to return home on the seventh day. This was true even though, in general, odd numbers were considered masculine and good for men, and even numbers were considered feminine. People feared that seven would bring evil and bad luck.

The number seven is used often in oaths. For example, *kuringa thengi,* an oath of innocence, requires the person seeking to establish innocence to insert an object into the anus of a ritual goat seven times. Similarly, another oath known as *muma wa gutagarara kaimba,* used to indicate a person accused of poisoning someone, requires the accused to cross the body of the dead victim seven times. (Women seldom do this, for they are rarely suspected of poisoning others, which, traditionally, is masculine behavior.) Yet another oath, *gucuna ruhiya,* requires the accused to lick a red hot knife blade seven times without being burned to prove innocence of stealing another's property and the falseness of charges. Numbers in Kikuyu culture have great symbolic importance. These examples are indicative, not exhaustive, of the wealth of symbolism that permeates Kikuyu culture.

6. If a Kikuyu circumcises Maasai-style, then ritual seclusion customarily lasts only four days. The first day is filled with ritual drinking and dancing. On the second day the circumcision occurs. On the third day the circumcisor stays with the initiates to instruct and comfort them and to administer to their medical needs. Finally, on the fourth day the initiates return home. Because of its brevity, many urban Kikuyu are turning to this ritual format.

7. One major function of circumcision is to impress upon the initiates that, as mature adults, they must be prepared to face and overcome trials and ordeals that might imperil the Kikuyu people. They are expected to face these with stoic determination and unflinching courage. Withstanding pain bravely is believed to prepare them psychologically for the rigors and difficulties of adulthood. The Kikuyu see pain and suffering as a normal part of life. While they do not encourage unnecessary pain or suffering, not to prepare the next generation to overcome such trials is considered irresponsible and negligent.

8. Many leading Kikuyu alleged that Kenyatta loved traditional culture so much that he and his son Peter Kenyatta had all of their male children circumcised, and all of their daughters underwent clitoridectomies. Such stories were heard in elite circles, as well as in impoverished urban communities such as Kawangware and Mathare Valley. I was unable to confirm these stories, so I report them here as hearsay requiring substantiation through further investigation. Mere circulation of these stories strengthened and encouraged those eager to restore African traditions and customs. The end result was that many dying cultural practices were revived and given a second life. This note refers to the postindependence (1963 on) era when Kenyatta became independent Kenya's founding father. As a legendary cultural hero, most of his deeds and the things he encouraged were respected and imitated by the masses. Such imitation was limited only by access to resources, and some consider it the ultimate compliment.

9. Since performers were paid for each appearance they developed a vested interest in maintaining certain traditions. Without doubt, this arrangement was equally advantageous for politicians eager to funnel spoils to supporters who may not have had the formal educational credentials to qualify for high-paying jobs in the modern sector. Nevertheless these people were thought entitled to rewards for delivering blocks of voters.

10. Luo initiation involves removal of the lower incisor teeth, not circumcision. Luo identity is not linked to this issue. Daniel arap Moi is presumed circumcised by Kikuyu because this was a major feature of Kalenjin culture. Thus, on cultural grounds, they consider him a mature and responsible man, capable of leading a community to prosperity and peace. Many tradition-

oriented Kikuyu and Maasai began to doubt the depth and sincerity of Moi's commitment to African culture when, in 1982, he banned Maasai clitoridectomies and labeled them barbaric after several Maasai girls died during an initiation ritual. Some observers feel that cultural clashes fueled the outlawed Mwa Kenya Movement, which opposes Moi.

## REFERENCES

Al-Saadawy, Nawal
    1977    *Woman and Psychological Conflict.* al-Mu'assasa al' Arabiya lil-dirassat wa'l-nashr.

Arthur, J. W.
    1942    Female Circumcision Among the Kikuyu. *British Medical Journal* 2: 498.

Assad, Marie-Bassili
    1980    Female Circumcision in Egypt: Social Implications, Current Research, and Prospects for Change. *Studies in Family Planning* 11(1): 3–16.

Bardis, Panos D.
    1967    Circumcision in Ancient Egypt. *Indian Journal of the History of Medicine* 12(1): 22–23.

Bean, G.
    1984    Neonatal Circumcision: When Is the Decision Made? *Journal of Family Practice* 18(6): 883–87.

Berardi, J. C.
    1985    Obstetrical Consequences of Female Circumcision: Study of 71 Circumcised African Women. *Journal of Gynecology, Obstetrics, Biology and Reproduction* 14(6): 743–46.

Bingham, Marjorie, and Susan Gross (eds.)
    1982    *Women in Africa of the Sub-Sahara.* Melbourne, Fla.: Gem Publishers.

Caplan, Pat
    1981a    The Hosken Report: Genital and Sexual Mutilation of Females. *Africa* 51(4): 877–79.
    1981b    Female Circumcision, Excision and Infibulation: The Facts and Proposals for Change. *Africa* 51 (4).

270    DALLAS L. BROWNE

Cook, R.
    n.d.    Damage to Physical Health from Pharaonic Circumcision Infib-
          ulation of Females: A Review of the Medical Literature. Alexan-
          dria, Egypt: *World Health Organization*, Mediterranean.

Cutner, L.
    1985    Female Genital Mutilation. *Obstetrics, Gynecology and Survival*
          40(7): 437–43.

de Wolf, Jan Jacob
    1962    Circumcision and Initiation in Western Kenya and Eastern
          Uganda. *Anthropos* 78(3–4): 369–410.

El Dareer, Asma
    1983    Attitudes of Sudanese People to the Practice of Female Circumci-
          sion. *International Journal of Epidemiology* 12(2).

Ellenberger, H. F.
    1980    Body Mutilations Inflicted on Women: A Victimological Study.
          *Criminologie* 13(1): 80–93.

Falk-Moore, Sally.
    1978    *Law as Process: An Anthropological Approach.* London: Routledge
          and Kegan Paul.

Grassivaro, Gallo
    1985    Female Circumcision in Somalia: Anthropological Traits. *An-
          thropological Annuals* 43(4) 311–26.

Hayter, K.
    1984    Female Circumcision—Is There a Legal Solution? *Journal of So-
          cial Welfare Law* 6(2): 323–33.

Heise, Lori
    1989    The War on Women. *Washington Post* (April 9): B1, B4.

Hodgkinson, Darryl, and Glen Hait
    1984    Aesthetic Vaginal Labioplasty. *Plastic and Reconstruction Surgery*
          74(3): 414–16.

Hosken, Fran P.
    1981    Female Genital Mutilation in the World Today: A Global Re-
          view. *International Journal of Health Services* 11(3): 415–30.

Kenya, Cheche
    1982    *Independent Kenya.* London: Zed.

Kenyatta, Jomo
    1938    *Facing Mount Kenya.* London: Routledge and Kegan Paul.

Kidd, Ross
  1983    Popular Theatre and Popular Struggle in Kenya: The Story of
          Kamiriithu. *Race and Class* 24(3): 287–304.

Levin, Tobe
  1980    Unspeakable Atrocities: The Psycho-sexual Etiology of Female
          Genital Mutilation. *The Journal of Mind and Behavior* 1(2): 197–210.

Lowenstein, L. F.
  1978    Attitudes and Attitude Differences to Female Genital Mutilation
          in the Sudan: Is There a Change on the Horizon? *Social Science
          and Medicine* 12(5): 417–21.

Macpherson, R.
  1970    *The Presbyterian Church in Kenya*. London: Presbyterian Church
          of East Africa Press.

Mazrui, Ali (ed.)
  1986    *The Africans: A Reader*. New York: Praeger.

Morgan, Robin, and Gloria Steinem
  1980    The International Crime of Genital Mutilation. *Ms. Magazine*
          (March): 65–100.

Murray, Jocelyn
  1976    The Church Missionary Society and the "Female Circumci-
          sion" Issue in Kenya, 1929–1932. *Journal of Religion in Africa*
          8(2): 92–104.
  1981a   Women of Omdurman: Victims of Circumcision. *Africa* 51(4):
          879–80.
  1981b   Against the Mutilation of Women: The Struggle against Unnec-
          essary Suffering. *Africa* 51(4).

Mustafa, Asim Zaki
  1966    Female Circumcision and Infibulation in the Sudan. *Journal of
          Obstetrics and Gynecology, British Commonwealth* 73(4): 302–06.

Myers, Robert, Francisca Omorodion, Anthony Isenalumhe, and Gregory
Akenzua
  1985    Circumcision: Its Nature and Practice among Some Ethnic
          Groups in Southern Nigeria. *Social Science Medicine* 21(5):
          581–88.

National Archives of Kenya
  1927    Watu Wa Mungu—The Murder of Trader Dick. *Confidential
          Papers* DC/KBU/3/2.

Ngugi wa Thiong'o

1983   *Barrel of a Pen: Resistance to Repression in Neo-Colonial Kenya.* Trenton: Africa World Press.

Odile, Frank

1984   Sisters in Affliction, La Mutilation Génitale des Femmes Africaines. *Canadian Journal of African Studies* 18: 441–44.

Ozturk, Orhan M.

1973   Ritual Circumcision and Castration Anxiety. *Psychiatry* 36: 49–60.

Ranger, T. O.

1972   Missionary Adaptation of African Religious Institutions. In *The Historical Study of African Religion,* ed. T. O. Ranger and I. Kimambo. London: Heinemann.

Rosberg, Carl, and John Nottingham

1966   *The Myth of Mau Mau; Nationalism in Kenya.* Nairobi: East African Publishing House.

Shandall, Ahmed A.

1967   Circumcision and Infibulation of Females: A General Consideration of the Problem and a Clinical Study of the Complications in Sudanese Women. *Sudan Medical Journal* 5(4): 178–212.

Sindzingre, Nicole

1977   Plus and Minus: Concerning Female Circumcision. *Cahiers d'Études Africaines* 17(1): 65–75.

1979   Excess and Loss: Excision and Representation of Femininity. *L'Homme* 19(3–4): 171–87.

Smith, Eleanor W.

n.d.   Female Circumcision: A Study of the Knowledge and Attitudes of Nurses in Alexandria toward Female Circumcision. The Mission Council of the Church of Scotland. Unpublished.

Wallerstein, Immanuel

1979   *The Capitalist World Economy.* London: Cambridge University Press.

Waruiru, Christopher

1971   *Female Initiation Controversy At Tumutumu, 1912–1937.* B.A. Thesis. University of Nairobi.

Weiss, Charles

1966   Motives for Male Circumcision among Preliterate and Literate Peoples. *Journal of Sex Research* 2(2): 69–88.